The Guest List

Also by Ethan Mordden

Ziegfeld: The Man Who Invented Show Business

All that Glittered: The Golden Age of Drama on Broadway, 1919–1959

Make Believe: The Broadway Musical in the 1920s

Sing For Your Supper: The Broadway Musical in the 1930s

Beautiful Mornin': The Broadway Musical in the 1940s

Coming Up Roses: The Broadway Musical in the 1950s

Open a New Window: The Broadway Musical in the 1960s

One More Kiss: The Broadway Musical in the 1970s

The Guest List

How Manhattan Defined American Sophistication—
from the Algonquin Round Table to Truman Capote's Ball

Ethan Mordden

St. Martin's Press
New York

Frontispiece: Stars and authors of *DuBarry Was a Lady,* a classic instance of New Yorkism in its rich vein of minority styles, mainly Irish, Jewish, and gay. Left to right: co-librettist and producer B. G. De Sylva, Betty Grable, Bert Lahr, composer-lyricist Cole Porter, Ethel Merman. Note that Lahr and Merman carefully support Porter, already crippled by his horseback-riding accident.

THE GUEST LIST. Copyright © 2010 by Ethan Mordden. All rights reserved. Printed in the United States of America. For information, address St. Martin's Press, 175 Fifth Avenue, New York, N.Y. 10010.

www.stmartins.com

A portion of Chapter 11 originally appeared in *The New York Times.*

All photos courtesy of private collections.

ISBN 978-0-312-54024-1

First Edition: October 2010

10   9   8   7   6   5   4   3   2   1

Acknowledgments

The author wishes to acknowledge his very good friend and agent, Joe Spieler; Jon Cronwell; Matt Callaway; Ken Mandelbaum; copy editor Angela Gibson; John Morrone; Vicki Lame; and his golden-age editor at St. Martin's Press, Michael Flamini.

Table of Contents

The Guest List

Introduction

This is a look at an early-middle-twentieth-century phenomenon, when certain leaders and opinion makers in the New York arts and letters scene seized control of the national culture on the elite level. This is why, for instance, Dorothy Parker and Cole Porter are in the book.

At the same time, a secondary theme runs through the narrative, treating the development and advance of three minority groups—Italian, Jewish, and black—in an environment that had favored only the Irish. Interestingly, the three "newer" minorities began to overwhelm the Irish in the sharing of power, taking influential positions in politics as well as the arts. This is why Fiorello La Guardia and Ethel Waters are in the book.

Yet more: the definition of "elite" changes in this time, as the precisely-derived celebrity of achievers evolves into the all-purpose celebrity of anyone who inspires chatter. "Talent" is replaced by that twenties term with an industrial quantity of meanings, "jazz," and fame expands to collect nobodies who commit outrages or become laughingstocks. Fame delights even in gangsters, previously society's unmentionables. But fame particularly seizes upon a new class, the "sophisticated"—glamorous, smart, tolerant folk who set the style associated with the New York arts scene. *Sophisticated* means more than merely worldly: a complex mixture, even (as Webster tells us) an "adulteration." An ethnicity, one might say, made of ethnicities.

Those in the heartland regard these evolutions angrily, especially in the way what we might call "New Yorkism"—the influence of these minority groups—affects their lives. In a tradition dating back to the Know Nothing (also called American) Party of the 1850s, Main Street periodically rises up to push back against what it sees as an aggressive transformation of the "meaning" of America. On the material level, immigrants compete with the native-born for jobs. Socially, they are Different: in dress, manners, vocal expression, and virtually every other way that shows. There is a religious divide, too, as many immigrants were the "other" Christians: Catholic, and thus supposedly in subversive conspiracy with Rome.

There is in fact a Fundamentalist Protestant identity in these uprisings, a demand that the nation adhere to someone's strict construction of what to believe and how to behave. The Prohibition movement, as we'll see, was more about a hatred of "modern" lifestyles than about liquor, and the current debate over gay marriage seems as much a holy war as a loony fantasy about what happens to heterosexual vows when homosexuals get to take them, too.

Even when religion is not overtly involved in a controversy—as in the isolationist/interventionist argument of the years before the United States entered the Second World War—one senses an undercurrent of bigotry, a suspicion of New Yorkism, in the otherwise political discussion. This is why Charles Lindbergh and Dorothy Thompson are in the book. Squaring off as if the designated spokesmen for the two sides, they came almost to embody two antagonistic views of American democracy, one closed to eclectic cultural transformation and the other embracing it. Or even: one hayseed and one sophisticate.

Thus, the present volume starts when scarcely anyone knows what an "intellectual" is or has laid eyes on an "artist," and it ends when half the country is talking of a masked ball given by a gay elf for the 540 most fascinating people he knows. An alternate title: *From Mrs. Astor to Truman Capote; or, The Rise of New Yorkism in American Life.*

Prologue
Did Mrs. Astor Attend?

By the late nineteenth century, the American city was in love with hotels—the big ones. Towers, palaces. These were not merely shelters, where travelers put up for a night on their way to somewhere. These hotels *were* somewhere: meeting places of the *nomyenklatura*, with banquet halls, salons, promenades, a caravanserai for the visiting notable and his retinue. The occasions of such a place were imposing, the toasts exhilarating, the guests tremendous.

There was a romance of the hotel, combining civic pride and the rhetoric of authority, for these buildings were not only instant landmarks but often the most important-looking structures in town. The events that transpired there were detailed in the newspapers and even novels. Virtually every major writer active around the turn of the twentieth century planned narrative around scenes in hotels. The hotel was the new enchanted forest, dragon's lair, den of thieves: where magic happens. Arnold Bennett built his novel *The Grand Babylon Hotel* (1902) on the greatest such place in the world, complete with a wine cellar richer than Fort Knox, a cloak-and-dagger plot involving European royalty, and—the new magician—an American millionaire. Denied a supper of steak and beer by a snooty headwaiter, the millionaire buys the hotel and sacks the waiter.

Hotels not only served fiction: they practically were fiction, reaching a climax in the cycle of works known as *Grand Hotel,* from Vicki Baum's novel *Menschen im Hotel.* (The title means *Hotel Guests,* but the meaning is *Life At the Top.*) Baum's imaginary Grand Hotel, Berlin is, once again, not just a hostel but a center of absolute glamor where human destinies intertwine. First a novel, then a play for Max Reinhardt's dazzling revolving stage, then a Broadway hit (and, much later, a musical), *Grand Hotel* moved on to the world's real-life center of glamor, Hollywood. And there it inspired MGM to invent the all-star movie cast, in 1932, intertwining Greta Garbo and Joan Crawford with Wallace Beery and Lionel and John Barrymore.

None of this was coincidental. Hotels really were, in the literal sense, fabulous. Boston's Tremont, Chicago's Palmer House, Kansas City's Muehlebach, and Philadelphia's Bellevue-Stratford were where urban culture showed off: with the latest in amenities for the rich, from hygiene to food. The hotel offered the best in living, and the Best People turned out to sample it.

Sometimes the Best People built the hotels themselves, as if wanting not only to enjoy the high style but control it. In New York, the hoteliers of note were the Astors. The richest American family in America's richest city, the Astors were Manhattan's slumlords, managing countless tenement blocks because the founder of the dynasty, John Jacob Astor, bought up cheap land obsessively. Lesser men sold their landholdings at a vast profit; Astor just kept buying. He never sold and he warned his heirs never to sell: that's what *richest* means.

Emigrating from Waldorf, Germany in 1780, Astor first established himself in the fur trade, launching a saga confused with recurring names—not only his own but those of his birthplace and his trading post in the old northwest, Astoria.* Thus, of the first five generations

---

* Someone else's birthplace enters the story here, for Ethel Merman was born and raised in Astoria, Queens, originally a rustic settlement that took its name in homage to John Jacob I, hoping for a legacy. In vain.

of Astors, there were six John Jacobs and two Waldorfs, not to mention four Williams and two Backhouses. ("Astoria" was reserved for objects, not people.) Further, a system of primogeniture recalling the hereditary practices of medieval barons created feuds between brothers that made the Astors not only wealthy and influential but colorful and scary.

Still, it was not brothers who tended the niceties of social status but their wives, and destiny decreed that if the Astor fortune could be joined to a glorious Old Knickerbocker ancestry, the resulting Mrs. Astor would rule New York society. There were, of course, various Mrs. Astors. But, as Max von Sydow puts it in *The Exorcist,* about the demons we hear assaulting little Linda Blair, There is only one. *The* Mrs. Astor had rivals—Mrs. Stuyvesant Fish, for instance, or Mrs. Ogden Mills. Yet her reign was absolute, proving that there really is no such thing as second best. There is only first, and she was the former Caroline Webster Schermerhorn (pronounced "Skermern," as if something out of Gilbert and Sullivan instead of Dutch Colonial), wife of William Backhouse Astor Jr. His niece, Mrs. William Waldorf Astor, habitually made motions of *lèse majesté,* and when the two ladies took residence as next-door neighbors in summer "cottages" in resort Rhode Island, each insisted on receiving mail as "Mrs. Astor, Newport."

The word "millionaire" is a nineteenth-century coining, because there hadn't been any need for it till John Jacob I came along—which is why the Astor millions placed the family at the center of New York society. And yet it was Astor hotels far more than Astor riches that engrossed New Yorkers. John Jacob built the Astor House at 225 Broadway, between Vesey and Barclay Streets, just across from the site of the old Federal Building that later became the city's main post office. In Second Empire style, the Federal Building seemed imported from Paris, with its stonework doodads, arched windows, operatic roofing, and surveilling cupola. The Astor House, by contrast, stared down the Federal Building with simple American power: a rectangular block of squared-off windows, flat roof, and storefronts lining the street floor, with only a big fat main entrance of stairs, columns, and lintel as rhetorical flourishes. Opened in 1836, the Astor House was a sensation, with interior plumbing (though guests had to share) and an around-the-clock gourmet dining room, unheard of at the time.

It was the greatest hotel in America by popular acclamation, and it stayed open till 1913, long after the commercial district had moved to the north. John Jacob had died sixty-five years before in any case, but his descendants carried on the work of aweing the town with great hotels: the Waldorf; the Netherland; the Astoria; the Astor and the Knicker-bocker, both in Times Square; the St. Regis; and, after the amalgamated Waldorf and Astoria were demolished to make way for the Empire State Building, the present Waldorf-Astoria, on Park Avenue.

These stand among the city's greatest hotels, past and present, truly historic places. Presidents stay at the Waldorf-Astoria, and lodging in the Waldorf Towers was once regarded as possibly the city's top address. The Astor used to host New York's most gala New Year's Party; at one of them, Florenz Ziegfeld met his second wife, Billie Burke, as they danced a Paul Jones. And the original Waldorf and Astoria buildings created objective co-relatives for New Yorkers' favorite family feud, for William Waldorf Astor erected his namesake, in the early 1890s, directly over-looking his aunt Caroline's house, with all the attendant upheaval of con-struction noises and the to and fro of foot and vehicular traffic. When the Waldorf Hotel was finished, Aunt Caroline was to be left hemmed in by the thing she dreaded the most. You know . . . people.

She moved to a mansion on Fifth Avenue at Sixty-fifth Street, shared with her son, William Waldorf's cousin Jack. For revenge, Jack planned to replace his mother's old house with a block of stables, thus to diminish the Waldorf Hotel's glamor with smells and smithing clangor. Then Jack realized that his cousin would resent something even more than horses: more of those people. So Jack built the Astoria there instead. Duelling hotels! Yet, from the start, a wary truce was called, so that the two build-ings might merge via connecting hallways. Should personal antagonism overwhelm commercial considerations, the connections could be stopped up and the two hostels operate separately. That never happened, because the newly named Waldorf-Astoria was so resplendently New York—so eloquent in its manifestation of the expensive excitement that the town loved in its leaders—that even the battling Astors had to look pridefully upon the sheer richness their fragile peace had created.

The Astors and their hotels were a gift to all New York. Celebrities of that day were reticent about making headlines, yet the prominent had a way of getting into anecdotes, and those hotels were so public! Any family can enjoy a feud or even, like the Astors, multi-generational feuds, inherited like their fortune. But poor Jack attained notoriety as one of the millionaires on the *Titanic* who failed to secure a lifeboat seat, gaily saw his wife off in hers, then calmly awaited a terrible death.

The Astors couldn't help making news, even if The Mrs. Astor had such a horror of being Known About or even glimpsed that she never went up to the windows of the Fifth Avenue house that Jack had built for her. Its ballroom held four hundred even—or is that an urban legend? Still, there *was* a Four Hundred, at least in the mind of Mrs. Astor's fervent toady Ward McAllister. He coined the phrase to delimit the socially reliable. "If you go outside that number," he told the *New York Tribune*, "you strike people who are either not at ease in a ballroom or else make other people not at ease."

A southern Anglophile with a Vandyke beard and mustache points, "Mc," as he was known to intimates, became the first of America's great social arbiters. Indeed, the grand folk who called on Mrs. Astor and were called upon in return needed Mc's help in sorting through the proprietors of the many new fortunes flooding Manhattan after the Civil War. There was railroad money, war-supplies money, retail money, stock-speculation money. Yet what was more relevant to what we might call the Ballroom Lifestyle—riches or family? Mc would advise. Better, he formed the Patriarchs, whose purpose was not only to give balls but, said Mc, to make it "extremely difficult to obtain an invitation to them."

Men tended to distrust McAllister; social conniving and categorizing was women's work. But Mrs. Astor gave him protection, and he squired certain of the "new" families into social prominence; and they were grateful. Giving their first balls in 1872 and 1873, when the doings of Society were literally the town topics, the Patriarchs included very distinguished local names, including two Astors and a Schermerhorn—the very dynasties that found themselves united in Mrs. Astor. Thus, like Truman Capote a century later, Ward McAllister got to be what he needed to be: the coddled little thrill of glamorous women. And then he made the mistake that Capote was to make: he told.

McAllister's book, *Society As I Have Found It* (1890), was not an exposé in any real sense. An anecdotal autobiography, it serves as a dos and don'ts of snobbery: whom to know and whom to cut, how to handle oneself in Situations, what to serve dinner guests (which turns out, over and over, to be canvasback duck). The writing is obsequious in praise of the author's social set—"the best people in the city," we read, or "ladies of established position," "born of noble race," "one of our oldest families." Who was gay first, Ward McAllister or Oscar Wilde?

It's a silly book, although there is one telling scene. McAllister's father and a friend—"the greatest swell and beau that New York had ever known"—are in London, in McAllister's favorite place to be, "a brilliant assemblage of people." The two men know no one and no one knows them, when suddenly the Duke of Wellington comes in. Surely the room goes stone-cold motionless: Napoleon's master himself! (McAllister, a feckless storyteller, leaves out this essential detail.) It happens that the duke is acquainted with our boys, comes right up to them, walks them up and down arm in arm, and leaves. Now, of course, the pair are mobbed, presented, welcomed. It's a hollow victory, however much the junior McAllister basks in it, but he's by no means alone in valuing such shallow attention. Switch from English ballroom to Hollywood, change the Duke of Wellington to, say, George Clooney, and the tale could have happened yesterday.

As the anecdote reveals, McAllister named some people and left others anonymous; who *was* the swank with the senior McAllister, anyway? McAllister also carefully left unidentified a certain woman he called "society's leader." She was "a true and loyal friend in sunshine and shadow," and even that much, that little bit of sheer admiration, was enough to turn Society from McAllister. Everyone knew that Mrs. Astor was society's leader. But saying it to the general public—to any parvenu or, worse, nobody who bought the book—was presumptuous. Saying it offended also the pretenders to Mrs. Astor's throne. And saying it offended

Mrs. Astor, because she hated being written about in any way whatsoever.

McAllister's membership in the club of First Families and Fancy Fortunes was not absolutely terminated. But he lost many an ally, and now those who had always disliked him yet had to be careful of Mrs. Astor's circle could cut him at will. The sunshine went all shadow when Mrs. Astor herself failed to attend McAllister's funeral, in 1895, at society's tabernacle of choice, Grace Church. (It's still very much in use, at Broadway and Tenth Street.) No Mrs. Astor? In the old joke, had McAllister been alive, this would have killed him. Even the Patriarchs were off McAllister by then, and Mrs. Stuyvesant Fish, in social historian Eric Homberger's words, "was positively incandescent in her absence."

In the end, McAllister's influence is hard to gauge, as there already was a Four Hundred being rich, exclusive, and, to some, fascinating. All McAllister did was give us a name for them. He did, at least, put some sort of imprimatur upon the concept of ballgiving as Society At Its Best, so he may have inadvertently created one of society's great embarrassments, the Bradley-Martin Ball of 1897.

This brings us back to the Astors, for the Martins' ball was held not at home, as society demanded, but in the Waldorf Hotel. (Its Astoria mate was not to open till later in the year.) Most of the Waldorf's public rooms were bound over to the festivities, attended in costume according with the theme, the court of Louis XV of France. For some reason, Bradley and Cornelia Martin had become known as the Bradley-Martins, and this Bradley-Martin Ball, in its turn, became known as the kind of thing that inspires French Revolutions. The United States was suffering the economic depression caused by the Panic of 1893, and an evening of rich loafers pantywaisting ostentatiously around seemed to bait controversy and even acts of violence by radicals.

Yet the ball went ahead, with boarded-up windows along the Waldorf's two lower floors and hundreds of law-enforcement officers guarding the surrounding streets. It was something new in balls: a very publicly private affair. Mrs. Bradley-Martin had determined to climax a series of notable parties with this one, to place her name as Society's Hostess in competition with that of Mrs. Astor, and the ball really was grand.

Receiving as Mary, Queen of Scots, Mrs. Bradley-Martin sabotaged her own theme, but at least Mr. Bradley-Martin dressed as Louis XV himself. There were various Madames de Pompadour and a few Marie Antoinettes, though her court waited upon Louis XVI. Some of the men came dressed as members of the *noblesse de l'épée* (in the French designation of the old feudal families, as opposed to the parvenue *noblesse de la robe,* ennobled for service to the crown). They actually bore arms, lumbering around with sword in scabbard. And, of course, there's always an enfant terrible; this night it was Anne Morgan, the liberal-leaning daughter of J. P. Morgan, who showed up as Pocahontas. Above all, we must ask the first question that anyone would have asked at the time: Did Mrs. Astor attend? And the answer to that is yes.

Interestingly, among the several sources of music that evening was Victor Herbert's Orchestra. It sounds like society's idea of a class hire, but in fact this first of Broadway's immortal composers was at the time all but unknown. The serious side of his career had barely got started; his first important job, as conductor of the Pittsburgh Symphony, would not begin till the following year. On the lighter side, as a composer for Broadway, Herbert had enjoyed a single hit, *The Wizard of the Nile* (1895), and this was regarded as the triumph of its star comic, Frank Moulan. In fact, Herbert's reputation was just about to break with *The Serenade* (1897), which had its world premiere out of town almost exactly on the night of the Bradley-Martin Ball. (Herbert's first lasting successes, *The Fortune Teller, Babes in Toyland, Mlle. Modiste,* and *The Red Mill,* all appeared in the following decade.)

One might want to credit the Bradley-Martins with musical taste so exquisite that they knew a coming champ when they heard one. However, one of the identifying marks of New York's aristocracy, in this era especially, was a lack of interest in the arts both high and low. These people were operagoers, of course, but not opera lovers: their musical habit consisted of looking fashionable in private boxes.

This is worth noting because—as we shall see—once New Yorkers begin to discern a more worthy elite in their artists and writers, Society will lose its hold on the public imagination. Talent, one might say, replaces family.

Still, the Bradley-Martins did create a notable happening of the Vanity Fair sort. As for criticism of such wanton spending in a time of public need, the Bradley-Martins pointed out how much work they had given to florists, dressmakers, cabmen, and the like, not to mention the players of Victor Herbert's Orchestra. Even so, the event left a sour taste, and eventually the Bradley-Martins gave it all up and emigrated to England.

Hotels, balls, and the Four Hundred: symbols of the impregnable caste system known as Society. In *The Anatomy of Revolution,* Crane Brinton defines "ruling class" as "the minority of men and women who seemed to lead dramatic lives, about whom the more exciting scandals arose, who set the fashion, who had wealth, power, position, or at least reputation, who, in short, ruled." Brinton goes on to observe that, "in a socially stable society," those not of this class "accept the leadership of those at the top of the social pyramid, and dream rather of *joining* them than of *dislodging* them."

But there must be flexibility at the top or one does, indeed, get revolution. As the lawyer Antoine Barnave bitterly noted, in pre-Revolution France, "the road [to advancement] is blocked in every direction." Nobles flocked to subversive salons and cheered the fiery democratic tirades in Beaumarchais' *Le Mariage de Figaro* (1781; first public performance 1784). Louis XVI bought the *Encyclopédie* (a second-hand set, albeit). Yet the rules of birth obtained nonetheless. To achieve "meritocracy," one must conceive first of individuals individually gifted; society's conception emphasized family. Your ancestors were your gift. Even Alice Roosevelt Longworth, daughter of Theodore Roosevelt and another of those enfants terribles, would speak intimately of "the Roosevelts" as if she knew them all right back to the little port of Nieuw Amsterdam. "Some thought the Roosevelts were entitled to coats of arms," she once said. "Others thought that they were two steps ahead of the bailiffs from an island in the Zuider Zee." It has the Alician charm of self-deprecation. Still, the attitude is dynastical.

In late-nineteenth-century America, many of those born out of society's ranks had distinguished themselves. Politicians are arguably far more of a "ruling" class than Knickerbocker nobs, and the clergy at this time held a commanding position in the culture. There was as well the *objets trouvés*, such as showman P. T. Barnum, or the writers, such as Mark Twain, the chairman of the board of American humor.

In particular, there were entertainers of various kinds, enjoying more impact than the others put together because they worked where you could see them. One such was the Pentecostal revivalist Billy Sunday. A former baseball player for the White Stockings (later White Sox), Sunday did not distinguish himself as an athlete save for unusual speed in base-running. But his preaching made him famous. In 1914, a poll run by *American* magazine placed Sunday among the top ten outstanding citizens; he tied with two other men (including Andrew Carnegie) in eighth place.

Nothing like a cleric per se, Sunday bobbed and weaved as he made his witness, using baseball metaphors and slang to turn worship into shtick just as he turned his "church" into a circus tent. Religion was big, but you had to serve it up with adventure and surprise. The master chef was General Lew Wallace, whose novel *Ben-Hur: A Tale of the Christ* (1880) preceded Billy Sunday's first revivalist tour by about ten years. The novel proved to be the biggest seller between *Uncle Tom's Cabin* and *Gone With the Wind* and, in due course, became a theatrical spectacle (1899) put on by the most powerful producing agency of the day, Klaw and Erlanger. The villain, Messala, was created by one of the first of the really big movie stars, William S. Hart, and the production roamed the nation on and off for over fifteen years, returning to New York for sizable runs in 1903, 1907, 1911, and 1916. Two elaborate film versions (1925, 1959) turned Wallace's intricate plot into a simple action fest with an inlay of religious awe, and they, too, were tremendous hits of the day.

All of this suggests an imbalance in cultural priorities: what energy from writers, showmen, performers! What an audience for not only the theatrical but the spiritual! Yet all we see aristocrats doing is giving balls. Exactly how elite *are* the elite? They're exclusive, but are they interesting? And how, precisely, do they rule? French aristocrats exercised genuine legal power of an almost medieval nature; the Astors didn't. At least Billy Sunday and Mark Twain had the power to make suggestions to a vast public about how the human condition might improve itself. That's power.

And then, suddenly, the notion of who was elite and how elitism worked underwent evolution, and the grid of power was unlocked. It took several generations, and some groups got their advancement faster than others. Nevertheless, it began to happen at about this time, and one may date it from . . . well, the Bradley-Martin ball, perhaps, in the public's rejection of its values. Or one might adduce the death of Mrs. Astor, in 1908, without question the end of an epoch. Living long enough to fall victim to the dreadful blur of the senses, she went on receiving callers and presiding over dinners, unfortunately to (in the words of social historian Lloyd Morris) "ghosts of the utmost distinction." She conversed in empty rooms. One could view this as an end to society, the etiquette feebly surviving the people themselves.

I prefer to mark notations of revolution in the popular arts, for they are quick to absorb shifts in the culture. Cole Porter was still a high-schooler at Worcester Academy when Mrs. Astor died, but eleven years later, already a Broadway veteran, he wrote his first score that was truly Porterian in style for an edition of Raymond Hitchcock's revue series, *Hitchy Koo 1919*. In "My Cozy Little Corner in the Ritz," Porter unites society with its favorite camping ground, the hotel. The song's verse promotes the sport of following the to and fro of the great world:

> Now, when I was but a baby Father took me upon his knee,
> Saying "Son, you must let Town Topics be your Bible;
> For I want my little boy to be as well brought up as can be,
> Yet never, never, never brought up for libel."
> So under the eye of Mother
> I was taught all my childhood games,
> Such as betting with baby brother
> As to dowagers' maiden names.
> From then on, I've followed the same old plan
> Of spotting the real "Who's whos."

But it wasn't Town Topics that made me a man,
For now when I want the news . . .

Town Topics was a precursor of the modern scandal rags, and its mention warns us that more than geneological data is at stake. Now comes the refrain, a gleeful schottische, as wicked Cole perpetrates the first gay double meaning in Broadway history:

I simply adorn a secluded corner,
A cozy corner in the Ritz Hotel.
When I wander each afternoon for tea,
'Cause I like to see the Kings and let the Queens see me.

Note that we aren't gazing at society but at celebrity, people they talk about because secrets have been exposed:

And if you want to meet the girl
That's got the latest complexion on her;
If you'd like to see the fellow
That your favorite prima donna
Cashes checks on
Just put your specks on
And try my cozy little corner in the Ritz.

And now it begins: "society" must give way to a more open system. Family becomes irrelevant, because ancestors are no longer as interesting as talent, and the ruling class can now include . . . well, anybody. The entertainers prosper while religion becomes supplementary, even optional. Frederick Townsend Martin, the brother of the ball-giving Bradley Martin, noted this turnabout with a certain resigned alarm. "After Mrs. Astor," he told *The New York Times,* "there was chaos."

The 1920s

1

Grand Hotel: The Round Table

The revolution collected its poster children in yet another hotel, the Algonquin, just a few months after Cole Porter claimed his cozy little corner in the Ritz. Here, at 59 West Forty-fourth Street, in Frank Case's twelve-story inn of special appeal to the performing arts and literary worlds, one gazed upon a clutch of truly familyless celebrities.

Some were the offspring of people only recently settled in America after emigration from unglamorous parts of Europe. Others came from geographical footnotes in the midwest or a city like Pittsburgh. One was even raised on a commune modeled on the Fourier phalange. Imagine the child of such eerie utopia mixing with the Astors! But the revolution thought nothing of it; if anything, it flavored one's résumé positively. It was only old Society that feared novelty.

None of the these newcomers to the great world had any money to speak of or was ever likely to—not in the way Society understood money. As Mrs. Stuyvesant Fish put it, "We are only moderately well off": because the Fishes had no more than "a few million dollars." Nor did this new group assemble in places thought elite—in the opera box or at Grace Church. Instead, the Algonquinites were theatregoers—especially on first nights, because many of them were theatre critics or knew a few—and essentially heathen. While society's leaders sought prominence within their set but anonymity elsewhere, the Algonquinites wanted to make their names, magnify them. The core group were all writers, but over the decade or so of its existence the Algonquin Round Table hosted actors, publishers, musicians, publicists, and sidekicks of various kinds. Achievers and the friends of achievers were welcome. Those whose achievement consisted in having great-great-grandfathers were not.

The whole thing got started by accident, in late 1919 or early 1920,* at a celebratory lunch more or less devoted to Alexander Woollcott. There were speeches, toasts, and insults both teasing and cutting, and everyone had a wonderful time. Someone said, "Why don't we do this every day?," and they began to, meeting in the Algonquin's main dining hall at a long table, with side tables attending as needed. Then, sensing an angle for publicity, manager Case moved the gang to the smaller Rose Room, seating them at a round table right in the center of every other diner's view. Some of the Round Table came often and some now and again, with wives, friends, or new talent ready to be Introduced and take the town. The also theres included actress beauties Margalo Gillmore, Peggy Wood, and Ina Claire; playwrights Robert E. Sherwood, Laurence Stallings, and Marc Connelly; novelist Edna Ferber; and comic Harpo Marx. But the Round Table proper counted a sextet:

ALEXANDER WOOLLCOTT, overbearing merrymaker. Best assault on Woollcott, by Gertrude Stein, who keeps interrupting: Woollcott: "People don't dispute Woollcott." Stein: "I'm not people. I'm Gertrude Stein."

ROBERT BENCHLEY, spokesman for the Little Fellow Eternally Puzzled By Life. Characteristic observation: "I seem to be behind on my parades . . ."

DOROTHY PARKER, wit, lover, and occasional failed suicide. Essential first line of a Parker short story: "Please, God, let him telephone me now."

---

* The date of the first lunch is unknown; writers treating the Round Table blithely skate around it.

GEORGE S. KAUFMAN, the fastest draw in the east in sarcasm. Typical un-Algonquinlike gallantry, in a curtain speech at the first night of *Once in a Lifetime,* a collaboration: "I would like the audience to know that eighty percent of this play is Moss Hart."

FRANKLIN P. ADAMS, the mentor, already famous in his late thirties when the others were more or less starting out. Another assault on Woollcott, who toys with one of his own books and sighs, "Ah, what is so rare as a Woollcott first edition?" Adams: "A Woollcott second edition."

and HEYWOOD BROUN, the one no one remembers anything about. Typical Broun line: "   ."

Socially breakaway to the point of mania, the Algonquinites first of all registered their importance for not only their work but their lives. Gossip was no longer relegated to *Town Topics* and the like; gossip was becoming news, even history. Some of the Algonquinites are read little if at all today, yet they remain famous for their eccentricities, and for doing things that writers don't normally do. A highly theatrical bunch, they actually put on a one-night-only revue called *No Sirree!* (1922) at a Broadway house, the Forty-Ninth Street Theatre. They took over on a Sunday evening, when the regular tenant, the Russian potpourri *Chauve-Souris,* wasn't playing. Some 750 guests and *their* guests—no critics were asked—sat through the usual revue of spoofs and specialties, but what a cast! The opening chorus was sung by Woollcott, Benchley, Kaufman, Adams, Connelly, and John Peter Toohey. There was a goof on a recent Theatre Guild offering, Andryeyef's *He Who Gets Slapped,* as "He Who Gets Flapped." He was the six-foot-seven-inch Robert E. Sherwood in straw hat and cane, dwarfing a line of flappers in gingham that included Helen Hayes and Tallulah Bankhead; the girls sang lyrics by Dorothy Parker. Benchley created a comic classic in his bumbling "Treasurer's Report." ("Mr. Rossiter, unfortunately our treasurer—or rather Mr. Rossiter, our *treasurer, unfortunately* is confined at his home tonight. . . .") Opera baritone Reinald Werrenrath sang "Johnny Weaver," on writer John Van Alstyne Weaver, the Algonquin's resident Extremely

Cute Boy and later Peggy Wood's husband. A. A. Milne's play *Mr. Pim Passes By* got the "Down with British Whimsey!" treatment. And, in a bow to Ziegfeld, Beatrice Herford took the next-to-closing* as "The Algonquin Girl."

Staged as "An anonymous entertainment by the Vicious Circle of the Hotel Algonquin," *No Sirree!* led to a full-fledged Broadway production, *The '49ers,* this time with sets, salaries, and critics. But it was still an amateur night, however full of personality. The non-participating Woollcott, who hated it, likened it to "a dinner consisting of five courses of perfectly splendid lemon meringue pie."

The '49ers bombed. Yet it is worth observing that, of its cast, Kaufman, Connelly, and Benchley all distinguished themselves later as performers on Broadway, as did Woollcott as well. The Algonquinites were showoffs, trading in eccentricity in life as well as in work, like actors who never quite made it to the wings.

For instance, wasn't Benchley always "on," always that bumbling treasurer? The word for him is "mild"; but it's the only word. It was probably Benchley more than anyone else who infused *The New Yorker* magazine, in its early years, with that zealotry of the trivial that has haunted its reputation ever since—that feeling that its writers seemed unaware of global cataclysm but fell to pieces when they had to change a typewriter ribbon. For *Vanity Fair,* the old *Life,* and *The New Yorker,* Benchley would prosper in the "casual," on problems with shoelaces or taxis or "Your Boy and His Dog." These pieces cannot even be called frivolous, because they lack the focus that, say, Noël Coward could bring to rhapsodizing about silly things. Benchley's pieces are curlicues of smoke, a way of writing without saying anything.

---

* The penultimate offering on a vaudeville bill, invariably taken by the top headliner or, on the small-town circuits, the least terrible act available. The last offering was known as The Chaser—something grisly, to "chase" the public out of the house, freeing seats for the next show. The next-to-closing survives in the concept of musical comedy's Eleven O'Clock Song, an exhibition piece before the last scene, reserved for the star. In old-fashioned shows it tends to the extraneous, such as *Bells Are Ringing*'s "I'm Going Back" or, when two stars share the spotlight, *DuBarry Was a Lady*'s "Friendship." The reconstructed musical absorbs the convention more thematically, as in *Gypsy*'s "Rose's Turn."

Benchley in person made the whole act charming all the same. Coward's art is brittle because it's a pose; Benchley isn't faking. Nor is his good friend Dorothy Parker, whose act was Miss Helpless, always short of the carfare home. Taxis seemed to bring out extremes in this set: George S. Kaufman, who made his act out of being imperturbable even when most biting, would become choleric in his dealings with cab drivers.

Yet Kaufman handled anyone else with ease, maintaining the smoothest irony in the business. Out of town with the Hollywood spoof *Merton of the Movies,* co-written with Marc Connelly, Kaufman found his partner holding tight to a laugh line that got no laughs. Night after night, the line went dud as Connelly kept explaining how it couldn't miss stopping the show as the public roared in delight. "There's only one thing we can do," Kaufman finally said. "We've got to call the audience in tomorrow morning for a ten o'clock rehearsal."

Oddly, these newfangled Round Tablers with their disdain—perhaps simply disregard—for received values could be conservative in their own way. Franklin P. Adams' famous newspaper column The Conning Tower actually anticipated the Internet blog in its printing of contributions from outsiders. Post comments here. Yet Adams himself wrote in an imitation of Samuel Pepys, complete with outdated syntax and bewigged observations. Also oddly, the Jewish Algonquinites were unbelievers yet married strictly within the parish. Further, when Kaufman and his wife, Beatrice, adopted a child, they applied to a Jewish organization for the baby. But if one has no use for the religion qua se, why make a point of expanding one's family under its jurisdiction?

The outstanding conservative in the pack—and, if he had anything to say about it, its leader—was Woollcott, a figure out of a vanished age. Not the nineteenth century but the tenth: a front-parlor pasha, accusing and tiffing, now cajoling his favorites and now consigning the disobedient to an oubliette. In small-town America, Woollcott would have been chased out of the barber shop by the real men, not because he resembled a big fat owl but because he was an angry queen *avant le temps,* sarcastically abusive of friends and enemies alike and as eager to boost a passion as demolish a peeve.

You've met him. He's Sheridan Whiteside, the man who came to dinner in the Kaufman and Hart play. Mind you, the authors didn't write a version of Woollcott. They wrote Woollcott: domineering yet easily hurt, not only manipulative but manipulating with evil relish, exploding one's direst vulnerabilities then pretending it was a harmless jest. After taking all this in, you notice that he is, after all, innovative in one area: there are no women in his life in the romantic sense. There are the Algonquin women, of course: to play games with and fill out the dinner table. Or perhaps simply to charm the other men.

Was he homosexual? He was certainly gay: in style. But did he go for men? A rumor about some childhood disease removing him from consideration as a begetter of children was the excuse fronting his bachelorhood. But did one need an excuse? This was the age of the *mariage blanc*. It was almost the rage. Many a show-biz couple mated without mating—the Cole Porters, the Lunts, the Katharine Cornells. And everyone knew that, early on, the Kaufmans had stopped bundling in an open marriage without a thought of divorce. "Beatrice is always picking up these sensitive, ambitious young Jews," Kaufman told Woollcott, who promptly replied, "Sometimes she marries them."

So he's worldly, isn't he, our Woollcott? Infirmity was not likely the reason why he did not consort with women. He didn't, either, with men, though he seems to have had a very physical crush on Harpo Marx, who was not unappealing when out of his getup. Woollcott consorted, really, with himself: with his micromanaging of the getaway weekend, with his running commentary on croquet championships and poker marathons, with his grand entrance as drama critic, complete with swirling cape, Count Dracula first-nighting. And, above all, with his devotion to great traditions in the arts, the *old* masters or those who, like the Lunts, found new ways to make good old-fashioned theatre.

The only really new thing about Woollcott was his status as one of New York's first Famous Queens. Supplementary Algonquinites John V. A. Weaver and Peggy Wood married because they were young and beautiful and gifted. It was the kind of fairy tale that movies invent but untypical of the Algonquin circle and unavailable to Woollcott. His story was that of the Difficult Celebrity, an invention of the 1920s, of Manhattan, of the Algonquin. Here was a new format for the elite, because the Round Tablers were not only peculiar but insular and provincial—not just New Yorkers but the essence of that address. Kaufman always said that he would travel only as far as would allow him to get "back to Broadway and Forty-Fourth by midnight."

But then, the culture in general was becoming Manhattan-centric at this time. Except for cinema, the entertainment media were headquartered in New York—popular music, for example. As a business, American song lived on Tin Pan Alley, the nickname for a block of Twenty-eighth Street where most of the music publishers auditioned and signed up new ware. The acculturation of radio in the 1920s and the arrival of the talkie at decade's end produced, for the first time, a truly national music, vitalized by the arrival of the Gershwins, Rodgers and Hart, Cole Porter. Irving Berlin and Jerome Kern had turned up somewhat earlier, leading an evolution away from, say, "Ta-Ra-Ra-Boom-De-Ay" and toward something like "Night and Day."

Thus, the first of the movies' all-sound features with song—the first Hollywood musical ever, released in early 1929—is called *The Broadway Melody*. It opens with overhead footage of Manhattan's skyscrapers to the strains of the kind of music they're not going to write any more, Victor Herbert's "The Streets of New York." We move thence to the Gleason Music Publishing Company, situated of course in Tin Pan Alley, and amid the cacaphony we listen for the next tune to define the age. Which will it be? A soprano tries out something on the dippy side, so that isn't it. Piano, guitar, and clarinet sample something hot for a men's singing trio, but the singing's just a little *too* trio. Or something. That isn't it. An ebullient sister act sways to a lively ballad—but before we can collect it, Mr. Gleason himself appears in the main hallway. (This is in fact actor James Gleason in a small unbilled role, for Gleason is famous for his wise-guy attitudes, what they call a "New York part.") Gleason's going to let our male lead, Charles King, plug a new one he calls "The Broadway Melody." You only get one chance with these things, so King instructs the pianist, "The second chorus—a little jazz, a little pep, and everything. Ya know?"

Now everyone crowds in to hear, and if the verse is restrained, the chorus immediately starts swinging. The instrumental trio from before sits in, winging it; one of the ebullient sisters, mesmerized, takes on the rhythm as if a second skin, moving within the sound. Even the dippy soprano gets with it. "No skies of gray on the Great White Way!" King exults, as the gang around him revels in the latest show-biz thing: a song to sweep the nation, stimulate and unite it. That's the Broadway melody, and "Hot dog!" King cries, buttoning the number. That's the tune of the age.

So how provincial were Kaufman and his kind, in fact, in seeing New York as an identity as well as an address? Not only the arts but the press as well was centered in Manhattan, and all of the Algonquites were journalists. Today, we think of them rehearsing their ad libs as if reserving their spots in anecdote collections. But America thought of them as newspaper and magazine bylines. They weren't reporters, of course. They were opinion makers, versed in arcane matters and, in the new Manhattan manner, "cracking wise." It was a novel style, postwar and seemingly born overnight in 1919, the year historians love to conjure with: a twelvemonth of disillusionment, experimentation, and preparation for the Jazz Age, history as fun.

Perhaps there's too much fun in the concept of a suite of hotel jokesters polishing off a piece, a play, a novel only to rush off to the real work of the day, lunch at the Round Table. Oddly, the Algonquinite's idea of a vacation was to move the Round Table to a rustic setting and thus spend one's "getaway" still being bossed around by Alexander Woollcott. Only now he was barking at everyone from a canoe. Even more oddly, a national readership envied them this life. Like Cole Porter tagging the culture with the names of the fabled great Whom You Must Know, the Round Table created for those who were interested a kind of national get-together of habitués with all New York for neighborhood. Fittingly, one of Woollcott's several radio shows was called *The Town Crier,* and came complete with clanging bell and "Hear ye! Hear ye!"

One wonders how these people got any writing done. Edna Ferber dropped in to lunch but seldom, because it was such a superb waste of concentration. George S. Kaufman broke up his collaboration with Marc Connelly because it was Round Tabling that thrilled Connelly, not playwrighting. The two men wrote seven Broadway titles, including two smash-hit comedies, two musicals, and *Beggar on Horseback* (1924), a bizarre breakaway piece to set beside *The Threepenny Opera* and *Follies*. Kaufman and Connelly were making theatre history, yet Connelly kept retreating to that Table. It was always something—a costume to be built for the next soigné masquerade, or Margalo Gillmore's cat died and I promised to help bury it. So and so's arriving from Europe; so and so's leaving for Europe. Come on, George, we've got to say Bon Voyage!

Kaufman never quit the Round Table exactly. But he didn't let it slow him up. In fact, his next writing partner was Edna Ferber, who had no use for Margalo Gillmore's cats, dead or alive. Ferber even warned more than one starstruck youngster away from equating the quipping sweepstakes with achieving. It was as if Ferber had been seized by a premonition and visualized the non-existent second act of F. Scott Fitzgerald's life.

Some in the entertainment and publishing worlds looked disdainfully on the Round Tablers, whatever they were up to, art of life or art of work. George M. Cohan, who liked his men real and his women cooking lunch instead of ordering it in a hotel, called it "a Round Table without a square man at it," and Peggy Wood's newspaperman father thought it "a collection of first-rate second-raters." Others simply resented the Algonquinite habit of praising each other in book and play review and the like, however tart they might be at Table.

What no one ever mentions is the quality of the food, which—except for a reliable pastry cart—could be called "pleasantly vacuous." The cuisine wasn't bad, but no matter what one ordered, it all tasted the same. There was a ton of it: the menu offered everything you ever heard of, but also sauerkraut juice, huckleberries, Kuroki salad, stewed rhubarb, acidophilus milk. Just the choice of potatoes is somewhat boggling: cottage fried, lyonnaise, julienne, au gratin, French fried, mashed, fried sweets, candied sweets, hash browned, hashed in cream, and "Saratoga chips," the old term for the crisps you get in a bag.

Nowadays, when the word "legendary" has been debased to mean simply "well-known in show business," one hesitates to use it when discussing anything short of the Golden Fleece. But the Algonquin Round

Table has truly become legendary in its vast popular recollection, its store of riposte readily quoted, its interaction of hyper personalities, all still vivid when so much else of the twenties fame-shop inventory is forgot. Is Teapot Dome legendary? Peaches and Daddy Browning?*

What exactly was the Round Table's influence? First, its meeting of men and women on equal terms was, as I've said, unusual for the day, a kind of photo op for the Nineteenth Amendment to the Constitution. This was the one that gave women the vote, proposed on June 4, 1919 and ratified on August 26, 1920—just as the Round Table was getting organized. After it, as their freedom of movement expanded, more women went into law and politics, and the notion of the genteel Lady Novelist with her three names and fluttery attitudes began to vanish.

Then, too, there was the secular makeup of the group. They were not opposed to religion; they simply lived without it. Yet they somehow gave one the impression that the many freedoms they espoused—freedom to defy taboo, freedom to have sex without marriage, freedom to lunch—were bound up in a central freedom to giggle at convention. And religious observance, in the 1920s, was still conventional for most Americans.

This marked a break with the *Ben-Hur* and Billy Sunday generation, whose art was seasoned with Christian references, whether in the Biblical language of silent-movie intertitles or prayer-like utterances in fictional narratives. The Round Table was not unique in this—one thinks, for instance, of the only somewhat veiled criticism of the church that runs through Mark Twain's *A Connecticut Yankee in King Arthur's Court*. And Twain, remember, was a spokesman for America, quoted, popular, and beloved. Still, the suavely agnostic nature of the Algonquinite world-

---

* Teapot Dome, Wyoming was one of two federally-owned oil fields (the other being Elk Hills, California) that were handed over for private development through pay-offs to officers of Warren G. Harding's cabinet. Harding's Watergate, the scandal revealed an administration corrupt almost right the way through. It's a major piece of the American chronicle, yet the average citizen does not hear content in the words "Teapot Dome" the way he does in "Watergate." On the other matter, Daddy Browning was old and rich and Peaches was ripe; the tabloids had an outing on their affair.

view pointed toward a utopia liberated not so much from Christian text as from the hypocritical bullies who exploit it.

In fact, something oddly secular was stirring in the culture generally, something that had no connection to the kind of people who wrote novels or put on plays. It was a wish to modernize religion, even consumerize it. Bruce Barton's *The Man Nobody Knows: A Discovery of the Real Jesus,* a huge bestseller in the mid-1920s, partakes of this remodeled Christianity. The son of a Presbyterian minister, Barton views Jesus as a precursor of the businessman—as, even, a small-town Chamber of Commerce go-getter. Chapter titles scan the Christ as "The Executive" ("He had the born leader's gift for seeing powers in men of which they themselves were often almost unconscious"), "The Outdoor Man," "The Sociable Man," "His Method," "His Advertisements," and so on. Naturally, Barton reaches a bit. "He was the great advertiser of his own day" turns out to equate haranguing folks in the market square with concocting an insinuating ad campaign to start people smoking cigarettes. But then, it was Barton's father who preached God's word; Barton himself was one of the named partners in the Madison Avenue firm of B.B.D.&O. Thus, he helps himself to misleading italics in the book's epigraph, from Luke 2:49, "Wist ye not that I must be about my Father's *business*?" The Bible is not referring to moneymaking at this point in the Gospel.

The Man Nobody Knows is not an impious work, and, as Barton says, "Success is always exciting; we never grow tired of asking what and how." Still, in rating Christianity's leader for His organizational and manipulative skills, Barton was board-rooming the spiritual, co-opting myth and belief as a front for toothpaste blurbs. Does this popularize religion or coarsen it? Give the Round Table credit for their neutrality: they didn't have religion, and they didn't despoil religion.

Perhaps most immediately, the Algonquinites aided in the launching of *The New Yorker,* America's greatest magazine and the very reflection of its artistic and intellectual community. Not that the Algonquinites contributed much in the first years after its founding, by Harold Ross, in 1925. They were supposed to. They had promised to. But the magazine was financially shaky, and the gang had paying gigs elsewhere in publishing. Now it's time for one of Dorothy Parker's more famous quotes: Ross asks why she hasn't come down to the office to write a little something, and she replies, "Someone was using the pencil."

Ross was a Round Tabler himself, especially at the gambling sessions, known variously by prank adherents but most officially as The Thanatopsis Literary and Inside Straight Poker Club. One of George M. Cohan's real men, Ross has been mocked by four generations of writers for his bushy hair, eccentric locutions, obsessions with things like commas, and clueless bemusement at the nonconformist behavior that the Round Table took for granted. In a typical exchange, somebody reports that Ross has taken up the sport of tobogganing. General hilarity. "What," asks one, "does Harold Ross look like tobogganing?" "Well," comes the answer, "you know what he looks like *not* tobogganing . . ."

However, Ross singlehandedly created and developed the nation's most literary publication, one that grew as its writers grew. This is extraordinary; magazines almost always impose themselves upon their writers. Think of *The New Republic*'s official Positions, of *Time*speak. *The New Yorker* breathed with its bylines, letting them dictate the positions and speech. *The New Yorker* was surprising, too; what other major magazine was? Publishing Shirley Jackson's barbaric guignol "The Lottery" (in 1949) in the weekly fiction slot, as if it were just another fine read, an O'Hara or Salinger, is something only *The New Yorker* would have dared. Ross was still its editor at the time—so how much mockery does he deserve, after all?

Most of all, the gathering of the Algonquin clan emphasized a meritocracy as the elite. In place of Ward McAllister's Patriarchs giving balls, the Round Tablers were centering the public discourse on art and achievement. Yes, much of it was shallow—Benchley and his shoelaces. Yet it was this very personalized approach to writing that pointed toward the more richly autobiographical art of F. Scott Fitzgerald and Ernest Hemingway. Just as Mark Twain seems to build novels around people he knows, Fitzgerald, Hemingway, and many others write about themselves by other means. It freed fiction from the academic notion that authors should be self-effacing, like eavesdroppers. What, in their own stories? The nineteenth-century novel, from Thackeray to Tolstoy, teaches otherwise: the author is his novel.

The Round Table took this one step further: the author is his life. These writers re-embodied the authorial voice, merging it with the authorial experience to create the art of being on-site when the anecdotes occur. Yet for all their foolishness, these were intellectual leaders with standards. "They were ruthless toward charlatans, toward the pompous and the mentally and artistically dishonest," Edna Ferber wrote. "They had a terrible integrity about their work and a boundless ambition."

And, remember, she was not a fan—not to mention her on-and-off feud with Woollcott. She put up with him to go first-nighting on the back half of his complimentary critic's seats. Still, given two such highly-strung fiddles, one or the other would snap and they wouldn't speak for a year. One day in 1932, Ferber decided to make peace with Alec and, by the by, see what the old crowd was up to, and she made her way at lunchtime to the Rose Room.

There was the Table: occupied by a family of tourists. Frank Case hadn't turned against his prize exhibition. He simply had nobody else to seat there, for none of the knights had shown up. The Round Table was over.

2

Dorothy Parker and Edna Ferber:
The Loneliness of Smarty

One of them was lazy, selfish, irritatingly vague about responsibilities, treacherous, charming, needy, and sort of pretty. She wrote of ephemeral characters in a moment or two of life, all in little forms—light verse and short stories—and she lived by doing the unexpected all the time without knowing why. *Impetuous.*

She married her first husband on little knowledge or even affection, and married her second husband twice. Although she had no response to music, she wrote one set of lyrics to the most musical of shows, Leonard Bernstein's *Candide*. She became a recluse in an apartment fetid with booze and dog evacuations, yet she was irritated that Truman Capote didn't invite her to his ball. And, in a final gesture of non sequitur, she left her estate to Martin Luther King Jr.

The other was wedded to her writing, responsible and precise, cross as a snapping turtle, unwilling to charm, and not pretty. "Work, walk, read" was her motto. As a novelist, she wrote of big characters, Heroes and Heroines, biting off chunks of Americana in sagas that pass the sweeping into the epic. As regulated as a grandfather's clock, she led exactly the life everyone expected her to, without a single surprise. She even died in character: nearly eighty-three years old, physically weakened yet still hard and unyielding and planning a novel about another chunk of Americana, the Indian. *Imperious.*

Neither Dorothy Parker nor Edna Ferber was happy, but at least they were famous. They still are: except for George S. Kaufman, mainly for two of his collaborations with Moss Hart, *You Can't Take It With You* and *The Man Who Came To Dinner,* Parker and Ferber are the only members of the Algonquin circle to survive their age in any real sense. Woollcott and Benchley still have Names, of course, but as bylines they stand largely unread. By contrast, Ferber's novels keep getting reprinted, and their adaptations are very much with us; *Show Boat* is the Great (Old) American Musical and the movie of *Giant* is so young it stars the American Peter Pan, James Dean. And Parker is by now an icon, creator of the Dorothy Parker Type with the Dorothy Parker Attitude spouting the Dorothy Parker Wisecrack. The last is unique because Parker's wit plays flip with the truth, turning it into a gag without robbing it of point. She's not only honest but lovable, as when a concerned friend hustles the lushly middle-aged Parker off to a meeting of Alcoholics Anonymous, which she enjoys. *Good!* Now, will she join the group?

"Certainly not," says Parker. "They want me to stop *now!*"

In the 1920s, the best line of work for a woman who wished to make something of herself was performer, heiress, or writer. Writing was easiest, because there was so much publishing going on that one could fall into it without ambition, without vocation, even without talent. Why did you become a writer? Because it's there.

However, Parker may have had a reason to write. Some authors of fiction create to sweeten their lives with fantasy versions. Parker did the opposite, creating to confide to the point of embarrassment. She wrote tight in a day when windy was the going style, and she wrote small, as I've said—a breakup, a missed chance, ambivalent feelings on a living-room davenport. After her first book, a poetry collection called *Enough Rope* (1926), jumped onto and stayed on the bestseller list as poetry collections never do, her publisher, Viking, begged for a novel. Typically giving into the demands of men while telling others what maddening dolts they all were, she began a novel called *Sonnets in Suicide, or The Life of John Knox.* That is, she began typing doodle pages and spending hours getting the alignment of her name in an upper corner of the page just right. Parker would never complete a novel, or even start one, because her art was little bursts of despair at a world made of unappreciative men. It's not that a novel was out of her reach but that a novel was unnecessary, because she told her tales right on the quick. Stop the presses—this just in.

In fact, the precision and clarity with which Parker told her tales marks her as a craftsman where her colleagues were simply garrulous. Our friends Benchley and Woollcott often give the impression of friends who tell stories without ever filtering out the unnecessary. We all have them: conversations are repeated verbatim, nugatory incidents delineated in real time. On the contrary, Parker never clears her throat, does "evocations," or details trifles. She is uncuttable, and that is highest praise.

Interestingly, all three wrote theatre criticism, though only Woollcott was knowledgeable; he seems to have seen and remembered everything from starry classics to the most uneventful revue potpourri. Benchley and Parker are the flimsiest of amateurs. Woollcott can place a production or actor in theatre history; the other two mostly giggle. Every now and then, Benchley notes something, as when he christens Ethel Barrymore's vocalized acting "the Episcopalian Method . . . each line is chanted like a response, with no differentiation in tone between lines." Or, at the height of the revolution from hoofing to Dance in thirties musicals: "For me, a little ballet goes a long way, and there seems to be no such thing as 'a little ballet.'"

Still, most of Benchley's theatre writing is babble, and Woollcott, while knowledgeable, is unbearably verbose. In the fall of 1923, Eleonora Duse farewell-toured to New York for one night at the Metropolitan Opera House and some matinées at the Century Theatre. Huge halls, rapt public, much To Do. The Met performance sold out at over $30,000, the most profitable single evening in New York theatre history. The repertory was Ibsen and three modern Italians, and Woollcott was there:

Well, Duse has come and gone. Somehow this indefatigable playgoer, in a month not altogether destitute of other theatrical entertainment, managed to see eight of her ten performances. After the last one the great audience stayed on and on in the theater, seemingly loath to say good-by.

At that performance your correspondent gave up his own seats in order that John Barrymore and Madge Kennedy might sit at Duse's feet, and for the surrendered tickets he received a premium rather richer than those demanded by the regular scalpers along Broadway. It was the sight of those two in tears at the rueful beauty and great tragic truth of this Italian woman.

All those words! And half the paragraph was about performers in the audience! Little in the entire piece tells what exactly made Duse so wonderful. Oh, wait: it was something "the fairies had whispered in that third class Italian railway train in which Duse was born one October day sixty-four years ago."

Strangely, the author of these quaint effusions prepared for his press pass as a war correspondent, Sgt. Woollcott of the U.S. Army's newspaper, *Stars and Stripes.* But then, perhaps Woollcott saw the war as a form of theatre. He claimed that American offensives to push the Germans back from their lines along the Western Front "remind you of a big first night because you see everyone you know."

Dorothy Parker's theatre reviews couldn't have been more different— as if she was not just a better writer but the very opposite of Woollcott in every particular. Like many New Yorkers on the guest list, she first-nighted less out of love of theatre than for the social advantages. It was a relief to get out of the apartment, and one could always go out drinking afterward. Anyway, even without Woollcott's store of theatregoing experience, Parker sensed when to praise and when to ridicule. Smart people always seem to know things without actually *knowing* them: it's a matter of being, if not educated, au courant.

Thus, writing up the Barrymore Brothers in Sem Benelli's melodrama *The Jest,* Parker praises, singling out John's "morbid ecstasies" and Lionel's "roars of rage and reverberating bellows of geniality." Someone or other has warned Parker that Robert Edmond Jones' visual pictures are The Latest, and she duly notes. Then, moving away from the play itself to a world she really does know—the land of fascinating personalities—she writes, "One must present it to the Barrymores; they are, indubitably, *quelque* family."

In another part of the forest, at the Century for the spectacular called *Aphrodite,* Parker ridicules:

> Most of the feminine members of the cast were recruited from the Century Roof, where they were trained for emotional roles in ancient Egyptian dramas by a course of dancing around between tables, singing "Smiles." Then, too, there is Etienne Girardot as physician to the Queen of Egypt, [wearing] much the same make-up that he used in *Charley's Aunt*. . . . There is even a brand-new drop curtain . . . painted with the mystic letters AΦPOΔITH, which most of the audience take to be the Greek word for "asbestos."*

Parker's having fun and so are we, but *Aphrodite* only returns us to the salient Algonquinite act: wisecracking as performance art. "It *was* the twenties," Parker explained two generations after, "and we had to be smarty." *Aphrodite,* an import from France, is that odd mixture of art and kitsch that was about to go out of style in the West while America revitalized it, briefly, in overbuilt productions created for massive auditoriums like the Century or the Hippodrome. It might have been intriguing to learn what these colossal offerings were like in the days before miking, when performers had to hurl their portrayals at the public. John Barrymore played the last weeks of his Hamlet, after Broadway and London, at the Manhattan Opera House, five times the size of the Sam

---

*The Century Roof was the typical "extra" house erected literally on the theatre building's roof, usually for light fare in the summer. Most were at least partly unenclosed, open to the breeze. Roof shows could be anything—the first black musical performed on Broadway, for instance, or children's entertainment. Nonetheless, the very term "roof show" betokened a music-and-girls revue. Etienne Girardot was famous for playing Lord Fancourt Babberley in the farce *Charley's Aunt;* the "makeup" Parker speaks of is a drag disguise. *Charley's Aunt* separated the transvestite business from the title character; the musical version, *Where's Charley?* (1948) conflated the two for Ray Bolger. And the asbestos curtain was used as a precaution against theatre fires, which usually started when sparks from lighting equipment ignited scenery. Lowering the asbestos curtain contained the flames and protected the audience. One sees these curtains occasionally in old movies, with the key word spelled out in block letters. Cartoons tweaked the usage with curtains reading, WE DO ASBESTOS WE CAN.

H. Harris Theatre, where it had opened. Further, these productions enjoyed considerable musical accompaniment, as if they were spoken operas. What were they like? Parker won't tell, because, as Alexander Woollcott put it, "that bird only sings when she's unhappy."

Unhappy in love: because, again, Parker wanted to write about what she knew and how she felt about it. That did not include theatre, but rather something like her story "Dusk Before Fireworks," in which a young woman tries to pin a young man down: *Is* he serious? He is: just not about her. "He was a long young man," Parker tells us, "broad at the shoulders and chest and narrow everywhere else, and his muscles obeyed him at the exact instant of command." What other writer of the day was so candidly pictorial about the Beautiful Male? But if she doesn't make you *see,* how can you understand the stakes she plays for? Hobie, she calls him. "His voice was intimate as the rustle of sheets, and he kissed easily."

As for the girl, Kit, "There was a tension about her mouth and unease along her brow, and her eyes looked wearied and troubled." Now the damnation: "The gentle dusk became her." Yes, like mourning becomes Electra. And the damn phone keeps ringing, and *every single time* it's another woman. Finally, Kit storms out with "You damned—you damned *stallion!*"

"Dusk Before Fireworks" lasts one afternoon in a hotel in Paris, but "Big Blonde," Parker's most famous and anthologized story, is a biography in thirty pages. Naturally, it tells yet more of woman's unhappiness at the hands of men, complete with a suicide attempt. Writing didn't come easy to Parker, but such tales as these were less difficult than anything else, because she didn't have to make anything up. That was why Parker never did Write That Novel. Those detailed narratives are so filled with . . . details. So stocked with other people and their stupid problems. Parker's own stupid problems were art enough. For "Dusk Before Fireworks," all she needed was one of those male Kewpie dolls and the telephone bell.

Ironically, while Parker has become iconic as a woman who broke out and accomplished, and while she wedded herself unquestioningly to every leftist cause (even unto affirming the validity of Stalin's show trials), she was no feminist. What, with all those Hobies running around? Yes, they were jilting machines; but so *pretty!* Parker's twenties circle included a few members of the Lucy Stone League, women who deemed it unnecessary to take on a man's surname upon marriage. Wasn't it hard enough taking on the man? Harold Ross' wife, Jane, née Grant, was called not Jane Ross but Jane Grant. She bobbed her hair, too.

Dorothy Parker wouldn't have been caught dead in her maiden name. She was née Rothschild, and "Dorothy Rothschild" suggested a girl from the neighborhood. An anybody. Marrying Edwin Pond Parker II turned her into "Dorothy Parker"—and *that* sounds like someone!

We wonder what Edna Ferber thought of the Lucy Stone option. Certainly, Ferber never met an issue she was neutral toward, and she didn't have to think twice. But Ferber never wed. She saw through the Hobies even while building them bigger than Parker did, in those monumental Ferber romances with monumental titles. *Show Boat. Cimarron. Saratoga Trunk.* And listen to the heroes' names: Gaylord Ravenal. Yancey Cravat. Clint Maroon. Beautiful and faithless, like Hobie, but big men, not only in size but in the grandeur of their self-conception. They're gamblers making magnificent gestures, such as betting down to the last chip on a bluff or building an empire. You don't find these men lolling about a hotel room answering girl friends' phone calls.

This is because Ferber saw men not autobiographically but historically. She saw women that way, too, often making them the protagonist, the central actor, of the work. *This* could be called feminism, but only on a technicality, because like many writers of her time Ferber saw ism thinking as malarkey à la mode. It was wishful thinking, propaganda, lies. You didn't hear Ferber doting on Moscow show trials. Anyway, Ferber wasn't using fiction to pursue an agenda. She was as caught up in her yarns as her readers were, playing make believe about America and how it got that way. Chicago and the midwestern prairie: *So Big* (1924). The Mississippi: *Show Boat* (1926). The old west: *Cimarron* (1930). Northeastern Society as Ward McAllister Had Found It: *Saratoga Trunk* (1941). The new west: *Giant* (1952). Ferber wasn't writing a map; she was singing the American experiences—farming culture in *So Big,* the theatre in *Show Boat,* journalism created on a single printing press in a frontier town in *Cimarron,* landgrabbing, crashing Society, oilrigging, goldrushing. How far from Dorothy Parker can one get? And to Ferber's "Work, walk, read" Parker's motto might have been "Dish, drink, fuck." It doesn't matter how much work you accomplish, because your masterpiece is you.

Ferber's masterpieces were fairy tales of America, which tells us why Parker dated and married while Ferber may not have had as much as a summer romance. Ferber was a professional professional, dedicated to not just her work but her oeuvre. Parker lived like a member of the leisure class, forever going out when she wasn't praying by the telephone. And neither woman was easy to know. Ferber, as gracious as nails, ripped into fans who accosted her in public. "I don't owe them anything," she would declare, when chided. Parker took compliments at a certain polite remove—though "What fresh hell is this?" she would murmur, as a grinning enthusiast approached.

Parker's background, centered on one of those unhappy families and based in New York City and its surroundings, was ordinary, the kind biographies need to race through in as few pages as possible. Ferber, however, logged unusual experiences while attaining the metropolis. Her family had fled the Chicago fire to fetch up in Kalamazoo, Michigan, where Ferber was born. Raised then in Appleton, Wisconsin, Ferber set out as a stringer for the local newspaper—but not genderized in Society tattle or an etiquette column. Ferber was a *reporter.* She learned, she said, "to read what lay behind the look that veiled people's faces . . . to observe, to remember." In short: "I was the town scourge."

After trying Milwaukee at its *Journal,* Ferber made it to Chicago and started publishing fiction, especially short stories about a traveling saleswoman named Emma McChesney. They made her name, and *So Big,* in 1924, won her the Pulitzer Prize. The far more expansive bestsellers *Show Boat* and *Cimarron* followed, and by then Ferber had become a key player in the pop-culture industry of the Hollywood Bestseller. This consists of a big-money book, sometimes followed by a big-money play, and absolutely succeeded by a big-money movie and, possibly, a remake or two. Ferber's titles in particular were a movie mogul's dream children, with their PR tags of "sprawling," "romantic," and "the life and death of an era." Tragedy at its best!

Culturally the inferior of literature and theatre at this time, Hollywood maintained a resentful respect for New Yorkers. The only thing that topped a big hit movie was a big hit movie based on a novel—especially a new one, because you could cast it with movie stars. Charles Dickens and people like that were good for prestige, but then you had to hire *actors*. Colin Clive and the like.

Cimarron was all-American and the third talkie to win a Best Picture Oscar. There were nominations as well for its leads, Richard Dix and Irene Dunne; its director, Wesley Ruggles; and its writer, Howard Estabrook—and still Ferber thought Hollywood the dumbest place on earth. She was there as seldom as possible. "It has no virility," she thought. "It sprang from almost pure vulgarity." Universal's Carl Laemmle, who made *Show Boat* that year's Picture of the Lot, was so unimpressive that Ferber's description of him suggests the disdainful telegramese of early *Time* magazine: "gnomelike little Oshkosh storekeeper."

Dorothy Parker spent years in Hollywood—not being adapted but actively writing scripts. She didn't like it there, either. However, unlike the bestselling Ferber, Parker and her byline-sharing husband, Alan Campbell, needed the money. "It always takes more to live on than what you earn," Parker once complained, in the batty yet irrefutable logic of Lorelei Lee. Parker and Campbell, too, got an Oscar nomination, for the Janet Gaynor–Fredric March *A Star Is Born* (sharing the citation with Robert Carson), and Campbell enjoyed going Hollywood because of the plentiful opportunity for work.

Still, Parker and Ferber were New York Women, used to spending afterhours with an intelligentsia, not riffraff drawn from the dirt roads and soda fountains of rural America because of their looks—not to mention the Oshkosh storekeepers who managed the place. Ferber even thought Hollywood "not American," about the worst insult she could throw at it. The movies manufactured visionary stylings of what the nation meant *as a* nation. Yet Hollywood itself had no content. There was no place there: it was one big movie studio, all sets and lighting. Orange groves: a set. Downtown: a set. There were film crews there every day. When a series of sex-and-drugs scandals threatened to destroy the movie business with a bluenose boycott, reporters applied to Hollywood sage Elinor Glyn (in more *Time*speak: gala English love-plot novelist) to ask what will happen next. Capitulation? A change in tone? More scandals? Quoth Madame Glyn: "Whatever will bring in the most money will happen."

There we remark a salient difference between New York and "coast" culture. Parker was righter than she knew when she observed that you never make enough to live on: in her Manhattan, you didn't. You wrote those savvy little poems and stories not because they'd make you rich but because, if you didn't, no one would know how you felt, including yourself. One almost suspects that Parker got into the more lucrative work of screenwriting simply because, once one showed up at one's office in the writers' building, one didn't really have to accomplish anything to qualify for a payday. Freelancers have to write.

Isn't that why so many New York writers put in at least some time on studio salary: because New Yorking their way through a writing career gave them little material security? Those "sellouts" we sometimes read about who gave up Real Writing for movie work weren't pushing for Enron swag. They just wanted room to live in and their health care paid for. Even Ferber, an outstanding earner—and an avid reader of publisher's royalty statements—never wrote for money instead of love.

Oddly, for all Ferber's insights into the national panorama, she is at her best on the intimate scale, watching the interaction of her characters in what they need and what they cannot say plainly—the look, as she noted, that veils people's faces. She writes about feelings, not about history. *So Big,* telling of an idealistic and independent young woman resisting for life a social system that takes women for granted, is like a serious *Auntie Mame*. A farmer's wife, Ferber's heroine, Selina, spoils her beautiful son, trying to save him from the vanities of the rich and social. But he is weak; he wants to be lured. "How big is my man?" Selina asks her son, Dirk, when he is a toddler. It's a game they have, a way of loving without having to say it, and the answer is Ferber's title. But *So Big* is also Chicago, industrial America, perhaps even Ferber's own sense of where she and Dorothy Parker and others are taking their customers. After 1919, we are in a new age, a Big One.

Ferber can catch minor characters in a sentence, as with the two aunts who bring Selina up: "Mitts, preserves, Bible, chilly best room, solemn and kittenless cat, order, little-girls-mustn't. They smelled of apples—of withered apples that have rotted at the core." Or Ferber can wound you with the hurt of those who aren't cute enough to keep up with the popular kids, as when Selina tries to cultivate a plain girl, one of her son's friends, while he is busy throwing this girl over for fancy people: "Selina wrote Mattie, inviting her to the farm for Thanksgiving, and Mattie answered gratefully, declining. 'I shall always remember you,' she wrote in that letter, 'with love.'"

A kind of Mattie herself, redeemed by her own ambitious talent, Ferber bestows judgment like a Fundamentalist. *So Big* ends with Dirk arrived and prospering, with a Quite So flat and a Japanese houseman. But that's not enough after all, is it?, and the novel ends as he throws himself across his bed in despair.

He has everything but a life: just like Dorothy Parker. But Parker had a mission, whether she knew it or not—the same one as Edna Ferber, and Ferber, at least, knew it. They helped lead the first generation of women who took position in the great world not by giving balls but by looking at the human condition and publishing what they saw. Parker's art was the mezzotint, nicely shaded with erotoemotional longing. Ferber's was a Wild West Show, treating, as she put it in *So Big,* "the theatrical way in which life speeds in America."

The two women helped lead as well the first influential generation of American Jewry emancipated from the ghetto—culturally evolved from immigrant parents and their Old Country accents, their clueless wonder at everything from escalators to crossword puzzles. Parker waved it all away. Baggage. Ferber, though spiritually agnostic, insisted on being Jewish in worldview. She knew anti-Semitism as Parker did not, having come from a part of the country rife with it. Parker saw bigotry as nonsense to busy a babbitt. Ferber saw it as dangerous.

This was the generation of Al Jolson, Eddie Cantor, Sophie Tucker, Fanny Brice, Nora Bayes: entertainers breaking free by nuancing their assimilation with racial signifiers: blackface, comebacks in Yiddish, a Second Hand Rose or Jazz Singer with a synagogue cantor father. They seize the Dixiana "coon song" as a gizmo of racial myths, then turn it inside out. In the movie musical *Say It With Songs* (1929), a radio back-stager with a manslaughter-trial subplot, Jolson is offered yet another Mammy number. This one is "I'm Going To Smother My Mother With Kisses When I Get Back To My Home in Tennessee." No, says Jolson, countering with "I'll Smother My Father in Gedaemfte Rinderbrust When I Get Back To Odessa." Indeed, Jolson was born over there—in Lithuania or Russia (the biography is cloudy). Headlining on Broadway by his mid-twenties, he launched the talkie as Hollywood's first singing actor, and for *Say It With Songs* he was paid half a million dollars. Isn't that the most potent of American dreams—to redirect the definition of an elite toward the contribution of talent?

This was Ferber's role as well. She was virtually the spokeswoman for the theatrical nature of that American speed: of the way, for instance, the notion of an elite changed like coin in the hands of the moneychangers in the temple. So Ferber's novels are sensitive to people but excited, enthralled by history. And that is why she is still around. Her major Coolidge-Hoover era titles, *So Big, Show Boat,* and *Cimarron,* have scarcely ever been out of print and claim among them eight different film versions. Dorothy Parker is even more current, because her warning of Women, Beware Men! anticipates each era's peculiar take on the gender war. Parker says the system doesn't work. Ferber says the system works—it's love that's the problem. *Time* styles an imaginary caption of the Ferber and Parker lives: intrepid New York writer gals getting what they wanted never.

Still, Ferber and Parker were, like others in this book, summoned in some important way: Cole Porter, Fiorello La Guardia, Ethel Waters, Dorothy Thompson, Arturo Toscanini. Some answered a social or political need. Some ended their career in the grandee phase, like Ferber, or in despair, like Parker. And, in our next chapter, one started off with a feat while the other was doing what comes naturally.

3

The Marriage(s) of the Century

In the years just before World War I, dancing became the passion of a couple's night out. Bandleaders egged them on, and songwriters introduced New Dance Sensations by the week—turkey trots, fox trots, grizzly bears, the something walk, the something toddle, the something rise, the something rag. Irving Berlin summed it up in 1921 with "Everybody Step." Syncopation, liberation, revolution. Decades later, they called it "Sex, drugs, rock and roll." In the 1910s and '20s, they called it "jazz."

To the authorities, it was the ultimate affront, literally "sex" in black slang. "Jazz me, daddy" is simply "Everybody step" in another language. Worse, it caught on as a universal one. As another Irving Berlin number pointed out, "Everybody's Doin' It Now!"

It wasn't only the impressionable working class or the usual college daredevils. Even Society must take a chance. So Vernon and Irene Castle—the official progenitors of the ballroom-dancing craze—were invited out one night to a Long Island estate, met at the railroad station by chauffeured car, deposited at the mansion, led to a closet, and told to wait. Broadway stars and pathfinders of fashion, the Castles were nonetheless treated like curiosities. Like objects. Instructed to partner the guests so that all could experience the Castle style in dance, Vernon led the ladies while Irene was "passed from gentleman to gentleman, like a football." Looking back years later, Mrs. Castle noted how Society kept "entertainers" at a distance, lest distinctions of caste be compromised. "Celebrities of today," she tells us, "have no idea how socially unimportant you were in the old days."

Yet in 1925, in one of Harold Ross' earliest *New Yorkers*, a debutante named Ellin Mackay published "Why We Go To Cabarets." The young Mackay's notion was that Society was breaking down and that the nightclub offered, if nothing else, the sheer honesty of melting-pot openness. It was a new sort of community, Society without ancestors. Virtually anybody could win the dance contest, or break the bank at Monte Carlo, or even achieve something meaningful. Suddenly, notable people were coming from what Society thought of as "anywhere," and the place to meet them was cabarets. One danced with the Castles on their turf now.

The late 1920s marked the height of this transition, from the New York of the Astors to the New York of—for instance—two men from anywhere who made Society marriages. One was an action hero and the other an artist. The artist was the best-known American songwriter after Stephen Foster and Victor Herbert. The hero, an aviator, was the greatest hero America had ever known.

Alone? . . . Does solitude surround the brave when Adventure leads the way and Ambition reads the dials?
                    —Editorial in the *New York Sun* during The Flight

He was Charles Augustus Lindbergh, who piloted *The Spirit of St. Louis* from Long Island to Paris in May of 1927, when aviation—and transatlantic flight in particular—had become an excitement of the day. As myth demands, Lindbergh not only acted but looked heroic: tall, trim, and shining. Still, however rustic and bashful, he had not precisely come out of nowhere. His father was Charles August Lindbergh, a Progressive Minnesota congressman who served five terms and to whom young Charles was very close. The two traveled together on the senior Lindbergh's campaigns, so the youngster would have heard something of the issues of the day. His father's pet issue was the House of Morgan, which, he believed, manipulated the global economy to benefit the rich. Father and son presumably had conversations on it; this is worth noting because the younger Lindbergh's apologists call his later love affair with the Nazis "politically naive." On the contrary, as we'll see in a later chapter, Lindbergh's political views were basic, not naive.

Oddly, considering the intense scrutiny given each new attempt to cross the Atlantic by air in 1927, fliers had already done it numerous times. Granted, every trip was by dirigible or taken in stages, following the land-based route from Nova Scotia across Greenland and Iceland to Ireland. But the mid-1920s saw new interest in the Raymond Orteig Prize, first offered in 1919 and now, suddenly, the rage of the aviator community. Orteig promised twenty-five thousand dollars for a single aeronautic trip between New York and Paris—and no dirigibles or rest stops allowed. Because the amount of fuel that one plane could carry was dangerously finite, the relatively safe but much longer northerly land route previously favored was hors concours. Thus, whoever won the Orteig Prize would make a transatlantic flight in the most literal sense.

The entrants focused the public's attention while the press ran through a prefabricated cycle of stories on each new pilot and his crew, his aircraft, and various niceties. One read that René Fonck and his Sikorski boasted a convertible sofa-bed and elaborate meals kept ready in specially-heated cellules. There were evil accidents, too, frighteningly good copy: the Sikorski crashed on takeoff, killing half the crew. Even more fascinating was the voyage of two French pilots who left Le Bourget airfield near Paris and may have traversed the ocean, because there were alleged sightings over Newfoundland and Maine. The pair never arrived, and even today no one knows what became of them.

Lindbergh wasn't good copy: he had nothing to say, especially to idiot questions more relevant to a high-school yearbook profile than to a death-defying aerial adventure. What's your favorite pie? Got a sweetheart?

Yes, yes, we know this—the feud between Lindbergh and the press, the hero who refused to adhere to PR etiquette. Still, Lindbergh had blundered into an exponentially self-aggrandizing media structure, a near-tyranny of reporters. The less he showed of himself, the more curious everybody got. Who was this guy? He didn't even field a crew, and for sustenance he packed a water canteen and sandwiches. Shortly before eight o'clock on the morning of Friday, May 20, 1927, several hundred journalists, fellow pilots, Lindbergh helpers, cops, local wellwishers, and the usual "Is somebody here famous?" moochers watched *The Spirit of St. Louis* get off to a wobbly, just-cleared-the-telephone-wires start. Lindbergh steered northeastward up the coast to Newfoundland, and this time the sightings weren't merely alleged.

Then Lindbergh cleared land and flew into the last genuine news blackout he would know for many years after. For everyone else, the suspense was distracting to a fault. Remember, in 1927 aviation was still extremely romantic and even implausible, more a magic than a science. There were no airplane passengers, at least in the modern sense, only the pilots and a few daredevils who went up for a few minutes and then talked of it for the rest of their lives.

So all America went into an uproar of bemusement, worry, and prayer. (Yes, there was plenty of prayer then, though not as an adjunct to zealots' intimidation of agnostics.) The waiting lasted till six minutes after Lindbergh touched down at Le Bourget, when the scoop was flashed to New York and thence through the nation's media circuits. The flight had taken thirty-three-and-a-half hours and covered 3,500 miles, and while the papers could not banner the story till the Saturday editions, word had spread viva voce as everyone tried to be the first in his loop to tell the others.

LINDBERGH DOES IT! was the start of *The New York Times*' headline, over four separate articles on the event, a map of the trip, and a headshot of the hero himself. They dubbed him The Lone Eagle but they called him Lindy, sheer twenties property, an epochal term like "jazz" and "bunk." A generation of boys was called Charles Lindbergh Something, and there were Lindy poems, Lindy books, Lindy songs.* The Lindy

---

* So much music was written in Lindbergh's honor that there were reportedly over two dozen pieces entitled "The Spirit of St. Louis" alone. The hit was Abel Baer and L. Wolfe Gilbert's "Lucky Lindy!," written and published within two days of the landing. The most distinguished author of the Lindy numbers was George M. Cohan, for "When Lindy Comes Home." The title has irony. The Lindberghs felt so endangered by press attention that for a time they exiled themselves in England.

hop lasted into the 1960s, enormous staying power for a New Dance Sensation, swamping the Varsity Drag, the Peabody, and the Big Apple. Lindbergh could even have gone Hollywood had he accepted William Randolph Hearst's offer from Hearst's Cosmopolitan Pictures, at a salary of half a million dollars and percentage points.

Lindbergh is not a New York figure in any sense, even if he raised his children largely in New York suburbs, from New Jersey to Long Island and then Connecticut. His importance in these pages, for now, lies in a Manhattan-centric culture's redirecting its admiration from wastrels like the Astors to the achieving parvenu. Interestingly, Lindbergh joined the catalogue of elite names as the most uninflected of public personalities— someone bizarrely simple after Algonquin sophisticates, for instance. Or so it seemed. More truly, Lindbergh was The Man Nobody Knows. Powermongers were already fingering him as presidential material, having no idea how stubbornly self-directed he was. Lindbergh had no use for diplomatic accommodation; when he felt like speaking, he spoke his mind. Bruce Barton saw his Carpenter flattering and teasing acolytes to whip them into business formation. Lindbergh wouldn't have flattered heaven.

"Puttin' on the Ritz"

—song by Irving Berlin

Now we come to the artist in this pair, Irving Berlin. He was in some respects the very opposite of Lindbergh: outgoing, worldly, and even previously married (and a widower). Yet the two share the distinction of supplying, at this time, the household name in their respective fields. The famous pilot was Lindbergh—but the famous songwriter was Irving Berlin.

He seems less so today only because the 1920s hosted the debuts of the Gershwins; Vincent Youmans; Rodgers and Hart; De Sylva, Brown, and Henderson; and Cole Porter. And Jerome Kern preceded them. Nevertheless, the squad crowded in only after Berlin had established himself as the leader of the generation that replaced "After the Ball" and "Ta-Ra-Ra-Boom-De-Ay" as the music of the nation.

This new sound is hard to define. Greatly to simplify: the start-up verse got less important and the refrain longer and more essential; an urge toward waltz and ragtime gave way to a general use of dance rhythms; the lyricists grew more resourceful; and the music sounded great on a jazz band, with banjo, piano, and drums supporting fizzy brass solos, a playful clarinet, and the devious saxophone, a bastard instrument, part reed and part brass. In other words: while your parents dote upon Victor Herbert and the summer bandshell concert, stiff-collar music, you've pushed back your suspenders and sneaked off to hear a pickup group getting giddy on "Blue Skies."

Lindbergh didn't just fly planes: he comprehended their technology. Berlin, by contrast, lacked even basic skills. For one thing, he was musically illiterate and couldn't record what he composed. An assistant would take down his tunes and notate the harmony under Berlin's supervision, in observance of the imaginary symphony that Berlin could "write" but couldn't write down.*

When necessary, Berlin could bang out his songs at the keyboard in his one key, F Sharp. Commentators fasten upon Berlin's custom-built piano, with a lever placed just above the right knee that allowed him to play in any key without adjusting his hands. Some of these writers seem to feel that this invention empowered Berlin, even freed him to compose as his colleagues did. In fact, the transposing piano was a silly toy devoid of creative purpose. It freed Berlin to accompany singers in any key they wanted if they were entertaining at one of his parties, and it had no other use.

That piano doesn't even work any more. In 2008, *New York Times* critic Jesse Green sought out the instrument. He found it in the offices of ASCAP—a suitable venue, home of the songwriters' association that allocates royalties based on public performance of songs. However, the piano was sitting unhallowed in a hallway under a tarpaulin. And lo, the transposing mechanism was jammed. But the melody lingers on:

---

*Berlin's musical illiteracy helped create the urban legend that "a colored boy in Harlem" was writing his songs. Besides, how else to explain the phenomenal run of hits? *One* man wrote them all? Given the sudden prominence of black musicians in the 1920s, it was if nothing else symmetrical that this output be in part of black origin.

Berlin is, after all, the author of two Tin Pan Alley titles that virtually every American knows, "White Christmas" and "God Bless America." In conclusion, Green asks, "Did his lack of training somehow make his style universal?"

Perhaps because he couldn't notate, Berlin started as a lyricist only. Yet how was he to stifle the "raggedy melody, full of originality" (to quote one of his lines) that he kept hearing in his head? He took up composing, the music a-frolic to the conversational idiom of the words: as if Berlin were extemporizing songs in your front parlor. He flirted and joked as you did, in dance tempo. Everybody's doing it now!, yes, we got that. Still, what is *it,* exactly?

It's a euphemism, of course, and Berlin explodes it in "They Call It Dancing":

> *If it's a ballroom, she doesn't mind his embrace.*
> *But in a hallroom, she'd slap him right in the face.*

Dancing—even music itself—is sex. The serene "Say It with Music" advises the courting beau to woo classically:

> *Somehow they'd rather be kissed*
> *To the strains of Chopin or Liszt.*

Yet we suspect that something more urgent than sonatas is at stake. Indeed, one of Berlin's characters skips the musical phase of the euphemistic structure entirely. "He isn't much at a dance," Berlin admits, "but then when he takes you home":

> *You'd be surprised!*

So it was Berlin's knack to sing what everybody else was merely saying, effecting a kind of neighborhood poetry. He made the ordinary sound exotic while domesticating the fanciful: daily life in a show-biz getup. "An Orange Grove in California" comes off as your own backyard, but "The Girls Of My Dreams" inspires with delightful peril.

Then, too, while retailing all the available genres from the ethnic stereotype novelty to the "girl's name" or "railroad" or "hometown" number,
Berlin innovated. In quodlibet style, he sounds a ballad, then a jagged
piece, then runs them simultaneously—and he seems to have been the
first to do it in just this way.* Berlin even almost invented the Cole Porter list song. Porter did get there first, but Berlin's list song appeared not
long after, in "When I Discovered You":

> Columbus discovered America,
> Hudson discovered New York . . .

This number comes from Berlin's first complete Broadway score,
Watch Your Step (1914), when Berlin was twenty-six, one year older than
Lindbergh was when he made The Flight. A major production by the
very prominent Charles Dillingham at a first-choice theatre, the New
Amsterdam, *Watch Your Step* boasted a score entirely in dance time: fox
trot, galop, tango, waltz. The show was a dance itself, ever in motion
and unwilling to light as its characters went nosing about New York
City much as the three sailors were to, thirty years later, in *On the Town*
(1944). In 1914, everyone thought *Watch Your Step* a delightful novelty.
In fact, it invented a new kind of musical, up-to-the-minute and full of
Manhattan sass. Last week, *Naughty Marietta*. Next week, *Lady, Be Good!*.

More innovative even than the giddy tempo of the narrative was the
set and costume design, shared by Helen Dryden and Robert McQuinn.
Major artists on the staff of *Vogue* magazine,† these two gave *Watch Your*

---

*The quodlibet, a venerable musical genre, entered the musical with Gilbert and Sul-
livan. They used it in choral numbers, usually counterpointing two melodies more
or less similar in style though differentiated in rhythmic emphasis. It was Berlin who
took the two strains to their extremes, working a smooth tune against a hairy one.
His masterpiece in this line is *Call Me Madam*'s "You're Just in Love." First comes the
dreamy "I hear singing . . ." and then comes the "Now it's *Merman's* turn!" bounce of
"You don't need analyzing . . ." When the two collide, it creates a union of contrasts
beyond anything in Gilbert and Sullivan.
†Dryden's reputation was so imposing that Studebaker's print ads for its 1936 model
caroled IT'S STYLED BY HELEN DRYDEN at the top of the page, dominating a color rendition of a gala yellow roadster.

Step a facetious high-fashion look new to modern-dress musical comedy. Squandering glamor, McQuinn set a scene in a "law office de danse" as a swank temple with sleek columns separating checked and cross-hatched panels, the whole colored with paintings of showgirls in fanciful costumes. It sounds Ziegfeldian—but *Watch Your Step* appeared a year before Ziegfeld's key designers, Joseph Urban and Lucile, joined the *Follies*. (Urban made his Broadway debut, in a non-musical play based on Hans Christian Andersen's "The Little Mermaid," just a month before *Watch Your Step* opened.) No, Dillingham and Berlin were genuine revolutionaries in this "syncopated musical show made in America," as they billed it in the program. And it was surely they who dreamed it up, because *Watch Your Step*'s librettist, Harry B. Smith, and director, R. H. Burnside, were no more than capable journeymen.

One thing about the show was old-fashioned: its legacy-with-a-catch plot premise, a cliché for a generation. At least the catch was nutty, for the fortune goes to the one who can resist falling in love. What, in a *musical*? The would-be heirs and their friends tour the local hot spots in terms any American might understand, based on making noise and acting important in a spoofy way:

> *Let's go 'round the town.*
> *And where a band is playing*
> *We'll go hip-hurrahing,*
> *And we'll turn things upside down.*
> *Our heads will grow dizzy*
> *Keeping headwaiters busy . . .*

Of course, what these young people really do is hold an evening-long "dancing party," of the kind already notorious in the culture because they encouraged boys to pet and girls to let them. You knew it was good because it so riled your parents.

Watch Your Step's cast included Vernon and Irene Castle, those mentors of a dancing nation, as we know. Vernon played one of the legatees, a dance instructor by profession, and Irene played . . . well, a girl who wants to dance. (The librettist's credit ran "Plot, if any, by Harry B.

Smith.") So, as the refrain of the show's central number started, most unusually, on the dominant seventh:

IRENE: *Dancing teacher, show us how to do the fox trot.*
VERNON: *You'll have to watch your step.*

And so on, till Irene and the girls master it:

IRENE AND CHORUS:
> *Dancing teacher, once again,*
> *Show us how it's done and then*
> *We'll do the fox trot*
> *The whole night long!*

Amid all the rumpus, Berlin pauses for the quodlibet. The first strain is tender:

> *Won't you play a simple melody*
> *Like my mother sang to me?*

and the challenge stalks it like a front-porch sheik:

> *Musical demon, set your honey a' dreamin',*
> *Won't you play me some rag?*

Again, it was conversational yet lilting, grounded in the old ways yet fairly jumping with novelty. It was this ability to address a wide public with his surprises that enabled Berlin to lead the breakaway generation in songwriting. His tricks were so deft that they reassured.

One might say as much about Lindbergh, a daredevil who nevertheless seemed the kind of boy your daughter brought home when she wanted to please. No dancing parties for this sober chap, though he did nurse a penchant for sadistic practical jokes that no one else thought funny.

Berlin was at once more excitable but more sociable. There is a more telling contrast yet in their respective worlds. Berlin's was music, almost as basic to life in Western Civilization as food and sport. But Lindbergh's world was fantasy. He was the man in the moon, going around the world in eighty days. However, the pair conquered these worlds on the highest level, absorbing their success with ease. The more typical American success story is a crashup: F. Scott Fitzgerald, Marilyn Monroe, Michael Jackson. True, Berlin was so defeated by the way rock had taken over as the national music that he went into a reclusive retirement for the last twenty years of his life, and Lindbergh destroyed his reputation with unsavory political militancy—again, as we'll see. But success qua se did not destroy either man.

PARENT DISAPPROVES SOCIETY GIRL'S MARRIAGE TO JAZZ COMPOSER
—Headline in *The New York Times*

Berlin and Lindbergh expanded in such a positive way the sociology of the parvenu that it seems logical today that they would contract prominent marriages, though Berlin's was a scandal. He made his match, in 1926, with the socialite Ellin Mackay, whom we last saw writing that *New Yorker* piece on cabarets. The pair met at one—a speakeasy, really, though in the 1920s synonyms for "nightclub" were used interchangeably.* Berlin was fifteen years older than Ellin and forbidden to her as husband material: Jewish, from the raffish world of entertainment, and socially self-taught rather than well-bred. Instead of Family, Berlin had a mother who, at the opening night of *Watch Your Step,* said, "Dot's nice, darling."

Interestingly, the Mackays were parvenus as well. They were Instant Society. Ellin's father, Clarence Hungerford Mackay, cooked his recipe for Arrival with a few dubious ingredients. Cole Porter would later identify America as "a nation where people go from Poland to polo in one generation," and Mackay did work fast. He was Catholic, too; Society

---

* One heard nuances of class rather than of meaning. *Speakeasy* was the street term, *cabaret* a bit ooh-la-la, fit for the bon ton, and *café* was favored by Algonquinite wags, whose class was talent.

demanded Protestant standing, preferably Episcopalian but, if necessary, one of the adjacent affiliations such as Congregationalist. Further, the Mackay fortune derived in part from a silver-rich miner father and his sordid rise in lawless Nevada. And—*and!*—there was a family disgrace, as Mackay's wife, Kitty, had carried on an affair with Mackay's physician. Came then heartbreak, divorce, the abandoning of her children, and, worst of all, headlines.

However, Clarence Mackay himself was not a silver miner. His millions depended on telegraph cable, a secure and impressive source of wealth. And Mackay had style: his estate was a showplace, a vast construction called Harbor Hill, overlooking the quaint old town of Roslyn—with duck pond, clock tower, and library named for William Cullen Bryant—from the highest geographical point of Long Island. To show how prominently Mackay socialized, Harbor Hill is where the young Edward VIII—the Prince of Wales—went to be fêted on his first visit to New York, with all Society eager to fawn. The heir to the only throne that mattered in all the West allowed Mrs. Vanderbilt to take him to the *Ziegfeld Follies,* but he partied at Harbor Hill.

This is a tribute to just how close to polo Mackay had got. Edward VIII was not only the most eligible bachelor alive but the most written-about of young men. Like all British royals of the day, he could not put a foot wrong in bearing and manners, and while his family had the utmost in past, he was thought to hold the utmost in future. A popular song of 1927 presented the gleeful yet awed report of a young woman who "danced with a man who's danced with a girl who's danced with the Prince of Wales." In a daze, the singer recounts the words the prince and his partner spoke: he remarked, "Topping band," and she answered, "Delightful, sir." Of course, the joke is that he in fact has said absolutely nothing, just as he was to say absolutely nothing for the rest of his wasted crybaby life. In the late 1920s, however, the prince was Charming and swept everybody away.

And somehow Irving Berlin swept Ellin Mackay away. Forbidding their marriage, the senior Mackay hustled Ellin off for a year abroad. It was the usual cure when pedigreed offspring took up dating in the neighborhoods, and it usually worked. With the story presumably over, Mackay came home first—but when Ellin followed, she found a squad of reporters waiting to interview her as she stepped off the boat. The story had scarcely begun.

In Mrs. Astor's day, of course, a lady never spoke to a reporter, much less a gaggle of them *en plein jour,* as a spectacle for porters and waterfront loafers to enjoy. But then, Mrs. Astor wouldn't have set foot in a cabaret, while Ellin Mackay had celebrated doing so in *The New Yorker.* Some in Society might have observed that the Mackays lacked the proper purple in the first place. But the general public's perception of who exactly was crème de la crème was changing, instructed by the media's ever more tolerant and even doting view of revolutionary attitudes. Ellin Mackay was seen as a belle of the age, smart and lively. She had a sense of loyalty as well: because she *did* speak to the press, saying that she would not marry without parental blessing. "I have not met the young man I would marry," she announced, "to give up my father."

Even so, four months later, on January 4, 1926, the plot thickened: Ellin and Berlin were married in a civil ceremony in what New York terms "downtown": the quartier of courthouses and bureaucracies clustered around City Hall. Didn't Society weddings occur in Grace Church or at home as a rule? Word of the secret event spread rapidly, and the senior Mackay thrilled tabloid readers with a narrative bump worthy of the Heavy Father in *Way Down East:* he called his attorney and revised his will to disinherit his daughter. Be it said, though, that Ellin had followed up her first *New Yorker* piece with one entitled "The Declining Function," setting forth the notion that "Modern girls are conscious of their own identity, and they marry whom they choose, satisfied to satisfy themselves."

So off to a European honeymoon on the SS *Leviathan* went Mr. and Mrs. Irving Berlin, disembarking at Southampton to take the train to London. At Waterloo Station, they were confronted by not reporters but the cast of Sigmund Romberg's operetta *The Student Prince,* whose West End production was just nearing the end of its rehearsal period. Clearly intending to serenade the Berlins, the performers rendered selections from the Romberg, irritating Berlin to no end. What a twist in the story: it turned out that the actors had mistaken Berlin for Mr. J. J. Shubert.*

Meanwhile, the American public followed the mésalliance of Park Avenue and Henry Street with fascination, because there was yet more story. The press narrated with the usual tweaking, including the entirely false report that the Berlins were to soothe daddy's wrath with Berlin's conversion to Roman Catholicism and a second wedding, this time in church. Show biz, too, narrated the saga with songs, revue sketches, and even a play. Crane Wilbur's *The Song Writer* (1928) offered the once famous but now forgot "second Jolson," Georgie Price, as a certain Daniel Bernard in love with debutante Patricia Thayer (Mayo Methot, later Humphrey Bogart's third wife). The *à clef* piece, a fixture on Broadway at this time, denoted entrenched fame: they didn't write plays about the Celeb in Passing.

The Song Writer was not a hit, and Price himself left show biz to become a stockbroker on Wall Street—just before the Crash. Yet Price made it through the Troubles nicely, while both Irving Berlin and Clarence Mackay suffered the dire trimming of the day. Mackay even had to give up Harbor Hill's lordly appointments and move into the gatekeeper's cottage. Then, in 1931, Ellin gave trial testimony favorable to her father in a lawsuit against him, and she and Berlin together attended Mackay's marriage to opera singer Anna Case, his longtime mistress. With a skittish reconciliation in the making, the headline fabulists realized that the plot was about to run out of action and, as the French put it, left the Berlins tranquil.

"After You Get What You Want You Don't Want It"

—song by Irving Berlin

---

* Shubert, the producer of the Broadway *Student Prince* as well as this London mounting, a replica of the New York original, had also been on the *Leviathan*. He was of course in town to supervise the final rehearsals of his pet project, for *The Student Prince* was arguably Broadway's biggest musical hit to that date. Apparently, Shubert didn't get off the train quickly enough, the Berlins appeared, and a keyed-up music director gave the cue. "To the inn we're marching for our throats are parching," the actors gleefully caroled—the very opposite, in words *and* music, of everything Berlin stood for.

As it happens, the press was by then busy with the other marriage of the century, that of Charles Lindbergh and Anne Morrow. The Irving and Ellin Story had lots of crazy parts to it—the various Mackay scandals, the truly big numbers of the Mackay fortune, the *Romeo and Juliet* tattle of the heiress and her cavalier from Jewish show business. The story was romantic and socially unruly at once, a storybook itself, filled with throughlines.

But Lindbergh's courtship of Anne was *Cinderella* in a paragraph. In his unadorned midwestern way, Lindbergh was the American Prince of Wales. And, like Prince Charming organizing a bride-finding ball, Lucky Lindy was looking for a princess.

Actually, it was Ellin Mackay who sounded the royal note: in her hilltop palace and with a family banking résumé that tilted the room at the grandest soirées. Anne Morrow represented a new kind of "society bride," middle-class rather than aristocratic and of a family rooted in duty and public service rather than private exhibitionism.

Come to that, the Morrows were barely middle-class in origin. Dwight Whitney Morrow, Anne's father, came from a family with a bookish but impecunious background. However, young Dwight's resourcefulness and ambition led him to a spectacular undergraduate career at Amherst College, where he made Phi Beta Kappa and was elected "Most Likely To Succeed." Physically short but a natural-born achiever, Dwight was a man to impress other men: brainy, creative, fair, and diplomatic. His wife-to-be was a match, Elisabeth Reeve Cutter, also brainy and ambitious, and an undergraduate at one of the so-called Seven Sisters, Smith College. Back then, Amherst dated Smith as Clark Gable dated Joan Crawford. The Morrows had three daughters and a junior, while Dwight Sr. went into corporate law, made partner in his firm, and was then brought into the House of Morgan—the very outfit that Charles Lindbergh's congressman father held accountable as the source of all evil in the industrialized West.

Note a certain adaptability in the upper echelons of Society as it welcomes Morrow into the halls of power, though he was of what was then called "humble" family. Of course, a finishing at a place like Amherst helps one to crack the top clique, and a corporate lawyer—Wall Street's favorite kind—is certainly easier to absorb than, say, a member of the Algonquin Round Table, with his jazzadoo comportment and unreliable enemies list. Still, Morrow's success story is that peculiarly American kind that was becoming very prevalent in the years after World War I.

One wonders how Charles Lindbergh and Anne Morrow might have hit it off if Morrow had stayed with Morgan. In fact, he was there just long enough to advise Lindbergh on investing his hero's fortune after The Flight. Because just then—as if destiny needed to remove an obstacle to the fulfillment of its fancy—Dwight Morrow's Amherst classmate President Calvin Coolidge asked Morrow to resign his Wall Street affairs and serve as Ambassador to Mexico.

If Clarence Mackay's greatest achievement was throwing the ball for the Prince of Wales, and if Mackay's sense of public obligation was expressed in his enlivening it with Paul Whiteman, the top-okay bandleader of the time, Dwight Morrow's achievement was genuinely patriotic. Our relations with Mexico had declined badly, and rather than post a major party contributor or spoils-system incompetent, Coolidge called upon Morrow's salient qualities of ingenuity and tact. And Morrow, in his turn, invited Lindbergh to fly The Spirit of St. Louis to Mexico City for Christmas of 1927. It was a public relations event to strengthen Morrow's cultivation of Mexican-American relations, because Lindbergh's presence worked a wild magic all over the Western world. And of course there was the romantic subtext of Prince Charming seeking his bride. "Girls were everywhere," he noted; he could have his pick. But they tended to get gooey on him, to freeze and just . . . stare.

Anne knew the feeling. "He is unbelievable," she raved to her diary, "and it is exhilarating to believe in the unbelievable." Naturally, Lindbergh had taken the Morrow women up in his plane, which amounted to something between witnessing miracles and having sex. Bohemian wags routinely got double meanings out of the very notion of Lindberghian flight. Cole Porter wrote a song on it, "Pilot Me," the cri de coeur of a bottom. "Cast away your fears," he or she pleads. "Strip my gears!" What dance music was to Irving Berlin, Going Up In My Airplane was to Lindbergh—or, rather, to his image. It was part of why he was admired as Everyman and Prometheus at once: the ultimate top man.

Any of the Morrow girls would have been acceptable, perhaps: Lindbergh was in Mexico to make a deal. And yet Lindbergh wanted Anne just as Anne wanted Lindbergh: a love match after all. Two years passed as the two collected their thoughts on the future and Lindbergh set about, in his words, "getting out of the hero business."

By now, in the spring of 1929, the press had begun hounding and crowding Lindbergh's every step and had to be baited and outwitted if the Lindbergh-Morrow marriage ceremony was not to be made a hurly-burly. In the event, the wedding surprised even the guests, who had been invited to the Morrows' New Jersey home for an afternoon of bridge. The handful of callers must have thought it piquant that Charles Lindbergh's mother and a chaplain were on hand; maybe this was Mexico City bridge. Then the doors to the living room were opened upon Anne, in a white chiffon wedding gown, on her father's arm. Her mother and sisters moved forward (brother Dwight could not join the party because of health reasons), and now Charles, in a blue-serge suit, joined his bride before the minister. The scarcely two dozen witnesses had figured it out by now: this was The Wedding. It was May 27, 1929—just about two years after The Flight—and following a very brief reception in the Morrows' garden, the newly-married Lindberghs hid in the back seat of a getaway car, heading for the groom's new forty-foot cruiser, the *Mouette*. A friend of Lindbergh's, tall and slender enough to resemble him, dressed in Lindbergh fashion to lead reporters on a wild goose chase after taking off from the local airfield in Lindbergh's Curtiss Falcon. The press caught up with the honeymooners soon enough, but the couple had nearly the first week of their marriage to themselves—and, arguably, the most romantic wedding of the decade.

The 1920s may have introduced the more or less penniless celebrity, for if Mark Twain earned a fortune, the Algonquinite writer's lifestyle depended a great deal on getting onto the free list, whether for theatre-going or to nosh dinner at press receptions. Even so, people were still fascinated by the lives of those with money. Irving Berlin was prominent enough in a lucrative field to be supposed a millionaire; before the Crash, he was one. And his wife, of course, was born an heiress. So was Anne Morrow, with trust fund capital of $500,000. Lindbergh himself, through the flash success of his tale of The Flight, *We;* from various advisory posts; and from investments handled by, yes, the House of Morgan, was even better off than his bride.

Why the rich? The answer is the obvious one: they have money—which is to say: they have freedom. All they have in common with the rest of us is death. Otherwise, they can do whatever they want. They can give balls and know other rich people. They have lots of room and great eats. They fear no one. They can fly.

And they can break rules the rest of us have to live by. No, they can't cheat death, but they could cheat life. Everybody "knew" that rich women never gave birth if disinclined to. As the popular song "Ain't We Got Fun" chortled, "The rich get rich and the poor get children."

Most people never knew *what* the rich did, because they were so good at keeping secrets: except when they weren't and a scandal broke out. Today, of course, scandals are the acts by which the famous stay famous, from pharmacopoeial breakdown to violence. In the 1920s, generally, the famous only got married. The Berlins' *Romeo and Juliet*ing and the Lindberghs' *Cinderella* marked a kind of apex, hot stories that were really just about couples in love.

Still, there were all those headlines whipping up interest—but in what? After The Flight, Walter Lippmann took to the pages of *Vanity Fair* to count off such twenties exhibits as the Mackay ball for the Prince of Wales, the riot at Rudolph Valentino's funeral, and a couple of murder cases to inveigh against "the publicity machine." We know all about it now, but in 1927 Lippmann was making a discovery of this "mechanical device" that hashes up the inspiring and the loathsome alike. "The machine," he wrote, "is without morals or taste of any kind, without prejudice or purpose, without conviction or ulterior motive." It not only corrupts culture by seeing fame and not morality as the first virtue, Lippmann warned. The machine also rules the very order in which things are allowed to happen, in effect controlling history: "It is no use trying to tell the public about the Mississippi flood when [murder suspect] Ruth Snyder is on the witness stand. . . . The opening of the Hall-Mills [murder] prosecution had to be delayed two weeks . . . until the front pages could be cleared of the clutter of news about a subway strike."

It hasn't quite happened yet, but we are about to witness the advent of what came to be called "publiciety." In Mrs. Astor's day, Society went where it couldn't be seen; publiciety will go where you cannot miss it. Thus, the marriages of the Berlins and the Lindberghs became scandals by other means. All the fun "news" was scandal, as colorful as the musicals flooding movie screens in the first year of sound yet rowdy as a Spielberg dinosaur. A marriage of the century all but erased Algonquin writers' luncheons: with real life, and life on the run at that. It was like a western. The Lindberghs came to feel that it was the gleefully relentless pursuit of the press, focusing so much attention on them, that led Bruno Hauptmann to kidnap and kill their firstborn child, Charles Augustus Jr., in 1932.

The Berlins, at first, were followed but not hounded. Ellin, further, was not even dropped from the *Social Register,* the annual listing, in different volumes for different cities, of those thought socially important. People could be dropped from the books for various reasons; Jane Wyatt got deleted when she took up acting. Well, the stage was wicked, once. At that, while Ellin maintained her listing, her marital status barely got a look-in, in a supplementary note. Why? As a spokesman for the *Social Register* put it, "Irving Berlin has no place in society."

Yet when they asked Jerome Kern what place Irving Berlin has in American music, Kern famously replied, "Irving Berlin has no place in American music. Irving Berlin *is* American music."

It all depends on what one means by the word *elite.*

The 1930s

4

Jimmy Walker, Fiorello La Guardia, and the War of the Minorities

In 1929, the first year of regular sound production in Hollywood, each major studio offered at least one Big Musical, a calling card for the newly-discovered virtues of All Talking! All Singing! All Dancing! Sometimes the Big One idealized elements of a studio's style, as when Paramount unveiled Ernst Lubitsch's *The Love Parade,* an operetta for Maurice Chevalier and Jeanette MacDonald in Paramount's characteristic dressy erotica. RKO, formed specifically to make talkies, had no style as yet and simply borrowed from Broadway, filming a Ziegfeld stage hit, *Rio Rita,* with large portions of the original work intact. William Fox's studio, the home of Will Rogers and John Ford, offered *Sunny Side Up,* an urban tale so folksy it seems to take place on a farm with sidewalks.

Universal, the most *passéiste* of the studios, blundered into its Big One, filming *Show Boat* as a silent and then, in a panic, tucking in sound sequences here and there. "Universal's talking and singing triumph!" the ads promised, quietly adding that the film could be seen both "silent and in Movietone," though the Movietone prints were pretty silent, too.

Then Universal suddenly released a genuine Big Musical, in mid-1929, an adaptation of the stage hit *Broadway* (1926). The play, by Philip Dunning and George Abbott, told of crime and show biz in a cheesy

New York nightclub, the Paradise. What is the true meaning of this place—gang war or entertainment? It's both at once: all shooting, all singing, all dancing. Yet Universal's film expanded *Broadway*'s modest hooch parlor into an art deco palace of sin. "The biggest set ever built!" the ads crowed. It wasn't—not after D. W. Griffith's Babylon in *Intolerance* (1916) and Douglas Fairbanks' *Robin Hood* (1922) castle. But *Broadway*'s Paradise stood seven stories high, a half-moon of band, staff, and patrons behaving like Old Testament revellers in one of the most constructed interiors imaginable, the Chrysler Building turned inside out. And to emphasize the mad energy of it all, the movie's director, Paul Fejos, shot from a camera crane mounted on a truck bed capable of panning six hundred feet a minute and climbing or diving four hundred feet a minute. This is literally a *movie*.

Fejos is one of cinema's lost wonderboys, because all of his famous titles survive in scraps. To this date, no Fejos masterpiece has been fully restored, but *Broadway*'s opening sequence is still alive, and it's a tell. Hollywood loves New York's music and wisecracks, but Hollywood absolutely cannot resist New York's lawlessness. This leaps into view even before *Broadway*'s credits, as, to portentous soundtrack exhortation, we see the night lights of the metropolis, urging us to come and buy. Lucky Strike! Chevrolet! A miniature of Manhattan appears, complete with tiny working automobiles, while a giant Bacchus strides in, shuddering with glee as he pours out wine—the symbol, in those late Prohibition years, of anarchy and sin.

Now the credits roll in to raucous dance strains, and presently we enter the Paradise Club itself. There!: its tough manager surveys his magnificent grotto of Here You May, where even music loves crime. Oh yes, it does: because later in the story one crook shoots another to death only to take his own fatal slug from his victim's girl friend. But the cabaret is roaring just then, and nobody hears a thing.

The Paradise's manager is Greek, the usual Nick, surnamed Verdis, because no one in New York is "American."* Besides the floor numbers,

* The Paradise's band, ironically, is a real-life Hollywood outfit, Gus Arnheim and his boys, who had been attracting notice at the Cocoanut Grove.

such as "Hittin' the Ceiling" and "Hot Footin' It," putdowns and come-backs fill the ear, right from the stage script, and riot fills the eye. The Paradise's patrons are as crazed as Fejos' hurtling camera while gangland evil quietly makes its deals in the back rooms. It's Hollywood's New York: Babylon with a dollar sign.

The play *Broadway* was one of a cluster of late-twenties stage hits that saw a connection between rich-and-famous glamor and crime, in not only outlaw subculture but municipal corruption as well. Whether in speakeasy or courtroom, everyone was guilty, from the paperboy to the Board of Aldermen. *Chicago* and *The Front Page* were two more such titles, in 1926 and 1928, respectively, but the concept arguably derives from early in the century in the work of the so-called muckrakers, especially Lincoln Steffens' series for *McClure's Magazine* on New York, Chicago, Philadelphia, Pittsburgh, Minneapolis, and St. Louis. Collected in book form as *The Shame of the Cities* (1904), Steffens' reports were filled with food-chain bosses ruling as despots while the citizenry could not or even would not evict them. "Corrupt and Contented" was the heading of Steffens' piece on Philadelphia.

Though the muckrakers were influential, their viewpoint was entirely political, amassing dry data. Even the scandals were boring. What the reform movement needed was personality, "hot" crime rather than graft, and show biz, and sex. "Will the people rule?" Steffens asks. "Is democracy possible?" Films like *Broadway* phrase it better: Will the people party? Is the union of glitter and power possible, hidden behind chorus girls and hotcha?

Adding the unenforceable *Thou shalt not* of Prohibition to the already vulnerable moral structure of urban government seemed virtually to greenlight the growth of crime, of its increasingly sophisticated organization and its adulterous union with legal authority itself. Who wasn't in on it? Who, if innocent of involvement, didn't accept it? There was a word for that attitude: *jazz*. Everything twenties was jazz—everything that wasn't a waltz, a preacher, or water was jazz.

Arnold Rothstein, a gangster of gangsters, was jazz. He was so jazz that he maintained connections to not only all of the underworld but New York's rulers, too, even the mayor. Rothstein was so jazz that he's a character in F. Scott Fitzgerald's *The Great Gatsby*. In the original edition, Fitzgerald called him—in a clumsy Anglophonetic spelling—Meyer Wolfshiem, correcting it under advice in later printings to Wolfsheim: *Wolfs-hime*. "He's quite a character around New York—a denizen of Broadway," Gatsby explains to a more American Nick, surnamed Carraway. "He's the man who fixed the World Series back in 1919."

Indeed, that was Rothstein's most famous accomplishment. When Carraway, a midwestern innocent in the land of jazz, asks, "Why isn't he in jail?," Gatsby answers, "They can't get him, old sport. He's a smart man."

Yet he made a fool's fatal error. Running out of luck in an epic crap game, Rothstein emerged owing serious money. Though a multi-millionaire, Rothstein did not pay up promptly, an aggressive violation of the etiquette. Further, he made it no secret that he believed the game had been rigged. His host, George McManus, was more than peeved to hear this: and McManus was as much a thug as Rothstein was mild. So when McManus called Rothstein for a meeting, Rothstein should have sent an intermediary to pay off the I.O.U.

Here's the error: Rothstein didn't. On the contrary, he met with McManus, who had checked into Room 349 of the Park Central Hotel (on West Fifty-sixth Street) as a certain George Richards. We don't know how the conversation went, but it is certain that McManus was still peeved, because Rothstein took a bullet in the nether region. Staggering down the hotel's back stairs, Rothstein collapsed. A hotel employee found him and called the house detective, who got the cops to send an ambulance.

Now to another hotel—Rothstein's—where the police set up shop with a stenographer and Rothstein's outlaw cronies, eager to donate blood to the cause. If you can't be the man who fixed the World Series, you could at least be the man who gave the transfusion. Rothstein was conscious and able to name his assassin; but jazz has its code. ROTHSTEIN, GAMBLER, MYSTERIOUSLY SHOT, *The New York Times* reported. REFUSES TO TALK. The *Times* usually ignored gangland hits, but this story was *big*. It was more than scandal, as publisher Adolph S. Ochs remarked: "It's sociology."

However, Rothstein had not been mysteriously shot. The whole city knew that George McManus had been pursuing Rothstein—and McManus' coat, with his name sewn into the lining, was found in Room 349. Further, there was a witness to at least part of this event, a chambermaid. Then the District Attorney seized Rothstein's records, and someone close to the case predicted, "There are going to be a lot of suicides in high places." Everyone knew what he meant: gangsters + government = jazz.

So the police department went into official screw-up mode, chasing false leads and suffering amnesia at the very mention of the word "McManus." This kind of thing takes more than skill: it's an art, especially when the chambermaid is interrogated so deftly that she is no longer certain of anything. It wasn't McManus who got off, in the end. It was the custodians of civic order, gulping down their ocean of payoffs. It was the shame of the cities.

New York's unique system of intertwisted corruption—unique because it sneaked over into bigtime entertainment and media loops—was defined, ruefully accepted, and even "explained" in the term "Tammany Hall." Cliché of clichés, it is hauled out yet today when someone needs fighting words to describe city government, but "Tammany" is so ancient it goes back to the end of the eighteenth century. Chief Tamenend of the Delawares was a semi-legendary figure, a real-life personage absorbed into larger-than-life romance. As "Tammany," the chief became a symbol of just about anything patriotic or heroic and lent his name to a social club favoring Indian terms (sachem for "leader"; wigwam for "meeting place," which was usually a saloon). Adherents of Tammany dressed as Indians, and by 1820 or so the social club was a political unit, with an official meeting place built for the purpose, the first of three Tammany Halls, down near City Hall.

Tammany was at that time a WASP enclave, but expansive changes in the voting laws and an upsurge in immigration led it to a policy of welcoming new arrivals as a prefabricated voting bloc. Thus Tammany became a success story in the habilitation of minorities, in this case the Germans and Irish. The European visitor scarcely got through the screening process at Castle Garden and onto city streets before he was hailed by a friendly Tammany representative who would help him get settled. (In the time of the Great Famine, starting in 1845, most of the Irish arrived literally half-alive. Some might easily have died in the New York streets without Tammany's assistance.) There were jobs and other amenities, including a vastly expedited naturalization process, for which one had only to give Tammany one's vote—all five or six of them, actually, moving from precinct to precinct or changing one's look. The friskier hombres could help intimidate voters in unreliable precincts or simply make off with the counting boxes. Tammany grew as New York's immigrant population grew, eventually to buy the fealty of cops, lawyers, reporters, judges, public prosecutors.

So Tammany was a criminal enterprise, furtive yet arrogant as it skimmed profit participation off of every transaction backed by the city treasury. If Tammany could realize a percentage on the purchase of lamp oil, imagine what it could do with the erection of a new courthouse. This proved a kind of latter-day pyramid, something fabulous. Take one item, for instance: $179,729.60 . . . for three tables and forty chairs. "Brooms were a steal," historian George J. Lankevich jokes, "at $41,190.95." A horn of plenty, the courthouse somehow never seemed to near completion, till it cost nearly four times what England spent to build the Houses of Parliament.

By 1867, when the second Tammany Hall was opened, on Fourteenth Street between Third Avenue and Irving Place, "Tammany" could not be distinguished from the Democratic Party in a city that was largely Democratic in its voting: a perfect marriage. Sandwiched between the Academy of Music to the east and Tony Pastor's Olympic Music Hall to the west, the new Tammany Hall—boasting a replica of Chief Tamenend in a cupola on the roof—appeared to assert the power of its "friends" in a physical sense. On the one side was the opera house, catering to the Knickerbocker grandees who quietly assented to the corruption: the moneyed elite. On the other side was the theatre of the upwardly expectant, where Pastor was reforming a proletarian stag show into middle-class entertainment: the would-be elite.

But note an adjustment in Tammany's ethnic identity, which is why our narrative of the 1920s is pausing in backstory. German immigrants, mostly of peasant- or artisan-class, tended to assimilate rapidly, and many moved on to the heavily Nordic midwest. The Irish stayed in New York, but few had any labor skills to speak of; further, they were thought uncouth troublemakers. Tammany saw an opportunity. Expanding its social programs, the machine now adopted the Irish in particular, giving them the law-enforcement franchise and promoting some to offices in city government.

This cultivation of an immigrant group is the sociopolitical precursor to the socio*artistic* twentieth-century development of "New Yorkism": the absorption of the unique styles and attitudes of minority groups to create an innovative arts culture without parallel elsewhere in Western civilization. Tradition gives us *Romeo and Juliet,* the comedy of manners, Bach's Mass in B Minor. New Yorkism gives us *Porgy and Bess,* the Marx brothers, and Leonard Bernstein's *Mass.*

Perhaps the very first of these inventions occurred in 1848, when the Tammany enclave of Five Points anointed a new Manhattan hero in a primitive musical called *A Glance at New York.* Five Points was so named because of its central address, the intersection of Orange (later Baxter) and Cross (later Park) Streets, joined by Anthony (later Worth) Street, which dead-ended there, creating five radii, or "points." (All that remains of the original junction is where Baxter runs into Worth, at the south end of the present-day Columbus Park.) The Five Points neighborhood generally was bounded on the north by Canal Street, on the east by the Bowery, on the west by Centre Street, and along the south by Chatham running into Pearl Street. Within these borders lay a slum of notorious squalor and crime, although it stood but a short walk, to the northeast, from City Hall, "Newspaper Row" (where every major city daily was headquartered), and that first of the Astor family's gala hostels, the Astor House.

The local "hero" of Five Points was the so-called Bowery B'hoy, so spelled to conform to the local pronunciation: Ba-*hoy.* The b'hoys were street toughs favoring red shirts, wide trousers, and boots, with a top hat over a hairdo sculpted with wet soap. Those of ambitious self-definition took membership in a volunteer fire brigade, and *A Glance at New York* featured one such in Mose the Fire B'Hoy. Actor Frank Chanfrau made a career out of Mose in this work and its many sequels, all based on a historic moment: Mose's entrance. Theatre in those days was romance, plotty farce, or the classics; Chanfrau connected art to life in the shock of the familiar, for the audience at the Olympic Theatre that night included b'hoys right off the Five Points streets. Chronicle tells us that when Chanfrau appeared in full b'hoy kit to announce, "I ain't a-goin' to run with dat mercheen [i.e., tag along behind the "machine"—the company engine—to fight fires] no more!," the audience went wild with recognition. At last: a play about what was real. A new art, even. In a revision that expanded Chanfrau's role, *A Glance*'s author, Benjamin Baker, further delighted the public with utterances that might have been taken down on the Bowery itself. "I'm bilein' over for a rousin' good fight with someone somewhere" referred to the riots that kept Five Pointers on their guard, and for philosophy there was Mose's dismissal of everyone out of his social orbit: "Foo-foos is outsiders and outsiders is foo-foos."

There apparently was a real-life Mose. More legendary even than Tamenend, Mose was at some early point a gang member affiliated with the nativist, anti-Catholic Know Nothing Party and at a later point a gang member on the Irish side. It would seem that one's identity as a B'hoy outweighed other considerations, even the virulent religious bigotry of the day. And that mirrors Tammany's early history, from resisting the Irish to assimilating and finally becoming Irish. Thus, while Mose's vogue was dense but relatively brief, he created a theatrical archetype that lasted in various forms and venues for some four generations: the New York stock character that turned into the New York *Irish* stock character. Pugnacious yet charming, of narrow working-class worldview yet sometimes open to progressive enlightenment, the fire b'hoy kept getting rejuvenated—in George M. Cohan's Doodle Dandies (on the sentimental and patriotic side), for instance, or James Cagney's Hollywood characters (playful yet dangerous whether outlaw or lawman). Further, performers such as Al Jolson and Bert Lahr gave the figure a Jewish inflection, even as, a bit later, the "*Dead End* Kids" of Broadway and Hollywood reclaimed the original archetype. This troupe of latterday b'hoys even got back-to-the-source billing in their B pictures as the "East Side Kids" and the "Bowery Boys."

Tammany Hall had its archetype, too—the infamous "Boss" Tweed. Unlike most Tammany leaders of his heyday, the 1870s—and Tweed was the Grand Sachem, no less—William M.* Tweed was a third-generation American of Scots ancestry. Nonetheless, Tweed—who had started as a b'hoy, with a firefighting unit—was universally thought of as Irish, especially by the Irish themselves, who saw not a colossal thief but a success story.

No one can say how much the so-called "Tweed Ring" stole. It was at least thirty million in nineteenth-century dollars, but more likely one hundred million, perhaps twice that. In Tweedism, one actually spoke of "honest graft," meaning the orderly offering of bribes and charging of kickbacks, as opposed to the mad pickpocket chaos of dipping right into the city coffers. With the beard and belly of a comic-opera rogue, Tweed fell to the pen of cartoonist Thomas Nast of *Harper's Weekly* like rock to paper in the old fingers duel. Ironically, Nast came from New York's "other" immigrant minority, having left Germany with his family when he was six years old. Historian Leo Hershkowitz believes that Nast and the Tweed-hating newspaper editors in fact "saw in Tweed an outsider threatening their position by his supposedly championing the 'drunken-ignorant Irish,' the overly ambitious German-Jewish immigrants and those seeking to change the status quo."

Yet Tweed was not only "Tammany Irish," in his honorary way. He was as well a jovial, popular character, anything but a backroom con-niver, much less a thug. Tweed tried to bribe Nast out of the political cartoon business—and Nast bargained, just to see how high Tammany would go: five hundred thousand dollars! Nast turned it down, and Tweed dropped the matter. With all the boodle at stake, and given the

---

* Tweed's middle name is popularly rendered as "Marcy," though he himself never supplied anything but the initial. New York historians give the name—a relevant detail in an era when imposing men liked to expand in print—as "Magear," from his mother's family. The Marcy is thought to be derived from the statesman William Learned Marcy, who famously declared in the U.S. Senate that "the advantage of success" in politics turned on the rule that "to the victor belong the spoils of the enemy." Thus, dubbing Tweed with a "Marcy" is the equivalent of "William Blago-jevich Tweed": a mocking sobriquet.

air of criminal license that Tammany engendered, it is amazing that no attempts were made on Nast's life.

For Nast's cartoons were extremely effective. One such, in 1871, was captioned UNDER THE THUMB and showed a gigantic fist, its short digit pressing upon the island of Manhattan and the cuff link of its shirt reading "William M. Tweed." As Nast set it down, the Boss accompanied this gesture of oppression with the words, "Well, what are you going to do about it?"

The confidence of the challenge was pure Tammany, but Tweed never uttered the words: they were Nast's crystallization of Tammany attitudes. And one month later, when the *New-York* (as it was then spelled) *Times* published pages of spectacular overcharging lifted right from Tammany's books by a Tammany apostate, civic reformers appeared near to breaking up the Tweed Ring. "STOP THIEF!" was the caption of Nast's next drawing, showing Tweed and his cohort (including the mayor, A. Oakey Hall), racing down the street. As I've said, the Astors and others of what we might call the Hotel Set had been acquiescent in and at times supportive of Tammany misrule. Was it because, behind the facade of their Society leadership, they were as corrupt as Tammany? Did these bankers and lawyers see New York as a business that could turn fabulous profits even while being looted by its employees? Or was it because, in the words of William Waldorf Astor, "Politics is closed to a man who will not seek votes in the Irish slums"?

Thus, at an early stage in the campaign to oust Tweed, a special committee of what Ward McAllister would have termed "the best sort" was formed to audit the city ledgers: five titans of the Wall Street–Fifth Avenue loop. The chairman was John Jacob Astor III, brother-in-law of *the* Mrs. Astor and William Waldorf Astor's father. The committee declared that "the financial affairs of the city . . . are administered in a correct and faithful manner."

Of course, Astor and his fellow boyars remained socially aloof from Tammany politicians. True, August Belmont, socially prominent though of less certain Family and thus of greater vulnerability, hobnobbed with Tweed, even dined with him; a gentleman mustn't. But once the *Times* unveiled that excerpt of Tammany's account books, the aristos evaporated on Tweed and his Ring. After all, a money scandal of this size imperiled New York's banking credit. All that it took now was for one of the real powers in the state to take over the war on Tweed. And that would be Samuel J. Tilden.

Arguably the pack leader of the New York State Democrats, Tilden nourished Ambitions, intending to follow the lead of Martin Van Buren (and anticipate Grover Cleveland and the two Roosevelts) in leaping to the White House from the New York governor's chair. Tilden needed an issue, such as Throwing the Rascals out, and so he turned on Tweed and destroyed him, twisting the statutes and corrupting due process till the Boss was made martyr. These words Tweed actually did say:

They will never get a jury to convict me.

but then, less confidently:

I have got twenty more years of life yet. I'm only fifty years of age.

and finally:

I guess Tilden and [state attorney general Charles] Fairchild have killed me at last.

Tweed died in prison at the age of fifty-five, in 1878. However, of his equally guilty cohort in the Ring, none was punished, and only Mayor Hall was prosecuted, unsuccessfully.* Yet Tweed remained popular among working-class Democrats, the Irish in particular. They got their first Roman Catholic Irish mayor, William Russell Grace, in 1880 (albeit on an anti-Tammany reform ticket). It was a belated acknowledgment that much of the flavor of New York—its sense of humor, its rambunctious cynicism, and a great deal of its theatre people and balcony audience—was

---

* Tilden got his run at the White House: and he won, but he lost. It was the controversial election of 1876, when Tilden took the popular vote but failed in the electoral college. Rutherford B. Hayes was certified as president.

Irish. Still, many Irishmen held Tweed to be the man who had given them a voice in city government, and the day his death was announced, it was said, there wasn't an unused black armband to be found within ten blocks of Five Points.

The saga of the Tweed Ring asks, Who *are* the elite? If they are simply prominent people with more or less the life-and-death power of a pre-Revolution French aristocrat, then the elite is made of politicians. But if the elite are prominent people who are creative and glamorous—those who, to repeat, lead dramatic lives and set fashion—then the elite hasn't really appeared in the age of Tweed. It took the expansion of Communications in the twentieth century to publicize the Smart Set's sayings and doings—and doesn't that begin with the Algonquin Round Table? This explains why Kaufman, Parker, and company remain summoning terms: they're the base camp from which one scales up to the folk later known as "café society." This incomplete term refers to the boldface names of Manhattan culture, such as arts patron Otto Kahn, playwright and director Moss Hart, gossip Elsa Maxwell, and just about everyone who crossed their path.

However, the gradual rise of this new intellectual elite did not displace Tammany Hall—just as the *philosophes* of the Encyclopédie did not displace the aristocracy. Under Tweed's successor as boss, John Kelly—known by ironic detachment as "Honest John"—the organization thrived. In fact, it was Tammany rather than the various mayoral administrations that ran the city, and here is where we pick up the blended strains of jazz crime, jazz glamor, and jazz *jazz* that the *Broadway* film tells of. The Jazz Age gave New York something the Tweed Ring could not have imagined: a jazz mayor. He tolerated the crime and symbolized the glamor—and he, too, was Irish.

However, James J. Walker, who served as mayor from 1926 to 1932 (in a second term cut short by his resignation), was not merely Irish by family, like his predecessor William Grace. Though born in Ireland, Grace did so well in business that he ended up owning a steamship company under his name. In the era we speak of, how many New York City Irishmen owned ocean liners?

No, Jimmy Walker was leprechaun Irish, pure stereotype: irresistibly charming even when most irresponsible. *"Don't look him in the eyes!"* they warned Samuel Seabury when he interrogated Walker in the hearings that ended in Walker's downfall. That is: the very command of his appeal will confuse your sense of right and wrong. There's a reason why we have the phrase "Irish charm" and not, say, "Palestinian charm" or "hip-hop-lyric charm."

Jimmy Walker was, as Gatsby put it a few pages ago, a denizen of Broadway. Here was not just a first-nighter and bon vivant of the speakeasies: he had logged time writing lyrics to songs to be interpolated into musicals. The tiresome Walker cliché is his one hit, sentimental glop to the music of Ernest R. Ball,* "Will You Love Me in December As You Do in May?":

> *When my hair has all turned gray,*
> *Will you kiss me then and say,*
> *That you love me in December as you do in May?*

More relevant to Walker's biography was his longtime adulterous girl friend, Betty Compton, a Broadway starlet. Compton was the real thing, too—not a showgirl but a genuine performer. She played the second woman lead in productions for the Astaires and Bert Lahr and held her own in a distinguished ensemble in Cole Porter's *Fifty Million Frenchmen* (1929). Still, her great role was as Jimmy Walker's scandal, the hotsy-totsy of a man both married and Catholic. Compton was an open secret among the informed; what the general public saw was the handsome, trim, dressy

---

* Ball is one of the many early-twentieth-century songwriters whose work has survived his name. Two of his numbers, from the Chauncey Olcott show *The Isle O'Dreams* (1913), are still with us, "When Irish Eyes Are Smiling" and "Mother Machree." The latter has been guyed by show-biz wags for sixty years. Aficionados of the musical can hear its first strain ridiculed in *Do Re Mi* (1960), on the jukebox racket. For the original's "Sure, I love the dear silver that shines in your hair," lyricists Betty Comden and Adolph Green substituted "Sure, I love the dear silver they put in the slot," complete with bogus Irish tenor Olcotting up to a high A.

mayor with his wife, Allie. Unlike Boss Tweed and the mayors of *his* day, Walker was not readily cartoonable. Here was the nineteenth-century b'hoy turned out for good looks and an air of sophistication.

What a fraud. The man was lazy, uninterested, and up to his bow tie in graft. He was almost certainly incompetent at his job, but we'll never know because he never did his job. In Walker's first two years in office, he spent 143 days in Europe, the Caribbean, Atlanta, Hollywood, at the Kentucky Derby, and at other ports of call, and this total doesn't count Walker's generous math on the number of days in a weekend. Walker's New York ran on Tammany and jazz. Robert Moses called Walker "half Beau Brummell, half guttersnipe." But that isn't correct, because, if nothing else, Walker had class. And he had nothing else.

Walker's mayoralty coincided with the high point of a war among New York's minorities as well as a war by long-established Americans *against* minorities. The Immigration Act that Congress passed in 1924 had been in the making for over a generation: Grover Cleveland, William Howard Taft, and Woodrow Wilson vetoed laws instituting literacy tests (in the emigré's own language, not in English) for those entering the country. Wilson vetoed his bill *twice,* but the second time Congress overrode him because of tremendous popular pressure to limit immigration, especially from southern and eastern Europe.

One reason was economics: new arrivals clogged the job market. Another reason, the sociocultural one, was abstract: most people just do not like Different. Chicago and Boston had huge minority populations, but New York was the place that Americans blamed for thriving on Different: "too worldly, too self-assured, too dense and too ethnic," says George J. Lankevich, "to appeal to the average American." New York was an offense to their concept of an American living style. "Wall Street and Tammany!" ran the nativist's war cry, and some comments heard from public figures critical of New York would have been called hate speech if the notion had existed then.

The 1924 immigration bill went far past literacy tests, reappointing a reduced population influx to favor, for instance, the German farmer and not the Russian shtetl dweller. Nevertheless, to some nativist viewpoints, foreigners *generally* were Different. Some were radicals. Worse, many of them drank. And this is what Prohibition was about, at the dark center of its mandate—not liquor but foreigners.

"Well-meant" is the term often pasted onto Prohibition by historians, presumably because they need to discover reason or at least benign intentions in a law that was to prove encompassingly destructive. On the contrary, Prohibition was another of the periodic Fundamentalist uprisings that characterize the American interior's relationship with its coasts—with the wit and wisecracks of Manhattan, the erotic brinkmanship of Hollywood, and all that banking, law, glamor, and sheer unapologetic ethnicity. With sin.

The conflict of Prohibition and jazz wrote the sociopolitical text of the 1920s. Alain Locke—the first black Rhodes Scholar and a leader of the Harlem Renaissance—defined jazz as "the symptom of a profound cultural unrest and change, first a reaction from Puritan repressions and then an escape from the tensions and monotonies of a machine-ridden, extroverted form of civilization." That Puritanism was, in historian Lawrence A. Levine's words, "the work habits and morality of the old America." Prohibition thus "clearly told every immigrant and every urbanite what it meant to be an American; it attempted to make the American Protestant ideal of the good life national by enshrining it in law."

It sounds almost sensible, if overbearing, but Prohibition was as well a vengeful assault on freedom by religious zealots. Another historian assists us here: Richard Hofstadter said Prohibition was "carried about America by the rural-evangelical virus." It was a rebellion by those of narrow culture against those of broad culture, comparable to the current battles over gay marriage—Puritan repression, as Locke stated. This is what Italians call *campanilismo* (literally, "church bell towerism"): a worldview strictly conforming to the beliefs and values of one's parish and intolerant of all other beliefs and values. Whatever isn't compulsory is forbidden. "The movement," says historian Leo Hershkowitz, "brought together nativists, Whigs,* do-gooders, anti-Catholics, anti-immigrants,

---

* The Whig Party represented the ephemeral alliance of factions united only by opposition to the policies of President Andrew Jackson. Active during the early middle 1800s, it elected two presidents but had disintegrated by 1860.

Fundamentalists and assorted sour apples—generally the most conservative anti-urban, anti-democratic elements."

True, it was the drinkers who started the rumble, deep in the nineteenth century. Every town above the size of a village had its saloon, invariably functioning as a kind of Crime Central. Prostitution, swindles, and impulsive violence were headquartered there, and the so-called Maine Law of the 1850s, adopted by other states, marked the start of major dry legislation. Court challenges prevailed, however, and the Civil War sidelined the issue. Then, in Thomas R. Pegram's words, "the cavalcade of bland, humdrum presidents following Lincoln and preceding Theodore Roosevelt" discouraged pursuing the divisive question of dry law.

It is notable, then, that the resurgence of Fundamentalist support for Prohibition coincided with the height of European immigration and calls for restrictions. We do not hear "benign intentions" from the drys, but rather the rhetoric of holy war. Some dry leaders openly advocated suspending the drinking population from cages in public squares, or poisoning the liquor supply, or torturing wets to death. Yes, in those words. Not surprisingly, when in the late 1920s it was undeniable that Prohibition had failed—and that it had destroyed respect for law and created a criminal infrastructure on the national level—the drys became not conciliatory but terminally vindictive. In 1929, federal agents invaded the home of a suspected bootlegger, clubbed him senseless, and then turned a shotgun on his wife when she tried to help him. And Ella Boole of the National Woman's Christian Temperance Union snarled, "She was evading the law, wasn't she?" Or, as Billy Sunday put it, "I have no interest in a God Who does not smite."

Prohibition marked Old America's attempt to eviscerate New America: a crusade against jazz and its media infrastructure. Richard Hofstadter called this viewpoint "the one-hundred per cent mentality." He was speaking of Billy Sunday in particular, but he could have meant the Prohibitionist: "a mind totally committed to the full range of the dominant popular fatuities and determined that no one shall have the right to challenge them." It was not a question of liquor, but of the retreat of Revealed Religion in American life. Immigrants, intellectuals, women's rights, and Hollywood sexplay proved that America was getting Different in every direction. "Expanding education . . . and the development of a nationwide market in ideas," says Hofstadter, "made it increasingly difficult for the secular, liberated thought of the intelligentsia and the scriptural faith of the fundamentalists to continue to move in separate grooves . . . the two were thrown into immediate and constant combat." But with the repeal of Prohibition, in 1933, the coasts overwhelmed the heartland and the war against the minorities went into retreat.

And yet the war *among* minorities was just getting started, particularly in New York. In fact, by about 1910 New York was the largest Italian city, the largest Irish city, and the largest Jewish city.

In the world.

So there were shoving matches when Jewish and Italian blocs demanded identity equality with the Tammany Irish. These new groups had higher expectations than their parents because they had established a presence in the usual American manner: in the popular arts. Then as now, a visibility in entertainment (in its broadest sense, from vaudeville to television table talk) advances one's share in political power.

It couldn't have happened earlier, because show biz wasn't ready then, and immigrants were too busy building their citizenship to consider turning performer. Of what? Now, however, their offspring could make art out of assimilation, joke about how it felt to be an American from someplace else. Some of my readers will have seen this in our own time, when a proliferation of gay characters in theatre and film anticipated and expanded Stonewall liberation.

In the early 1900s, this was a Jewish operation. Following the break-in popularity of "Dutch" comics Weber and Fields—so they were known, like a line of cough drops—came Al Jolson, arguably the most famous name in old show biz. Fanny Brice and Eddie Cantor cracked the *Ziegfeld Follies,* whose annual opening was the biggest night of the New York theatre season. And, this time, the Irish were in uniform riding horseback in crowd control while Brice and Cantor held court.

The Italians had music, especially at the high end. Enrico Caruso, who debuted at the Metropolitan Opera in 1903 to sing 607 performances in thirty-seven roles to his death, in 1921, remained opera's most evocative synecdoche for fifty years—the name you thought of when you thought of opera. And Giacomo Puccini was not one of those dead classroom names like Mozart or Gounod, or the four others mounted on plaques above the Met's proscenium. When Fanny Brice joined the *Follies,* in 1910, the Met had been giving Puccini's *Madama Butterfly* for only three years, with Caruso and the house glamor diva, Geraldine Farrar. The latter had fans like a rock star; later, come summer she would go Hollywood with director Cecil B. DeMille and a squad of illustrious costar hunks from Wallace Reid to Milton Sills. Today, opera is an exclusive preserve; it wasn't so then. Opera was contemporary: the Met lit up 1910 with the world premiere of Puccini's cowboy opera, *La Fanciulla del West,* conducted by Arturo Toscanini and covered by an international press. If a Jewish-American success story was Irving Berlin's taking charge of Tin Pan Alley and charming his own personal heiress, an Italian-American success story was one of vaudeville's singing Ponzillo Sisters' moving to the Met to command the greatest soprano heroines, from Norma to Aida, as Rosa Ponselle.

Nevertheless, Jewish and Italian leaders envied the political success that the Irish enjoyed. In the second half of the nineteenth century, the population of New York tripled, and most of the latest newcomers were Jewish and Italian immigrants who had access to only the most exhausting jobs under appalling working conditions while the Irish were electing mayors. The Triangle Waist Company Fire of March 25, 1911, marked the crash-over line, at which the public and the state realized that legislation must end the practices of the sweatshop.

Triangle manufactured shirtwaists, tailored blouses with an expansive bosom tapering to a narrow base that were very popular among women with a progressive sense of fashion. They retired the dress for day-to-day wear, seeing the combination of shirtwaist and skirt as liberating, comfortable, and stylish as well. Triangle's factory occupied the eighth, ninth, and tenth floors at the top of the Asch Building, at Washington Place and Greene Street, a few hundred yards east of Washington Square Park. The structure was boosted as fireproof, and it was. Only its contents would burn: 146 human beings, 123 women and 23 men, virtually all young Italian and Jewish immigrants. Anna Ardito. Kalman Downic. Irene Grameatassio. Rosie Grosso. Augusta Kaplan. Jacob Kline. Annie L'Abbato. Israel Rosen. Gussie Spunt. Fires were not only a hazard in places like the Triangle Waist Company but a routine occurrence—yet there was no sprinkler system, no adequate fire escapes, no fire drills. Most fatally, crucial exits were locked, to control workers' mobility.

Ironically, the fire broke out just a few minutes before quitting time, on a Saturday, and while the fire department responded promptly, no ladder in the city reached higher than the seventh floor. Those who did not make it out of the building within the first moments were trapped; spectators watched in the horror of seeing the unseeable as those who were able to leaped to the street below to avoid the flames and die sooner. Some were already burning as they fell. Reporter William Gunn Shepherd, who had happened upon the scene by chance, wrote, "Girls were burning to death before our eyes. There were jams in the windows. . . . But one by one the jams broke. Down came the bodies in a shower, burning, smoking, lighted bodies, with the disheveled hair of the girls trailing upward. . . . There were thirty-three in that shower."

The fire became a national scandal on the all-devouring recklessness of industrialists, but in New York some saw it as a peculiarly ethnic victimization, what happens to helpless minorities. Communities must unite behind candidates who would protect them as Tammany protected the Irish—as, indeed, government would begin to do for all citizens in the aftermath of the Triangle fire. The New York State Factory Investigating Commission is a historian's point of reference in the battle to create safeguards and disburdenments for labor—shorter hours and free Saturdays, for one thing. Frances Perkins also witnessed the Triangle disaster by chance, as she had been socializing in a house on Washington Square and was drawn to the Asch Building by the fire sirens. Perkins later became Franklin Delano Roosevelt's Secretary of Labor, the first woman in American history to hold a presidential cabinet chair. "The New Deal began the day the Triangle Factory burned" is a common rendering of remarks Perkins made many years after. In truth, she did say as much, as did others in Roosevelt's circle. Most officially, however, Perkins said:

> We had in the election of Franklin Roosevelt the beginning of what has come to be known as the New Deal for the United States. But it was based really upon the experiences that we had in New York State and upon the sacrifices of those who . . . died in that terrible fire on March 25, 1911. They did not die in vain and we will never forget them.

One of the members of the Factory Investigating Commission was Alfred E. Smith Jr., an old-school Tammany kingpin who nevertheless took no part in the graft. Smith had the easy tongue of the born politician and, when roused, could turn an angry eloquence on those he saw as aligned against the welfare of the unempowered—working people generally but especially women, new citizens with few or no spokesmen—and on hypocrites like the factory owner who backed Prohibition laws to keep his employees docile while he enjoyed easy access to the contraband. The rich get rich and the poor get arrested.

Smith was as well a devoted listener when around those of informed intelligence, an unusual quality in a political boss. Someone once asked how Smith got so smart, and someone else replied, "He read a book." The title? "He knew Frances Perkins and she was a book."

Perkins is the link between Smith and Roosevelt, particularly in the early 1920s, when Smith was Roosevelt's mentor: before the patrician outstripped the cincinnatus in popularity and the latter turned publicly against the former's policies. As Perkins saw it, Smith's investigation of management's brutalization of labor transformed him. From the professional populist, he turned into a genuine progressive, and Smith made sure that Albany's commission would inspire dense reform, not cosmetics. Bosses in some industries conspired to try to stubborn their way out of worker relief. Incredibly, it took new law to free workers from labor on *Sunday;* even then, the canning interests asked for an exemption. Smith gave them reply, quoting the Fourth Commandment, the one with "Remember the Sabbath day, to keep it holy." And, added Smith, there was nothing in there like "except in the canneries."

Smith makes an interesting study in how close to the power center minorities could get in the 1920s. As an Irish Catholic* in New York State, Smith could rise to governor four times . . . but President of the United States? In 1924, when Smith made the first of two tries to run as the Democrats' national candidate, he found himself locked in a stand-off with the half of the party that supported Prohibition, the Ku Klux Klan, and rival candidate William Gibbs McAdoo.

By contrast, two weeks earlier, in Cleveland, the Republicans enjoyed a reasonably mild convention to unite behind Calvin Coolidge. Nothing united the Democrats: they were two different parties, one advocating a tolerance of Different and the other trying to revive a time before Different even existed. Comically enough, the Democrats assembled for their convention in New York, Different City itself;† an English tourist in the visitors' gallery commented to a reporter during the first day how sedately it was going.

"Just wait," came the reply. "Those are Democrats down there."

One writer described the convention as "Seventeen days of animal riots, slapstick hoopla, and popcorn anarchy." This was the famous "103

---

* Frances Perkins clarified, on her own research, Smith's complex genealogy: he was in fact German, Italian, and even English as much as Irish. However, such details could be prohibitively confusing on election days, and Smith rode out his career as the usual professional Irishman of Tammany Hall. This shows just how much a melting pot New York had turned out to be—and to texture Smith's faceted ethnicity further, his most trusted advisor was the Jewish Belle Moskowitz. This shows as well how important separate-but-equal identity management was to become in the development of New Yorkism, in politics and the arts.

† They gathered in the old Madison Square Garden, which actually was in Madison Square, unlike the later two sports-and-meeting centers bearing the Garden name. Designed by Stanford White, it stood at the square's northeast corner, from Twenty-sixth to Twenty-seventh Street on Madison Avenue. Many of my readers may know this bit of trivia. Yet there was another Madison Square Garden before these three, on this same site. Originally it served as the Union Depot of the New York and Harlem Railroad. When the station moved to the site of the present Grand Central (in a smaller building), P. T. Barnum took over the structure, a single-story square with a tower at its southwest corner. It was Barnum's Hippodrome in the 1870s and then became the very first of the four Madison Square Gardens in 1879. White's spectacular new edifice, in Spanish Renaissance style, rose in 1890. It, too, had a tower, but this one was a soaring barbican, one of the very highest structures in the city.

ballots" convention, which finally ended when the McAdoo and Smith factions accepted a compromise candidate in John W. Davis. A top hat with experience as ambassador to Great Britain and Wall Street lawyering, Davis made an odd sort of Democrat—but then, it wasn't clear by the seventeenth day just what a Democrat was any more. "Coolidge or chaos" was the G.O.P.'s slogan for the 1924 campaign.

Coolidge won, of course, taking even New York State by a huge plurality—but Al Smith, returning to the governor's mansion in November, achieved a winning spillover of nearly 110,000. Within his sphere, clearly, Smith was all but invincible; on the national level, however, he was Different. Out in the small towns and on the farms, throughout the south and the lower midwest, hatred of Different was at once an article of faith, an identity statement, and comfort food. "That thing can't live in this country," stated Smith in a speech in Boston shortly before Voting Day in 1924. That thing was the Klan, specifically—but wasn't Smith speaking as well of Main Street America's resistance to minority culture? "The Catholic can stand it," Smith went on. "So can the Jew and the Negro. But the United States of America can never stand it!"

Four years later, in 1928, Smith again sought and this time won the Democratic presidential nomination, unleashing a storm of shameless vilification. "My America against Tammany's" is how one private citizen phrased it, in the privacy of her diary. "Prairie, Plantation and Everlasting Hills against the Sidewalks of New York." Diary entries were the least of it. Smith was "Rum and Romanism," a slave of Papal command, and even, bizarrely, a would-be murderer of Protestants. Then, too, Smith cut a distinctly regional figure on this national campaign, for he refused to modify his b'hoy accent, his New York usages, his "raddio" and "horspital." What a great orator! "His voice quavered," said one listener, "his eyes flashed, his face crimsoned, Passion shook him." But what the sections saw, down south and out west, was one of those New York aldermen, corrupt and clannish, doing his little fixings around the ward, buying votes in saloons, scheming with cardinals. Middle America treated the election as a hate-speech field day, though much of it knew as little of Catholicism as the inner-city public-school kids who thought that nuns moved around on rollers attached to the soles of their feet. Herbert Hoover, Smith's Republican opponent, said nothing to uplift the campaign dialogue, though as a Quaker he was bound to tolerance. "Friends are urged," it says in the Advices, traditionally read aloud twice a year in Quaker Meetings, "to bear testimony against all forms of oppression."

As we know, Hoover won the election—because of "Republican prosperity"? Or was it in part the *religion* of Prohibition, the zealot's notion of culture as fixed and ahistorical? The voters of 1928 who rejected Smith because he was Catholic also had no real knowledge of the arts-and-letters figures we've looked at so far. They would have been aware only of Charles Lindbergh, and few would have sensed that Lindbergh's world of aviation was to prove far more revolutionary than anything happening at Algonquin lunches.

No, the revolution they discerned obtained in Hoover's successor, in 1932, Franklin Delano Roosevelt. It is impossible to imagine a politician less like Al Smith than FDR, patrician and debonair where Smith, in his Sunday Best ward-heeler suits and Five Points brogue, was virtually a cartoon of type. All the same, Roosevelt no less than Smith represented foreign, destabilizing, experimental New York, and liquor, and Different. A folk tune of the time shows us moderns how blunt Americans once were when they didn't like certain people, as Franklin serenades Eleanor:

> *You kiss the Negroes,*
> *I'll kiss the Jews.*
> *We'll stay in the White House*
> *As long as we choose.*

This, then, was what Jimmy Walker's New York represented to the resistant section of the nation: a scorning of what today are called "traditional values." A failure to go to church. The defiance of Father. New York was the place where heiresses married Irving Berlin, where Broadway was less a street than a catalogue of sins, where God had a name but His name was Jazz. Walker was indeed the ideal mayor for New York in the 1920s—an ingratiating greeter for the seductive decadence of the

Paradise Club. *Don't look him in the eyes!* Yet Walker wielded as much real power as the bridegroom poppet atop a wedding cake—which, in a way, Walker really was. All the content of government lay below him.

And above him was FDR, governor of New York State and about to play a very subtle—indeed, almost invisible—Samuel J. Tilden to Jimmy Walker's Tweed. In 1930, Samuel Seabury—always called Judge Seabury, though he was no longer on the bench—was appointed investigative counsel to look into the Magistrates' Courts and to pass on the findings to the governor. A kind of special prosecutor, Seabury expanded his survey as crime led to crime, taking in the police and the criminal courts. The press ate it with a spoon, as varlets, professional liars, and even bordello madam Polly Adler told how, among other things, the cops ran a business in blackmailing innocent women. Adler proved especially good copy in her answer to "How would you describe your employment?":

POLLY ADLER: I am a student of the human condition.*

The most famous sequences were those repopularized in "Little Tin Box," from the musical *Fiorello!* (1959). In fact, the boxes were of the safety-deposit kind, inclined to size. *Fiorello!*'s songwriters, Jerry Bock and Sheldon Harnick, added the "little" to fill out the scan of their soft-shoe music, but New York County Sheriff Thomas M. Farley specified "a big box in a big safe." It was there that Farley, cornered by Seabury's interrogation, claimed to have found a fortune as if by magic. "What did you have to do," Seabury asked him, "rub the lock with a little gold and open it to find more money?"

Not one of the "tin box" witnesses could explain his high-income lifestyle, and by now Seabury was looking into all "the departments of government of The City of New York," because Tammany had got into everything. This story was not just another Tammany rowdydow, but a national scandal. In the summer of 1931, Seabury graced the cover of *Time* magazine, that weekly arbiter of membership in the American elite, as clerics across the land made mephitic New York their Sunday

---

* *The New York Times* fussily corrected this to "vice entrepreneuse."

text. Soon enough, the Seabury team was bound to confront the mayor himself. "Let them come," Walker told reporters on one of his countless vacations, and in the spring of 1932 they came.

On the stand, Walker was as evasive and sophistical as his minions had been. It was an art, a jazz. "Everybody is wondering what Governor Roosevelt will do," said a *New York Times* editorial, "when a transcript of the evidence is laid before him." At one point—in a murmur, so the court stenographer couldn't take it down—Walker told Seabury, "You and Frank Roosevelt are not going to hoist yourself [*sic*] to the Presidency over my dead body!" Then, too, even now Walker was wildly popular. Perhaps some saw him as the opposite of Prohibition, of the despotic interference in basic freedoms by those living in a slavery of their own design. Or had Walker simply "come by large amounts of money with minimum effort," as *The New Yorker* cynically suggested, and "spent it without stint"? As the magazine concluded, "He's the man we all dream about being."

What Governor Roosevelt did about Walker was: nothing. He had let Walker destroy himself, not least with his spats-and-waistcoat swash-buckling on the witness stand. The mayor's plan was to turn the pro-ceedings into a circus, another "Well, what are you going to do about it?" Laugh, town, laugh. Still, it was all over but the paperwork, though Walker held on to his job with shameless determination. Meanwhile, Roosevelt finessed his way to his party's 1932 presidential nomination, settling a quarrelsome convention (in Chicago) by making deals in Texas (with his soon-to-be vice-president, John Nance Garner) and California (with its king, William Randolph Hearst). Both Walker and Al Smith were in Chicago as Roosevelt-hating spoilers, impotent ones. And in the end it was Smith who gave Walker the news that Roosevelt had beaten him. Walker had to go, for the sake of the Democratic Party and be-cause, finally, Walker's regime had become intolerable. Privately, Walker spoke of it using a joke of the day: "Daddy made me eat my spinach." Publicly, Walker was bitter. Headline: WALKER RESIGNS, DENOUNCING THE GOVERNOR: SAYS HE WILL RUN FOR THE MAYORALTY AGAIN, APPEALING TO 'FAIR JUDGMENT' OF THE PEOPLE. The subheads included CALLS TRIAL A TRAVESTY and ROOSEVELT NOT SURPRISED.

The symbolism is arresting: one Irish Catholic fires another at the behest of a WASP aristocrat. However, it's vastly misleading, because Walker ran an even dirtier shop than Tweed had done. For all that, Roosevelt appointed minority figures to his White House staff, including as we know the first woman cabinet member and, as Roosevelt's second Secretary of the Treasury (for eleven years), the Jewish Henry Morgenthau Jr. Aside from appointments to the Supreme Court, it was the first time that the political establishment had absorbed minorities at the utmost levels of power.*

New York itself broke with precedent in that same election of 1932, choosing as mayor someone neither WASP nor Catholic. It is often said that Fiorello La Guardia was half-Italian and half-Jewish, but in fact he was Italian on both sides, with a father from Foggia and a mother from Trieste, respectively as far to the south and the north of the Italian boot as one can get. But La Guardia's mother was Jewish, though he identified as Episcopalian and his wives were Catholic and Lutheran: a match for the New York melting pot.

Short and round, shrill when defied, and excitable to the point of violence against even the biggest aggressors, La Guardia was everything. Cowboy, aviator, attorney, congressman, polyglot interpreter for the Bureau of Immigration on Ellis Island,† three-times mayor of New York (from 1933 to 1944), and outspoken enemy of the "irresponsible rich," La Guardia—he himself said—was as well "an incurable insurgent." But why a Republican?

"Because," he explained, "I could not stomach Tammany Hall." After his election, surging into City Hall for the first time, a one-man crowd, Fiorello shouted, *"È finita la cuccagna!"*: *No more loot!* Like a severe new

---

* There had actually been a nineteenth-century Jewish cabinet member, Judah P. Benjamin, but his precedent gets drummed out of the annals because he served under President Jefferson Davis of the Southern Confederacy.
† One of La Guardia's gifts was a genius-level ease in picking up languages, and his Ellis Island experience idealized him later, when campaigning in the ethnic quarters. It is widely assumed that he learned Yiddish from his mother, but she spoke only a northern Italian dialect. La Guardia's Yiddish—like his other foreign tongues—was picked up on the job.

pope rehabilitating disused sumptuary laws, La Guardia made war on "the interests" and their system. Not just their graft but their cronyism and encouragement of slothful civil service. "Take your hat off when you speak to a citizen!" he cried at an arrogant relief-office supervisor, throwing the offending headgear to the ground. His cigar, too. La Guardia loved spot-checking his squad, and he thought nothing of naming as Fire Commissioner a grunt, John J. McElligot, because the ranking officers didn't impress him.

"Be good or be gone" was a favorite La Guardia warning. Here was more than a hands-on mayor: he *wrestled* with New York, tamed it, loved it, screamed at it, inspected it, threw its hat off when it got insolent. He made a point of showing up at calamities—not to stand there, but racing in to help. Fires were his passion. "Will someone get the mayor out of there?" cried one firefighter, as he and his comrades trudged out after terminating a blaze in a restaurant. La Guardia finally came out by himself; he had been checking the refrigerators for violations of the building code. "He was not only New York's greatest mayor," writes La Guardia's biographer Alyn Brodsky, "he was the nation's." What could such energy have created in private business? Yet La Guardia and his second wife, Marie, lived simply, because he had no time for the Jimmy Walkerness of life, the gallivanting around. When someone suggested that Mrs. La Guardia help lay some cornerstone, the mayor replied, "Her name's Marie, not Eleanor."

Even so, La Guardia maintained fiercely interdependent relations with President Roosevelt. Most important, La Guardia secured for New York a special status as the New Deal's showplace city. "The word 'dole' doesn't scare me," he once wrote. The word that scared him was "usury"—that of Wall Street and the banks. *No more loot!* And here, again, Roosevelt as the heir to entrenched WASP power deals generously with a minority-group politician.

True, there were sand traps to drive over. One was FDR's Secretary of the Interior, Harold L. Ickes, who dispensed the largesse with the reluctance—really, the bureaucratic *adagio*—of a Scrooge. More problematical was Roosevelt's hatred of La Guardia's most apparent associate, the unbearable yet strangely essential Robert Moses, whose various offices (some of his own invention) might be summed up as Public Works Tyrant of the City of New York.

Nonetheless, the New Deal married New York just as La Guardia had done, and the work of absorbing more first- and second-generation Americans could commence. On a ceremonial occasion, Al Smith said, "As I look around the room tonight, I see the Governor here, Herby Lehman. He's Jewish. Take the Mayor—he's half-Jewish. The President of the Board of Aldermen, my old job, he's Jewish. And so is Sam Levy, Borough President of Manhattan. I'm beginning to wonder if someone shouldn't do something for the poor Irish here in New York."

To put it another way, the contract between the Astors and Tammany Hall was over. The Democratic machine remained nominally active, moving into the third and last of its wigwams, around the corner and up the avenue from the second one, now overlooking Union Square, in 1929. Still, the organization never recovered its hold on the city after the Seabury hearings and La Guardia's three terms. As with Samson and his hair, Tammany derived its strength from one thing only: a unified Irish sub-population controlling the outcome of elections, policing the streets, and buying courts. La Guardia beat the monster down with diversity and meritocracy; they proved irresistible. Tammany even lost its hall, defaulting on the mortgage of the third building in 1940. (Today it houses the New York Film Academy.)

The names of Jimmy Walker and Fiorello La Guardia have remained illustrious, even if Walker's stands for no more than "charismatic scoundrel." La Guardia's reputation has actually sweetened, possibly because he really was one of the rare honest politicians and because he did so much for the city. But we tend to forget that, not unlike FDR, he had a tyrannical side. No doubt dragonslayers have to; they make war. On slot machines, for instance, the delight of the underworld because gangsters could blanket New York City with them by threatening the proprietors of innocent places, thus turning kids criminal, luring them into robbery to play. A performance artist in the truest sense, La Guardia didn't just drive the slots out of town (out of state, in fact, all the way to Louisiana) but took an ax to them, literally. But then, La Guardia was something of a puritan, and he closed down burlesque, too, sending its adepts scurrying to Hollywood and Broadway to survive.

Yet the lines between the bad guys and the good guys were starting to blur. No one could confuse Fiorello La Guardia with Jimmy Walker. But folks were confusing Jimmy Walker's fame with Jimmy Walker's moral value. The Cole Porter musical *Anything Goes* (1934), produced during the second year of La Guardia's first term as mayor, celebrated the twenties hedonism—Jimmy Walkerism, so to say—that La Guardia was dismantling. *Anything Goes* is set largely aboard an ocean liner, and when the passengers learn that Public Enemy No. 1 may be on board, they are not anxious but thrilled. A *celebrity!*

The show intends this satirically—but we see how, already, the American religion of fame is vitiating morality and common sense. Nowadays, even to notice this corruption of public judgment makes one seem corny, an antique lacking in cool. That was La Guardia, and he was open, abrupt, and even rude about it: to serve the people and respect only those who obeyed the law, not those who broke it.

The People, said Ernest Cuneo, La Guardia's secretary for two and a half years, "was a magic phrase with Fiorello. Whenever he used it, one could almost hear a military band playing 'The Battle Hymn of the Republic' in the middle distance." The Major, or The Maje, as La Guardia liked to be called (after his rank as a bombadier in the Army Air Service), sought to establish a host of social programs unheard of in his day that we now take for granted. Reforms such as unemployment insurance, securities regulation, the forty-hour work week, and bank-deposit insurance—part of FDR's legacy—were in fact introduced, if unsuccessfully, by La Guardia. This reminds us how encompassing is Frances Perkins' statement about the New Deal originating in the aftermath of the Triangle Fire: in the progressivist legislation that began in New York and was then taken, by its governor, Franklin Roosevelt, to the federal capital.

Even so, La Guardia is commonly known as a bullier of bullies, a power-slinging crime fighter. When he heard that law enforcement out west had been accused of beating an arrested kidnaper with a baseball bat, La Guardia said, "They should have put spikes in the bat first, and beaten the son of a bitch to death."

Not that every office-holder in his administration had broken with Tammany corruption. In 1935, a grand jury looking into the numbers racket realized that the district attorney conducting the case was shielding the guilty. In what is now called "runaway" style, the jury members called for the D.A.'s removal, and they knew whom they wanted as his replacement: Thomas E. Dewey. Governor Lehman, a Democrat, wasn't eager to give glory to Dewey, a Republican, but the matter became too public for a stonewall. Lehman appointed Dewey.*

In taking on the case, Dewey became the scourge of Dutch Schultz, the numbers mogul whom the corrupt D.A. had been safeguarding, in thanks for vast contributions to his election campaign. Schultz wanted Dewey killed, but gangland, like the courts, had its due process, and Schultz had to get permission to hit Dewey. Gangland said no: because the post-Tammany, post-Prohibition, post-Walker atmosphere wouldn't tolerate the assassination of a crime fighter as it might have done in the 1920s. The rule of Anything Goes was over.

Schultz was no team player. He decided to arrange a Dewey hit anyway—and Dewey made it easy for him by following a set routine every morning, starting with a phone call to his office. The tender husband didn't want to disturb Mrs. Dewey's sleep, so each day he and his two bodyguards would leave the Dewey apartment and head to the same nearby drugstore, where Dewey made the call while the guards waited outside.

Didn't anyone on Dewey's side ever question this clockwork vulnerability? Didn't the guards say something? What saved Dewey's life, oddly, was Schultz himself: he bragged. And gangland—or, as its secular arm came to be known, Murder, Inc.—heard. Rather than bring down

---

* Dewey's reputation in law enforcement was of Homeric majesty even among wiseguys with Tammany connections. Thus, when show-biz entrepreneur Billy Rose opened his Diamond Horseshoe nightclub, a gangster chief called to sell Rose "protection" for a fifty percent interest in the club. Where should they meet to conclude the deal? Rose replied, "Tom Dewey's office at noon," and Rose never heard from the gangster again.

upon itself the wrath of the authorities, Murder, Inc. hit Schultz before Schultz could hit Dewey.

Mortally wounded in the hospital, Schultz took nearly twenty-four hours to expire, now lucid and now groggy on "bonbons" (apparently the argot for morphine). Unlike that other victim of gangster-on-gangster murder, Arnold Rothstein, Schultz talked. But he couldn't identify his killer, and most of what he uttered has the rambling yet precise lunacy of Gertrude Stein stalling a bill collector. "Oh, oh, dog biscuit, and when he is happy he doesn't get snappy" is one remark, "French Canadian bean soup" another. This went on for hours, at one point reaching a height of a sort with "A boy has never wept, nor dashed a thousand kim."

Then Dutch Schultz died: a victim, one might say, of the way La Guardia's worldview had replaced Jimmy Walker's. It was a New Deal death, of absolute evil absolutely unmourned in an age rich in transitions: from grand hotels to nightclubs; from ghetto aliens to assimilated commentators on American life; and, coming up next, from a racially segregated show business to a racially integrated show business.

The man who really saved Thomas Dewey's life was Louis "Lepke" Buchalter, known as "The Judge" of Murder, Inc. Lepke himself would be pursued by Dewey only four years after Schultz was. In 1935, however, Lepke swayed Murder, Inc. against Schultz's petition to slay Dewey. And when Schultz went rogue on the firm and his inventory had to be terminated, it was Lepke who handled the account.

5

I Cabaret'd Last Night: Ethel Waters and the Black Emergence in Show Business

Elia Kazan once got an emergency call from Twentieth Century–Fox's chief, Darryl Zanuck. John Ford had been directing *Pinky,* about a young Caucasian-looking black woman caught between the races, and Ford was giving up. Would Kazan race out to the coast and complete the picture?

As it happened, Kazan was eager to endear himself to Zanuck. It was 1949, and Kazan had capped a decade of stage plays with Arthur Miller's *All My Sons* and *Death of a Salesman,* separated by Tennessee Williams' *A Streetcar Named Desire.* Kazan was Broadway's top director, but now he wanted to get really hot and go Hollywood. He had already directed four films, three of them for Fox, in particular *Gentleman's Agreement,* whose look at anti-Semitism offered obvious ties to the racism in *Pinky.* Kazan knew that Zanuck had a thing for socially progressive film; he had let William Wellman direct an anti-lynching work, *The Ox-Bow Incident,* despite a hatred for Wellman, simply because Zanuck felt the movie had to be made and no other studio would touch it.

So Kazan agreed to take over *Pinky,* on the condition that Ford's footage be discarded. Kazan wanted to start anew for the sake of consistency, and Zanuck said okay, giving it out that Ford was retreating for reasons of health. When Kazan arrived on the set, he discovered a hero-ine, Jeanne Crain, who had beauty but no interior vitality as an actress: a movie star. Kazan was startled to learn that Crain was a mom; she seemed so affectless that he assumed she was—as he delicately put it—"intact." Her romantic vis-à-vis, William Lundigan, was the usual banal but efficient Hollywood boy friend, and Ethel Barrymore, of a venerable stage tradition that Kazan fondly mistrusted, was nonetheless a superb technician. What was it about the production that had spooked John Ford?

"He hated that old nigger woman," Zanuck explained, "and she sure as hell hated him."

Ethel Waters. As Pinky's pious and self-sacrificing grandmother, Waters was perfect casting. In her youth, when she was tall, skinny, and full of sass, Waters was known as Sweet Mama Stringbean. Now, just this side of fifty, she looked far older: grey and heavy, bending to earth, her face carved of a thousand sorrows yet radiant with spiritual fervor. Pinky is the film's protagonist, but Waters' Aunt Dicey holds the story together, as Pinky travels a road of self-discovery in standing up to the casual fascism of the smalltown American south. That is, Pinky is what happens but her grandmother is why.

So Ethel Waters would be the director's leading player—the per-former whose work shapes the production and thus the prime recipient of John Ford's habitual sadistic *Personenregie*. No actor in Hollywood was exempt from Ford's brutalizing, not even John Wayne. But Waters did not respond to such treatment, and she and Ford were busy paralyzing each other's abilities to function when he quit. Kazan, who had a ma-nipulative side in his dealings with actors but—at least overtly—treated them with respect, won Waters over, saving the film and hundreds of jobs. At the wrap party, deep in the splendor of their cups, Kazan and Waters levelled with each other.

He said, "You don't really like any white people, do you, Ethel?"

"No, I don't," she replied—"her religion mask," he reports, "clatter-ing to the floor." More: "I don't like any fucking white man. I don't trust any of you."

Actually, Waters didn't trust men, period—and she had no use for most women. Many stars of this era came up the hard way, conquering family problems, deceitful managers, and bad luck—but they were playing what was known among blacks as "the white time": show biz, by whites and for whites. The black time, strictly ghettoized, was smaller and harder, makeshift and dangerous; it was just what the young Ethel Waters had expected of life in general when she started singing and dancing professionally as a teenager. Born of rape when her mother was but twelve, Waters later described "the kind of people I'd grown up with" as "rough, tough, full of larceny toward strangers, but sentimental and loyal to their friends and co-workers." As an audience, they were difficult to win over but idolatrous if you landed—none of that polite little clapping thing that whites did, as if appreciating a delightful new cozy at a tea party.

The black time: a maze of scams, local rivalries, and firetrap playing venues. Nonetheless, Waters' blues "shouting" and nimble moves sent her to the top of so-called "race" entertainment so surely that she found her act rivaling the paradoxically effervescent wail of Bessie Smith, the undisputed queen of the blues. But Smith was disputed now.

After the start of the Harlem Renaissance (at something like 1925), Waters arrived on Broadway, heading the cast of all-black revues. It was race entertainment on the white time, a tremendous breakthrough for black performers not only in enhanced earning power but in achieving influence in American art. There had been a little movement in this direction at the turn of the century, but the key event was Florenz Ziegfeld's tapping black Bert Williams for the otherwise all-white *Follies,* in 1910. Mixed-race casting was forbidden by unwritten law at the time, so this was raw history. To this day, no one knows how Ziegfeld got away with it (though he did have the protection of millionaire intimates, including William Randolph Hearst).

Williams' work in the *Follies* emphasized his blackness, because the *Follies* was a tasty ethnic dish, as Ziegfeld dipped Nordic-looking showgirls into a chowder of nationalities. A spoof of the Ballets Russes would find Fanny Brice applying Lower East Side attitudes to a frisky hymn entitled "Nijinski":

For when Nijinski start to beginski,
He leaps right upski in the air.
He is a bearski, beyond compareski,
His Russian styleski is so rare . . .

Then Will Rogers would lead a comic scene set around the cracker bar-
rel of a rustic general store. With the boys in Rip Van Winkle beards
and nor'easter accents, one started to wonder what race even they belonged to.

While Ziegfeld had many imitators, none of them joined in utilizing blacks in white shows, and Williams' early death, in 1922, left a
vacancy to fill. Instead, the all-black shows proliferated, narratives as
well as revues. Their salient innovation lay in dance, especially that of
the ensemble, whose fresh variations made their white counterparts
look a generation out of date. Audiences especially rejoiced when a
rogue chorister would dart out to improvise an unscheduled solo as
his or her buddies seethed in the background and the public sensed An
Occasion.

The significant advantage of the white time was that only there could
black musicals throw off national song hits. The classic in this line, *Shuffle Along* (1921), introduced "I'm Just Wild About Harry," which stayed
big long enough to be adopted as the anthem of Truman's presidential
campaign. Black shows even took over the white musical's most idiotic
convention, the New Dance Sensation, which promises to teach you the
latest ballroom craze and then doesn't. "Ev'ry step you do," it explains,
"leads to something new." Yes, but how do I execute it? This one is the
"Charleston," by Cecil Mack and Jimmy Johnson, from *Runnin' Wild*
(1923). It's one of the two most enduring numbers in the entire twenties
black-musical cycle,* so assimilated that no one thinks of it as a black
number.

Of course, this kind of assimilation happens by accident: however
one reads the Harlem Renaissance, it was not looking for opportunities

---

*The other is "I Can't Give You Anything But Love," from *Blackbirds of 1928*.

to go on the white time. Still, the issue is complex, because a number of whites wanted to take part—producer Lew Leslie, who in fact produced almost nothing but *Blackbirds* revues, was a white man. So was Carl Van Vechten, whose novel *Nigger Heaven* (1926) publicized the Renaissance in a way that, for example, Langston Hughes' poetry never could: as a shock. Van Vechten's 1,400 photographs of maximum leaders in the arts have created a kind of album of the elite in Manhattan (and beyond) in midcentury America. "Carlo," as he was known, caught both Ethel Waters (who looks strangely sedate, even content) and Bessie Smith, and such thirties artists as Paul Cadmus and Diego Rivera, and eventually Marlon Brando and Dave Brubeck. But Van Vechten's camera in the dotty little "studio" he set up in the apartment he shared with his wife, Fania Marinoff, didn't start clicking till 1932. In the twenties, Van Vechten was known for writing.

He was especially known for *Nigger Heaven,* as he no doubt intended to be. Some in the black community could not—would not—get past the title. Some did read the novel, in disgust, seeing nothing more than, in David Levering Lewis' words, "a copyrighted racial slur." There is a central romance of boy meets girl, boy abandons girl for pricey Other Woman, boy gets abandoned himself and tries to kill his replacement. But the book is mainly a Harlem travelogue, from middle-class Strivers' Row to gin joints. It was not the first such book, but everyone thought it was because its title was so . . . well, titley. It could be read as a pun. "Nigger heaven" is another term for the "peanut gallery": the cheap seats in the balcony. But "nigger heaven" might also refer to Van Vechten's personal view of the place, as a besotted pilgrim making his devotions. It was in any case a book you couldn't miss and a book you couldn't mention, to devour or boycott.

Another of those married gay guys, Van Vechten was also Manhattan's most apparent "jig-chaser," which he himself defined as "a white person who seeks the company of Negroes." One learned this in a glossary published with *Nigger Heaven,* because, whatever one thought of the novel—and many were those who thought it not only offensive but an act of treachery—it was meant to bring outsiders into Harlem culture, not least into its lingo. The compilation of terms includes such synonyms for black* as "shine," "smoke," and the baffling "spagingy-spagade" (to match, for a white, "fagingy-fagade."). The nineteenth-century "Mr. Johnson" (denoting the law, though it confusingly had other uses) was now "Mr. Eddie," to divorce is to "unsheik," and a white woman is "Miss Annie."

So black ethnicity, in the 1920s, was in a heyday of its own making even while attracting white analysis. In other words, the subculture was achieving breakout—and this is just when Ethel Waters hit the start of her mid-prime period, comprising her own personal breakout. From the all-black segment of Broadway, she went to Hollywood for a major event, a Warner Brothers backstager called *On With the Show!* (1929). Set during one night's performance of a book musical in tryout, it gave Waters no spoken lines, just two solos, "Am I Blue?" and "Birmingham Bertha." The songs tell us what she's playing: an Alabaman heading north to find an errant sweetheart. Waters took no part in the backstage saga, so southern cinemas could snip out her two spots without harming the continuity.

More essential to Waters' career than black revues or Hollywood was that corner of the Manhattan nightclub scene where black talent took the applause of all-white audiences, often giving encores to the swells who dropped in at dawn to close down their evening. The advantage of these bookings lay in those bons vivants and their circle, which included most of the nation's opinion makers of the late night. For a performer who lit the joint with these grandees at table, the column inches alone were worth two months' salary; better, you became exclusive, envied, the ritz. You became white: in power. Because whites wrote your numbers and whites capitalized your playing venues and whites loved your work. And while your own mother couldn't get in to see you, Walter Winchell could: at such famous Harlem spots as the Hot-Cha, Small's Paradise, Connie's Inn, Tillie's, the Yeah Man, and of course the Cotton Club. There was as well the Plantation Club, a "roof theatre" set up atop

---

* This is our word today. In the 1920s, "colored" was the exact equivalent, the "neutral" description. "Negro" was acceptable, but a little prim. Devotees preferred the slang used by blacks themselves, though this could be viewed as poaching.

the Winter Garden, in midtown. Lew Leslie of the *Blackbirds* was the massa here, and his pet star was Florence Mills, a captivating saucebox whose death at thirty-two left another vacancy in the history.

Black performers of this time would later comment on the shady bigotry of what we might call "colorism": favoring the lighter tints of skin. "Tall, tan, and terrific!" ran the Cotton Club's promise, of its chorus line. "And 50 copper colored girls!" Waters observed that this was more a black than white obsession, but everyone knew that when the Cotton Club occasionally admitted blacks as customers, it maintained a light-skinned colorist standard.

Even so, the Cotton Club, in the 1920s and 1930s, held the center of white-time blackness. If you headlined there, you had to be the best: Bill Robinson, Cab Calloway, Aida Ward, the Nicholas Brothers, the Dandridge Sisters (Dorothy among them), Nina Mae McKinney, Peg Leg Bates, and Duke Ellington leading the band. Calloway in particular left his mark, for his dressy capering and the nonsense syllables that he called out to the audience, who responded in kind. And Bill Robinson's informal presidency of black show biz was an obsession of Cotton Club songwriters. The 1937 edition of the *Cotton Club Parade* offered such numbers as "Harlem Bolero"; "Go South, Young Man"; a Calloway specialty, "Hi-De-Ho Romeo"; and a New Dance Sensation, "The Bill Robinson Walk." As always, everybody's doin' it: "Bankers, brokers, even shoeshine boys." Two years later, another *Cotton Club Parade* proposed Robinson—by his sobriquet, as Bojangles—as "The Mayor of Harlem."

But it was Ethel Waters who got the first song hit out of the club scene, at the Plantation in 1925, when a Tin Pan Alley trio handed her "Dinah." And it was Waters who filled the Bert Williams and Florence Mills vacancies, in the Irving Berlin–Moss Hart revue *As Thousands Cheer* (1933), sharing eminence with Marilyn Miller, Clifton Webb, and Helen Broderick. This late in theatre history, Waters was still only the second black to get a lead in an otherwise white show on The Street—and this was not just the white time. This was Big Broadway, comparable to the *Follies*—even if Waters had to take below-the-title billing.

As Thousands Cheer structured itself as a newspaper, each spot announced as THE FUNNIES or MAJESTIC SAILS AT MIDNIGHT or LONELY HEART

COLUMN. At some point early on, Berlin and Hart decided to enhance their stunt with something one might actually read in the papers, something serious. UNKNOWN NEGRO LYNCHED BY FRENZIED MOB would herald the number "Supper Time," as the victim's widow laid the table for her children's dinner. Berlin had never written anything like it before; no one had. Simply setting that headline into type in the playbill—early in Act Two, between METROPOLITAN OPERA OPENS IN OLD TIME SPLENDOR and GANDHI GOES ON NEW HUNGER STRIKE, with Clifton Webb as Gandhi and Helen Broderick as Aimee Semple McPherson—was incendiary. It defines Waters' standing that they couldn't have hired anyone else for it: no one but she was grand enough for the material and sympathetic enough to try the patience of those who don't like being preached to out of church.

Thirties revue plumed itself on above all versatile talent. While the previous generation's variety shows doted on specialists, New Revue required stars able to sing, dance, jest, and pull off celebrity imitations. Like Cole Porter, Moss Hart saw the famous as the decoration of life, and he decorated his stage with them, as Marilyn Miller tried out her Joan Crawford here and Clifton Webb his John D. Rockefeller there. Waters got to do Josephine Baker, complete with spitcurl and cigarette holder, singing "Harlem On My Mind" as she revels in *la vie parisienne*. One of Waters' sketches—NOEL COWARD, NOTED PLAYWRIGHT, RETURNS TO ENGLAND—cast her as a hotel scrubwoman going Mayfair and spouting epigrams with Miller and Webb, also menials transformed by exposure to The Master. "Well, I'll be goddamned!" cries housekeeper Broderick, for the blackout.

In fact, the show ran its stars ragged as they darted off after each sequence to be remade as their next "character," passing their scurrying colleagues to dart right back again. Worse yet was the difficulty of perfecting the running order. Musical numbers had to sit in balance with sketches, dances with songs. The evening had to build steadily, mounting to a stunning first-act finale—ROTOGRAVURE SECTION, opening on the ensemble frozen in tones of white and sepia in a re-creation of photographic reproduction from 1883. Then they all broke into motion for "Her Easter Bonnet"—or, to use its published title, "Easter Parade." An increasingly sensational second act must follow. All this while the stars bickered over who had the best numbers, most stage time, too much applause.

In terms of clout, Waters did not have a lot of wiggle room. Besides, she was in truly splendid company and making the most of it. Before the second act was frozen, Moss Hart (who seems to have been at least as much in charge as the production's director, Hassard Short) thought that "Harlem On My Mind" might have to follow SOCIETY WEDDING OF THE YEAR. This was a bright little gem for Miller and Webb, launched by bridesmaids and ushers before the traveler curtain, which then parted on the happy couple waking up in bed after a night of pre-nup. Came then a cute little vocal, "Our Wedding Day," followed by what the raw-tongued yet sexually puritanical Waters later called "a flippant bedroom dance." The audience would be enchanted, and Hart wondered if Waters feared trying to follow such a tour de force by favorite stars.

"Hell, no, Mr. Hart," Waters replied. "I like workin' on a *hot* stage!"

Then, too, Waters came out ahead of the curve in the laydown of the star quartet's last appearances before the finale. There was no way to contrive the prestigious spot, the next-to-closing, for all four at once; instead, they took turns. PRINCE OF WALES RUMORED ENGAGED offered Helen Broderick as Queen Mary in outlandishly dowdy white with veil and lacey outgrowths, brandishing a tabloid containing Winchell as she and the king interrogated the prince. ("George," Broderick told the crown, "you stay out of this!") Waters' Josephine Baker followed. And at last came SUPREME COURT HANDS DOWN IMPORTANT DECISION, which holds that musicals can no longer end with reprises of the top tunes. Miller and Webb obliged with a new number, the merrily lilting "Not For All the Rice in China."

So Broderick was happy because her Queen Mary dominated the evening's best sketch. Waters was happy because "Harlem On My Mind" was an extra number, written during the Philadelphia tryout. And Miller and Webb were happy because they got the eleven o'clock song.

As Thousands Cheer proved one of the decade's outstanding hits, with a damn-the-Depression run of 400 performances. Two years later, Waters was again in a quartet of stars, for the Arthur Schwartz and Howard Dietz revue *At Home Abroad* (1935)—and this time Waters was billed over the title, second only to Beatrice Lillie. A lesser hit, *At Home Abroad* did not stretch Waters with anything like a "Supper Time." But then, *that* Waters emphasizes the tragedian; at the time, she was celebrated instead for her fanciful comedy. It was only later, in film and spoken theatre but first of all in the play *Mamba's Daughters* (1939) that the serious Waters emerged in full.

A hit by the standards of the day,* *Mamba's Daughters* marks perhaps the most significant advance for black performers in the entire epoch, because Waters' apparently effortless transition from singer and comic to actress was all but unheard of in the white *or* black time. It happens often enough nowadays, but it created a precedent in 1939, and as it was a black woman who pulled it off, it sparked an awareness that imposing talent had been hidden from general view.

Like the play *Porgy,* the source of *Porgy and Bess, Mamba's Daughters* is Dorothy and DuBose Heyward's adaptation of a novel by DuBose alone on black life in Charleston, South Carolina. Some of the *Porgy and Bess* cast also appeared in *Mamba's Daughters*—Anne Brown (the original Bess), Georgette Harvey, Helen Dowdy, J. Rosamond Johnson—and there was some music. A tale of three generations of women, the youngest of whom seems destined to break out of the ghetto as a radio singer, the play told how Waters' Hagar protects the girl after she has been raped, then takes her own life after killing the rapist. The role is odd, for most of Hagar's dialogue is functional rather than dramatic or poetic; director Guthrie McClintic took advantage of Waters' unusual height to establish how gentle she is with her loved ones and dangerous to aggressors. It's an acting challenge advanced for its day, in which character is internalized in the very breath of life rather than indicated in stagey line delivery.

Looking at Waters' career, one sees several versions of her, one after

---

* It played 162 performances, toured, then revisited New York for a final two weeks. But it should be noted that in Chicago it lasted as long—five weeks—as Katharine Hepburn in *The Philadelphia Story,* quite an achievement.

the other, because unlike so many prominent American lives, Waters' did not lack a second act. On the contrary, hers runs to three or four, with enough twists to fill out an evening of Sardou. Back in the 1920s, she is the blues singer and purveyor of the shimmy, amassing titles for the race label Black Swan: "Oh Daddy!," "Midnight Blues," "Ethel Sings 'Em," and the like. By the late 1920s Waters has moved to Columbia, one of the nation's two major labels. (Victor was the other.) Billed as "America's Foremost Ebony Comedienne,"* Waters now sings mainstream pop, even covering Maurice Chevalier in "You Brought a New Kind of Love To Me." One can hear a laugh in her voice as she glides through it, because some of those white boys really can write 'em, even if they can't play blues for beans.

The straight-acting Waters follows, on stage and in film, and at the end there is a Pentecostal Waters, taking up the spiritual to tour with Billy Graham's revival show. Still, there's an arresting and little-known Waters in the middle of all this, when she really was a comedienne. Literally. A taste of this Waters is preserved in a film short of 1934 called *Bubbling Over,* from the black studio Official. As the wife of a man rich in freeloading relations, Waters shows off her sarcastic side. Yet another moocher ambles in through the open doorway:

NEWCOMER: Hi. Can I come in?
WATERS: (with the dangerous clarity of the terminally exasperated) You *is* in!

and he has brought his three brothers along. Waters asks what they do:

---

* The use of "comedienne" reflects the recording industry's inability, in the first decades of the twentieth century, to find a term for a woman singer who wasn't a soprano. We call them "belters" now, but in the very early 1900s they were known as "seriocomics." The word became antique by 1920 and bad for business, and when the soprano heroine gave way to Ethel Merman, how was one to categorize? From Nora Bayes to Annette Hanshaw, black or white, loud or lullaby, most of the girls were featured on disc labels as "comedienne" till Merman's 1930s found a solution in the emptily neutral "vocalist."

BROTHER: (keeping it nice and vague) We was travelin' men.

Okay, that's it. Grabbing all four and dragging them to the door—remember, Waters is man-size—she gives them a parting shot:

WATERS: I'm goin' to see that you pick up where you left off!

Waters has two song spots as well, including the wistfully lovely "Darkies Never Dream." What's odd about *Bubbling Over* is its lack of black shtick. Except for the dialect and a few *Amos 'n' Andy* malapropisms ("psychoannihilated" for "psychoanalyzed"), it's a universal tale.

Waters herself was becoming universal, albeit in her own way. The French class their pop singers as *réaliste* or *fantaisiste*: respectively, those who act their songs or those who have crazy fun with them. In other words, Édith Piaf or Maurice Chevalier. Making the analogy in Waters' America, that might be, say, Helen Morgan or Al Jolson.

But Waters falls into neither school: she has fun with the music while acting the lyrics. She can be conversational even while decorating, scatting in *nya nya* noises or singing a second chorus with almost completely different notes than the written ones. She has a broader tonal range than most pop singers, from bass to soprano, and she exploits it, for instance making "Midnight Blues" into a duet with herself, alternating phrases in high and low voice.

A prolific recording artist, Waters trifles with not only the notes but the lyrics as well, coloring key words by elongating vowels or jabbing at consonants. In "You've Seen Harlem At Its Best," a risqué Jimmy McHugh–Dorothy Fields list song, Waters fondles the lyrics like a French diseuse, getting especially bemused at a reference to—as she puts it—"the Elks' pee-rade." Ethel doesn't only sing 'em: she pronounces 'em. Yet she relishes her accompaniments, chiding that high-hat Fletcher Henderson when his keyboard gets too white and classy. On a Black Swan of 1923, "You Can't Do What My Last Man Did," Waters performs with nothing but the honkytonk piano of the song's author, J. C. Johnson. Between choruses comes a tasty quatrain:

Early this morning
You wanted to fight,
'Cause you heard
I cabaret'd last night.

These words were diluted two years later when Waters remade the number, with sax and trumpet along with the piano. But now she actually has that fight, with "Slow Kid" Thompson as the inferior new boy friend—and suddenly Waters is funning all over the place. "So I heered," Thompson avers at one point. "Oh, you *heered* that?" Waters snaps back. As if to reproach this unconscionable insult to the language, she then gets quite royal in tone, insisting, "You just cawn't do, *you just cawn't* do what that lahst man did," topping it with a provocative "Come get me, Ethel Barrymore!"

Waters is not only aware of other show-biz celebrities: she is intimately acquainted with rival vocal styles. On "(Not on the first night, baby, or) Maybe Not At All," she warns "a smalltown sheik" that he won't get lucky tonight, or possibly ever. Waters sings the second chorus imitating Clara Smith, and ramps up to the third chorus with "Now I'm getting ready for the Empress, Miss Bessie Smith!," and sails into another imitation. These are not spoofs, but flawless re-creations, revealing a sensitive ear unusual in the intensely competitive territoriality of the blues diva.

As with many blues singers, most of these early Waters numbers are hers alone, never covered by others. Yet once Waters takes up standard pop, she still claims an unusual number of titles as much "hers" as "Over the Rainbow" is Judy Garland's. "Dinah," "Stormy Weather," "Am I Blue?," and "Takin' a Chance on Love" can be covered, of course: but with caution. And "Supper Time" is virtually trademarked, not least by Waters' much-quoted statement that "If one song could tell the whole tragic story of a people, that was the song."

Still, one could make comparably expansive claims for Waters' casually blissful "Old Man Harlem (keeps me rollin' on)." The work of two white boys (Hoagy Carmichael and Rudy Vallee, arguably the whitest boy who ever lived), "Old Man Harlem" features the mellow Waters, with a serene first chorus, an irresistible dance break for the sidemen, and a second vocal chorus with variations. At the end, Waters rises note by note to a tonic tone so sunny and splendid that one is amazed to learn that is only a D Flat. Vallee made his own version with his Connecticut Yankees, and it's amusing enough, especially when he eats the "rollin' on" like candy. Yet it is Waters who finds the grin in this inverted homage to "Ol' Man River," making it as basic and lived-in as skin.

Waters' break with the more extroverted vocal styles of the Jolson school coincided with two other extremely influential musicians, Louis Armstrong and Bing Crosby. No wonder: all three found their individual voices just when the microphone was introduced, in the mid-1920s. This allowed music makers to tone down, so to say. They let electricity do their projecting while they enlightened music with niceties that would have been ineffective back when filling auditoriums was the singer's first responsibility.

Crosby's reputation is paradoxical, because his movie persona is lazy while his singing—though only in his early years—is very athletic, filled with games and curlicues. He'll launch a phrase with a single note that unfolds like a fan and he is absolutely obsessed with the upper mordent.* Louis Armstrong's influence is more abstract, as it depends on his playing as well as his singing. Thus, Waters' 78 disc of "I Can't Give You Anything But Love" follows Armstrong's own vocal styling on her second chorus, but she then imitates his trumpeted coda, singing the syllable "Dit" on the rising scale that Armstrong played.

Three great progenitors of pop music's lingua franca: yet Waters is unique in her "other" identity as actress, for neither Crosby nor Armstrong rivaled her as such. Crosby of course played many movie roles, mainly in his charming "just me" persona but also a few genuine dramatic challenges. Still, nothing that Crosby did compares to Waters' serious

---

* The upper mordent, or *Pralltriller* (German for "tight trill"), adds an extra two notes to the one the composer wrote. For example, on a C: you sing the C, leap up to the D above it, then fall back to the C again. Probably its most persistent memory in popular music recalls Ethel Merman's delivery of the first line of "There's No Business Like Show Business," applying the upper mordent to the "No" and the "Show." There is as well a lower, double, and prolonged (or extended) mordent.

parts; and Crosby never dared the stage. Armstrong's film appearances offer not acting but rather his ebullient music-making self, even back in Little Old New York in *Hello, Dolly!* (1969), where, in the title song, he assures Barbra Streisand, "This is Louis, Dolly," just in case you thought he was John Philip Sousa or someone.

It is worth noting that Waters' acting even in musicals relied on a palette of colors richer than what was usual in the form. She claims not only her songs but her show, *Cabin in the Sky* (1940), like Ethel Merman's *Gypsy* or Gwen Verdon's *Sweet Charity* unthinkable when conceived if not for the presiding diva. A fantasy about agents of heaven and hell wrestling for the soul of the ever backsliding Little Joe, *Cabin* gave Waters her only book-show role, as Little Joe's wife, Petunia. It was one of Broadway's experiments in the uptowning of the lowdown, setting the classiest auteurs—composer Vernon Duke, lyricist John Latouche, and director-choreographer George Balanchine—loose on tropes of Kongo Komedy. The material had all been introduced to Broadway in the twenties black shows—winning the lottery, evading shady companions, heaven as a fried-chicken picnic, and sin as the earthly mission of a certain Miss Georgia Brown. Yet in *Cabin* the clichés seemed, for once, clarified, mythologized in a parable that actually sang and danced like one. As Richard Rodgers said, of *Oklahoma!*, "It was a work created by many that gave the impression of having been created by one."

It was as well Waters' personal triumph, and not merely as a singer. Brooks Atkinson spoke of "the rangy warmth of spirit that distinguishes her acting."* This was unusual in reviews of musicals; no one spoke of Ethel Merman's acting at this time.

Moving to Hollywood for MGM's adaptation of *Cabin,* Waters made her farewell to her madcap side, for she would soon be physically too big to maintain her stock identity as the Vamp of Lenox Avenue. In a last pushout, fit for the Savoy Ballroom on 140th Street, she dances a

---

* The praise is especially noteworthy, because, one year earlier, Atkinson undervalued Waters' Hagar in *Mamba's Daughters,* forcing Carl Van Vechten to shame him with an objecting petition signed by heavy names.

jitterbug with John W. Bubbles (the original Sporting Life in *Porgy and Bess,* here billed under his family name of Sublett). But Waters was essentially giving up the fun stuff now, even if she later became one of television's first black sitcom stars, albeit as a maid, on *Beulah.*

In fact, everyone working on the *Cabin* movie was giving up the fun stuff, because Waters deeply resented having to share a soundstage with MGM's particular Georgia Brown, the twenty-something Lena Horne. What was the use of filling out your certificate of genius if they don't validate it until you've lost your looks? All those years! All that work to get on the white time! Striver's Row? They don't have that smarty crowd in the neighborhood *I* grew up in! And now that I finally got to The Place, they spring this . . . this twenty-year-old bedroom dance on me!

Right. So one day, Waters let loose with one of those Scenes. Everybody froze to wait it out, Waters finally went silent after a rant of some seven or eight minutes, director Vincente Minnelli closed down for the day, and that was the last of the geschrei.* Still, by the 1940s, Waters' complex sense of whom to trust and whom to challenge gave her a mixed press among show folk. She was motherly to some—the Nicholas Brothers, for instance, because two young dancing black boys were the least of her worries. She was a termagant to others, especially young black women singers, even as people like Lena Horne had to be aware that Waters was their George Washington. Much later, in an interview, Mahalia Jackson said, "Ella [Fitzgerald], Billie [Holiday], Sarah [Vaughan]. They all came from Ethel Waters."

Did Jackson mean that Waters' vocal style had so much content that artists as different as the affably dynamic Fitzgerald and the keening Holiday could learn from her, or simply that Waters founded the profession of black women whose talent becomes indispensable to the national culture?

Waters' primary contribution was to reveal anew the multi-tasking ingenuity of the best American entertainers. Her quixotic imagination

---

* In her autobiography, Waters waxes vague about the episode, admitting only that there was "snarling and scrapping" and "I won all my battles on that picture."

influenced on an incalculable level the national singing style in the first decade of the microphone (1925–35): that is, after Al Jolson and the Vaudeville Freakazoid school, in the new age of crooners and nuanced torch singers. Above all, her career taught us that talent declares its own limits, that a few of us absorb so well the show biz that permeates American life that they can move to and fro and up and down in it at will, like the devil on earth.

There was another major black singing-dancing-acting talent back then, and we should consider her as well, because like Ethel Waters she lucked into a historical moment, between Dred Scott and rap, when the meaning of the word "elite" was being expanded racially. She makes an interesting comparison with Waters, too, in that their careers went in completely different directions.

In fact, today Josephine Baker is more famous than Waters* for accomplishing less. True, Baker had more sheer life—repatriating to France, roaming through Paris with a leashed cheetah, adopting a slew of multiracial kids, and getting evicted from her château in a dire photo op. Yet of her art Baker left much less behind than Waters, though her films preserve a charmingly effusive and wondering quality. Her singing, too, is arresting, not at all what one expects: a plaintive, highly placed soprano.

Still, nothing in Baker's cinema compares to the moment in *Pinky* when Waters is reunited with her granddaughter. Kazan admitted that he was no movie director at this time: he incited the actors and let the photographer and editor manage the creation of film. Still, this scene is beautifully told, for while it takes in both women it somehow lets us feel what Waters feels. As she crosses to her laundry works from the house, Waters has registered that a white woman has arrived and, not looking at her, passes a few pleasantries. Then Pinky speaks. Bent over her tub, Waters stops, raises her eyes, and finally sees: her joy and worry,

---

*Born in 1896, Waters was ten years older than Baker. For most of her life, Waters was thought to have been born in 1900, but she herself corrected this when in her seventies.

the white-black girl closest to and most distant from Waters' world. She lets off thanks to heaven for this day, so long in coming, and as she goes to embrace her child, the entire movie is in her face.

Baker's films, by contrast, are, for instance, *Zou Zou* and *Princesse Tam-Tam*. It was her dancing that put her over. Clips have survived of Baker's locomotion in the late 1920s; they catch a perfect little devil. Twenties hoofing concentrated on the feet, but Baker dances with her body, all of it. She does not fear looking awkward—you'll get used to it, she says, jutting out her bottom, exploiting the elbow, crossing her eyes, having a ball. Much is made of Baker's erotic power, especially when she performed wearing nothing but a cincture of jungle ingesta, but Baker is above all a comic. You say "erotic," and she says "erratic." It isn't serious enough to be sexy.

There is a major difference between Waters and Baker in the latter's ability to enjoy her career. Both were difficult, but Waters was wary as a rule where Baker was unpredictable, never difficult the same way twice. She could be selfish and domineering, but also generous and forgiving. Baker, too, had had a hard upbringing, if not as rough a one as Waters—though both were first married at the age of thirteen.

At least Baker got big fast. She started in the chorus of the touring production of *Shuffle Along,* fired in New Haven for breaking out of line to show off. But then the show's composer, Eubie Blake, called up to find out how the premiere had gone and heard about Baker. Okay, but how did she go over?

"The truth is," the stage manager told him, "those crackers loved it."

"Put her back in," says Eubie.

Baker moved on to Broadway and the New York club scene, but Paris was her very next stop. Overnight, Baker was famous, late for everything, and the symbol of how show biz enriches emancipation as no proclamation can: she became the first *free* black American in the truest meaning of the word. "Paris has never drawn a color line," explained Janet Flanner, *The New Yorker*'s correspondent in Paris. Baker's first show there, *La Revue Nègre,* got a most prominent booking, at the Théâtre des Champs-Elysées. Analyzing the production's smash success, Flanner cited the sets of Miguel Covarrubias, "pink drops with cornucopias of hams and watermelons, and the Civil War did the rest, aided by Miss Baker."

Note, too, that her *Zou Zou* costar was Jean Gabin, eventually France's most essential movie star but already big at the time, in 1934. Directly after this, Baker played the heroine of a new version of an Offenbach operetta of 1875, *La Créole*. Indeed, it was revived for her, even if Sacha Guitry had to coach her for the dialogue scenes. Baker was aware of the honor of singing Offenbach to the French (and at another imposing hall, the Théâtre Marigny). Still, she said, "I prefer my playwrights living so we can discuss the work." This was not an instance of color-blind casting, for *La Créole*'s heroine is black in the first place. Yet it appeared that there was nothing that Baker could not do on the grounds of race—in France, that is—and now the idea came upon her to try Broadway.

"Will they make me sing Mammy songs?" she worried, as her husband, Count Giuseppe Abatino, went on ahead to make Baker's contract with the Shuberts. Abatino was neither a count nor Baker's husband, but that was part of the fun of being the Rage of Paris. What's "true" in show biz, when all the world's an Oz? If other stars have agents, *la Bakair* must have a count. And "If that boy sticks with me," she said, "he's got to bring home some bacon and buckwheat, too."

Note the southern (that is, black) references: if Ethel Waters worked on the white time but lived on the black, Baker merrily resided in both at once, as if a science-fiction traveler touring dimensions. There could be rude shocks along the way, for black and white cultures had been mixing for only a few years, and the etiquette was not yet in place. One thinks of that notorious moment at—of course—the Van Vechtens', when Carl's wife, the aforementioned Fania Marinoff, tried to kiss Bessie Smith goodnight. Picture the scene, mixed of the socialites of Broadway and Lenox Avenue. James Weldon Johnson will read his poetry; Gershwin will play. And Bessie has been knocking them back all night till the terrible moment arrives. Marinoff reaches for her affectionately, and Bessie shoves her to the floor with "Get the fuck away from me! I ain't never heard of such shit!"

Baker had a comparably bad experience at a dinner party at Lorenz Hart's. Apparently Hart's black maid, "Big Mary" Campbell, was one of those Characters, and when she heard Baker speaking French, the maid reared up with "Honey, you is full of shit. Talk the way your mouth was born!"*

These tales come in threes, but the third is less an anecdote than a headline: JOSEPHINE BAKER FLOPS IN THE FOLLIES BECAUSE NOBODY GETS HER. The event was *Ziegfeld Follies of 1936,* a Shubert affair renting the late showman's name and having little connection to the art of Ziegfeld. In fact, this *Follies* was in structure and style entirely coincident with post-Ziegfeld thirties revue—exactly like the two white shows Ethel Waters did, but without an overriding theme. Besides Baker, Fanny Brice, Bob Hope, Eve Arden, contralto pop singer Gertrude Niesen, and the Nicholas Brothers will head the cast,† all given material crafted especially for them.

All except Baker, perhaps. Vernon Duke and Ira Gershwin wrote the score, George Balanchine (for the higher dance) and Robert Alton (for hoofing) choreographed, and John Murray Anderson supervised the production: a lineup as good as any in thirties revue. But Baker's first number was an African belle sauvage dance dredged up out of her earliest Paris days. New York had never seen this novelty for itself, and it frankly wasn't ready for it now. Baker's giddy spoof confused them— wasn't this supposed to be Astarte Revealed? Later, a dashing number called "Maharanee" found her captivating the men at Longchamps race-

---

* Many writers repeat this tale, and no one questions it—but was Hart's maid really allowed to assault his guests? Had she been appointed that evening's chitchat monitor? And what happened right after—was she fired? Did Dorothy Parker or Irving Berlin, for example, take that treatment from an employee of the house? What business is it of *the maid* what language Baker speaks in?

† Note that Baker and the Nicholases meant that three lead black performers were featured in a white show—undoubtedly the result of Waters' two appearances. Then *Babes in Arms* (1937) reemployed the Nicholases (in a subplot involving racial bigotry), *The Cradle Will Rock* (1937) fielded a mixed-race chorus, and *Sing Out the News* (1938) built an entirely black production number—a Harlem block-party christening—on what turned out to be the show's song hit, "F.D.R. Jones." (Or, as the refrain phrases it, "Mister Franklin D. Roosevelt Jones, yessiree, yessiree, yessiree.")

track in a spangly, tight-fitting sari, cape, and headdress, but the gallop-ing music defeated her stringy soprano. "Five A.M.," a pensive ballad surrounding one of the first of Broadway's dream ballets, was more suc-cessful. Still, it lacked the exhibition-piece rightness of Fanny Brice's Baby Snooks routine or Hope's big number, wooing the icy Eve Arden in "I Can't Get Started."

Everyone got raves but Baker. Critics picked on her smallish singing voice—Brooks Atkinson called it "a squeak in the dark"—and while terming Baker "the most prominent Negress since Eliza in *Uncle Tom's Cabin*," Percy Hammond deplored "African displays too exotic for me to talk about." These were the opposite of the notices Ethel Waters invari-ably got, as if in sly agreement to deny the emigrée Baker the good will accorded the all-American Waters. Each woman used touches of black-time show biz to build her art. But if Baker was unique, it has to be said that Waters was universal.

So Waters served as the transitional figure in the racial integration of show biz: from separate to equal. Yet Waters is never appreciated in this role. Many squander this credit on Paul Robeson, who in fact did little more than sing "Ol' Man River" and play Othello.

Is this because those who write on the arts don't understand how a woman can function historically in something as complex as race rela-tions? Is it because Waters had religion instead of politics? Some are uncomfortable with leading figures who actually mean it when they say, "God bless you." Would Paul Robeson even have had his shot at Othello if Waters hadn't done the heavy lifting first in *Mamba's Daugh-ters*? There were important black actors before Waters, such as Charles Gilpin (O'Neill's first Emperor Jones, which Robeson also played later on) and Rose McClendon. Still, it was Waters' jump from musicals to drama, in a succès d'estime that was also a commercial hit, that called attention to the scope of her abilities, leading those of good will to ex-pand their perspective. Not that Waters ever asked for credit. On the contrary, she resisted admiration. All she wanted was respect, especially from white men.

So there's this story. It's late in the ramp up to the premiere of *Cabin in the Sky*, and everyone involved knows that the show is something special. However. In that maddeningly unknowable chemical process by which great musicals captivate, an ingredient was missing. Somewhere in Act One, just when the show should have hit liftoff, it remained helplessly *capable,* first-rate but fumbling the magic.

Then Vernon Duke pulled a number out of his trunk, "Fooling Around With Love." A former collaborator, Ted Fetter, had written the lyrics, and now *Cabin*'s poet, John Latouche, wrote a new set over Fetter's, so to say, as "Taking a Chance on Love." With days to go before the first performance, the song went in and so exhilarated the production that the evening seemed to float above the stage. At the premiere, the audience did the usual cheering and Latouche ran backstage to exult with his star.

"Ethel!" he cried. "We did it!"

"Miss," she told him, *"Waters!"*

The 1940s

6

Wise Guys

In Cole Porter and Moss Hart's musical *Jubilee* (1935), a character modeled on Johnny Weissmuller's Tarzan "aw, shucks"es his way through a personal appearance at his latest film, *Mowgli and the White Goddess,* then sings an establishing number, "When Me, Mowgli, Love." Only Cole Porter would dare: this prodigious jungle beast not only goes all night but does so in front of an audience of elephants who don binoculars as if at *Siegfried*. And in a line of enjambment sparked by an interior rhyme, Mowgli admits, "Me so provincial, me simply like entire knowledge of Winchell and O. O. McIntyre." Will Hays and Emily Post get a look in as well, and, like Walter Winchell, they maintain some reputation today, at least among the educated. But who was O. O. McIntyre?

Oscar Odd McIntyre was the man who started it all: he invented The Column. In a more recent musical, Marvin Hamlisch and Craig Carnelia's *Sweet Smell of Success* (2002), a press agent hustles a frail with "I can get you in J. J."—this being the first and middle initials of a Winchell figure. To be mentioned in his Column is to enter a warp to fame. And, of course, one imagines how many such men tried the line in the 1930s and 1940s, when Winchell enjoyed his widest reach. There were many other columnists as well, all working the beat of nighttown Broadway.

Yet all of them—Winchell included—owed their form to a country boy who became a professional gawker at, promoter of, and sentimentalist about the place that was The City as surely as Rome was in Europe two millennia ago.

McIntyre came from the midwest, born in Missouri and raised in Ohio. Famously—even comically—natty, he roamed through Manhattan collecting material for New York Day By Day, a feature of the *New York Journal-American* but syndicated in over five hundred newspapers across the land. Although McIntyre always played the yokel-turned-dandy while his imitators styled themselves as seen-it-all Broadwayites, their indentifying usages originate with McIntyre. He gives us the constant sighting of celebrities at first nights and restaurants, the blend of neologism and cliché, the favorite phrases ("in days agone . . ."), the plugging of newcomers ("The most perfect verbal silversmith, to my notion, is Christopher Morley"), even the acid observation ("There is no such thing as a 'little bit of garlic,'" which recalls Robert Benchley's comment about 'a little ballet').

Unique to McIntyre was his self-portrait as a doting flâneur (albeit in a chauffeured limousine), noting and eulogizing the most unnotable aspects of metropolitan life. The hot-chestnut street vendor, for instance: "I suspect some in their vacant gazings to be poets, or too clouded of mind to have truck with the world." Perhaps the best sample of McIntyre comes from that most unappetizing of columnists, the openly bigoted Westbrook Pegler. Spoofing McIntyre's incessant restauranting and name-dropping, Pegler catches his prey's style:

> The faint nostalgic nosegay of the Old World ateliers always assails me when my evening stroll takes me in the neighborhood of Le Chat Malade, that swank rendezvous of the cognoscenti in New York's Montparnasse.

Then comes Pegler's version of McIntyre's celeb sightings:

> Irvin S. Cobb, Fannie Hurst, Will Hays, Charlie MacArthur. Will Hays and Irvin S. Cobb. Sometimes, too, while browsing through my Petit

Parisienne, lingering over my Pour Boire, I spy Gene Tunney, Irvin S. Cobb, Will Hays, and Irvin S. Cobb . . .

McIntyre was precious and corny; his colleagues dropped that tone while adopting his format. And they added the spice of gossip with so heavy a hand that the Manhattan insider's column lost its impressionistic air to obsess about marriage, divorce, adultery, feuds, firings, and crime.

So it wasn't really gossip, was it? "Gossip" sounds so harmless: who's dating whom. But who's *killing* whom—and Winchell, for one, dipped into the topic more than once—stands beyond tattle. We recall Crane Brinton's definition of ruling class, with "dramatic lives" that "set the fashion" and figure in "the more exciting scandals," those with "wealth, power, and position." Does that include Vincent "Mad Dog" Coll, whose murder Winchell predicted to the day? Or our old friend Louis Lepke of Murder, Inc., who, when surrendering his freedom after two years on the lam, in 1939, went not to law enforcement but to Winchell personally? This particular columnist was so powerful—better, *connected*—that Lepke, the FBI's Most Wanted, thought it entirely logical to give himself up to The Column. Why not? Everyone else who needed to matter did, too.

I can get you in J. J., right. Yet nowadays, Winchell is America's Ozymandias.* But when Winchell handed Lepke over to J. Edgar Hoover (Winchell: Mr. Hoover, this is Lepke. Hoover: How do you do? Lepke: Glad to meet you. Let's go.), Winchell ruled American information. His sometime editor at two different newspapers,† Emile Gauvreau, thought him the lowest of men and, worse, an inept writer. Where but in the

---

* From Shelley's poem about a statue in the desert of a former super-monarch. Only the legs remain in place, with the head broken and half-buried nearby: "Round the decay / Of that colossal wreck, boundless and bare / The lone and level sands stretch far away." Ozymandias had a "sneer of cold command," and so did Winchell.
† The *New York Graphic* and the *New York Daily Mirror,* the latter a Hearst operation that came complete with a syndication network that vastly expanded Winchell's audience, starting in 1929. A year later, he was on NBC radio in a network of some fifty stations, his quick talk and raspy tone a sensation. To some in the Other Places, Winchell's was the voice of New York.

world of the New York tabloid could there have arisen such a monster of puffs and revenges, a busybody treated like an emperor? And on radio as well! Folks planned their week around Sunday evenings with Winchell. It's almost touching to report that O. O. McIntyre was so offended by Winchell's ratatat writing style that he sent anonymous denunciations to Winchell's publishers, unfortunately in his trademark green ink. Gauvreau, however, was offended by Winchell, period, seeing in him a dangerous coincidence of ignorance and arrogance. "By some form of self-hypnosis," Gauvreau reasoned, Winchell "came to feel himself the center of his time."

Which is exactly what Winchell was, for something like a generation. Readers were fascinated by the racy language, with coinings that had never occurred to O. O. McIntyre—"keptive," for example, meaning a married man's dish on the side. Perhaps they even liked the sudden shifts in tone, from vulgarity to boobish tenderness, as when addressing the wife and children he neglected except on vacations. "Daddy is making pennies," he once wrote in an aside to his two kids, "Huh, huh, lotsa pennies, so mamma can travel in [transcontinental railroad car] drawing rooms."

Then, too, the swirl of news and scandal kept The Column startling—though, as Winchell's critics now insist, his treatment of both as "items" of equal weight made a tizzy of the very concept of information. Worse, this knowitall really was one, with a corner on the national intel. Thus, his enthusiasm over various onthewayups and places and things appealed to the socially insecure: now they knew whom to speak of, where to be seen.

Other journalists hated him. His coarse language lowered standards, his claim to be a "reporter" instead of a snitch offended reporters, his power to boost with plugs made him a one-man consensus. And that dissolving of rumor into hard data! Winchell handled facts the way sloppy opera singers handle pitches and note values. They call it "swimming," and that's what Winchell did: he swam through the news. "Never spoil a good story," he once said, "by trying to verify it."

We're not done, because his personal style, too, offended. He was brusque and pushy, a scrapper dressed as a gent. He conversed like a public address system, eructating without listening. He lived on grudges, treasuring the misery he could create with his Drop Dead List. Worst of all, like many of the subjects in this book Winchell got a *Time* cover—this Desperate Desmond of a Peeping Tom, pounding out his ridiculous telegraph-key *Leitmotiv* as he opened his radio spiel with "Hello, Mr. and Mrs. North America and all the ships at sea! Let's go to press!"

Yeah, but what was he *really* like? Capitalizing on a row that Winchell was supposedly having with bandleader Ben Bernie, Twentieth Century–Fox starred the pair in two films. The first and better of the two, *Wake Up and Live* (1937), featured Alice Faye and Jack Haley, the latter as a golden-voiced singer spooked by microphones who can only deliver when he thinks nobody's listening. Accidentally hooked up to Bernie's radio show, Haley becomes the Phantom Troubadour,* so Bernie spends the rest of the film trying to sign his mystery star while Winchell tries to expose the scam.

Much of the script treats the fantasy feud:

BEN BERNIE: Good old Walter. Man after my own heart . . . with a knife.

Winchell does appear tough and unscrupulous, but not without charm. Trim, somewhat short, and wearing a cagey half-smile, he is surprisingly adept at playing himself, even natural and charismatic. True, Winchell started as a performer, in vaudeville, but strictly as a song-and-dance man. In *Wake Up and Live,* he reads dialogue well and embodies at all times that snappy style that, to the nation's moviegoers, authenticated a Manhattan mailing address. Most amusingly, we get a preview of a visual not to be fully acculturated till Winchell got onto television in the early 1950s: the man in the suit and hat and loosened tie—for that "this just in!" city-room feeling—frantically tapping his telegraph key in his *hurry! hurry!* sideshow barker's voice. And all the ships at sea.

In fact, playing opposite a bandleader—especially bandleader Bernie who at times conducts with fiddle and bow under his arm, as if he

---

*Haley's singing voice was a thin tenorino, useful but lacking in glamor; Fox dubbed him with the opulent baritone of Buddy Clark.

were Johann Strauss—gentles Winchell down from the megalomaniac he is remembered to be when remembered at all. Is this the guy whom everyone feared, who enjoyed wielding headsman's power over their livelihood? But do you know who was FDR's idea of the most dangerous man in the country? No, not Huey Long—Douglas MacArthur. Of course, Winchell was a passionate supporter of the New Deal. Whom would Roosevelt have thought most dangerous if Winchell had run with the opposition?

And what made Winchell so powerful? Perhaps it was his position as the First New Yorker at a time when the nation was deep in a resentful and even hate-speckled love affair with the city. In the south and Fundamentalist midwest, New York was still a Babylon of unreliable social elements, and The Column swelled with them: the squalid rich, showgirl keptives, squads of doormen parting like the Red Sea for entourages of hoodlums entering the we-never-close nightclub of human junk.

You knew who they were, too, because Winchell named names the way Cole Porter wrote list songs. It was niche gossip, like knowing what a *mariage blanc* was, and who had one for what reason. Picture poor Mr. Heinz, my dear, without a pickle! Reading or listening to Winchell, you could know what the rich knew, what movie stars and gangsters knew. You could know New York. Once again, the notion of an elite got redefined: it was anyone who could crack The Column.

You expect so unlikable a man to know thousands without a single friend among them. Yet Winchell had a few, including that other herald of Broadway lore, Damon Runyon. They did not hit it off till late in both careers, in the 1940s, when Runyon was dying of throat cancer and operations had left him silent with a writing pad and the stoic look of a guy who is doomed yet a gentleman. So Winchell and Runyon were perfectly suited, because the former liked to talk and the latter couldn't interrupt, crack wise, or even reply.

Damon Runyon was mainly what Winchell wasn't: a genuine reporter and a gifted writer. Though he is known today exclusively for his tales in patois of the gamblers and broads one might meet in the Paradise Club, Runyon was versatile. An outstanding sports writer, he wrote about many things, including following General Pershing's pursuit of

Pancho Villa after Villa's army perpetrated an outrage in Texas. Runyon also created a fiction milieu entirely apart from the guys and dolls that keep him in print today: the Joe and Ethel Turp series, about a working-class Brooklyn couple who somehow get into adventures almost as bizarre as Runyon's gamblers.

There was as well Runyon the Beau Brummell. O. O. McIntyre was a dandy, but of the silly sort; he wanted to be seen a mile away. And Winchell wore the standard outfit of suit, tie, and fedora. It was Runyon alone who dressed the swell, conservative in taste but fresh and immaculate to the point of obsession. Runyon also takes part in the myth of the provincial seizing destiny in the metropolis, but he never played the gawking hayseed in the McIntyre manner. Runyon acclimatized himself. Winchell's myth was that of the New York Native coming into his inheritance, yet, as the essential New Yorker, Runyon has outstayed him. *His* is the voice of the city and his subject is the outlaw.

But then, why not? The Column stacked newbies atop Names and the grand with the sleazy in Winchell's unique debauch of the notion of a ruling class. Runyon wrote about many people, but he immortalized a set of thugs and their assistants because he hung out with them. He thought them picturesque, good copy. And they were a part of the New York that he and Winchell were inventing, because both men came along in time to thrive in the second quarter of the twentieth century— the part that can be written out in the equation

(New York vs. Fundamentalism) + jazz
+ (second-generation immigrant culture)
+ notoriety = The Column Known As Broadway

In early days, Winchell collected the scuttlebutt by wandering along The Street, asking for the latest. A hustler. In his prime, however, Winchell was royalty: petitioners had to make kowtow at the throne, Table 50 in the Cub Room of the Stork Club. And when Winchell and Runyon became friends later on, Runyon was the most honored of the nobles in Winchell's feudal system, not only seated with highest prestige but spared the contempt with which the king generally ruled.

However, when Runyon started writing underworld fiction, he was more likely to be found in less savory hangouts, picking up material. Our old friend Arnold Rothstein's Table 50 was a booth in Lindy's delicatessen, at 1626 Broadway, in the center of what later could be called Runyonland. (The Stork was in a different neighborhood altogether, east of Fifth Avenue.) Lindy's, which Runyon renamed "Mindy's" in his tales, was where Runyon caught Rothstein at his exercises, and Jimmy Breslin tells the story: while Runyon and Rothstein are talking, Rothstein's business telephone rings. (This is, of course, the Lindy's phone-book number.) Rothstein goes up to the cashier to take the call; from what he's saying, Runyon can tell that the caller wants to borrow money. Five hundred dollars.

"I can't hear you," says Rothstein, in the provocatively nonchalant tone of one who can hear but won't lend.

The caller insists. Rothstein won't budge. "I can't hear you," he repeats. "The connection is bad."

At which the long-distance operator intercedes to clarify the dialogue, in that curious accent once favored by phone-company personnel: "He *say*-yud that he *nee*-yuds *fi*-yuv hundred *dol*-yurs."

So Rothstein tells her, "If you heard him so good, then you give him the money." And hangs up.

The story has a Runyonesque quality, to be sure, and Runyon was to use Rothstein as a character, called simply The Brain. "The Brain Goes Home" actually treats Rothstein's murder, though in the Runyon version he is stabbed, and by a debtor rather than, as Rothstein was, a creditor. Even the smallest touch of piquant naturalism lent color to Runyon's pictures, as when he watched a rambunctious card player calling out comments on his hands, his luck, his skill—and finally laid down his winning cards with "Nicely, nicely!" He became the character Nicely-Nicely Jones.*

---

*Readers familiar with the Runyon musical, *Guys and Dolls* (1950), will know him as the renamed Nicely-Nicely Johnson, a featured player who suddenly takes stage for the irresistible revivalist spoof "Sit Down, You're Rocking the Boat." Amiable to a fault with his Broadway tenor, Nicely-Nicely embodies Runyon's friendly view of the dice-and-track outlaw that—as we're about to see—is extremely romanticized.

It may be that taking down the diction and attitudes of these "characters" gave them a certain authenticity, but Runyon revised them in his writing, leaving out much of the sheer abandoned ruthlessness that marked them in life. Here was something else that Runyon had in common with Winchell: both palled around with gangsters. And if one is close to the crew one might as well be special-close with their captain, Owney Madden, the most powerful criminal in New York and, incidentally, the owner of the Cotton Club. Jimmy Breslin tells this one, too, explaining the origin of a certain phrase. It seems that there is bad blood between Madden and a con named Jigger McGrath. Madden lets it be known that they can shake hands and end this quarrel. Jigger agrees. The two meet up at Forty-seventh Street and Twelfth Avenue, at the very edge of Runyonland; two steps over and you're in the midwest. So McGrath holds out his right. "Shake hands," he cries. Madden takes McGrath's hand and holds on, and while McGrath struggles to break free, a Madden torpedo named Arthur Bieler steps up from out of gangland nowhere and shoots McGrath dead while Madden shouts, "Shake hands with the devil!"

So now we know where that phrase comes from; but there is nothing so concisely vicious as that anywhere in Runyon. There are murders, yes. We know what happened to The Brain, and a story called "Sense of Humour" is filled with killings. But no one in Runyon's world exults in evil power the way Owney Madden did. Runyon's very titles convey a breezy worldview incorporating characters who are essentially comic: "Dream Street Rose," "The Snatching of Bookie Bob," "Butch Minds the Baby," "Little Miss Marker," "That Ever-Loving Wife of Hymie's." And of course the obsessive use of the present tense,* along with the saucy jargon and the twist that ends a story with either an O. Henry–like surprise or an ironic envoi, have added to the air of mythmaking.

---

* The original story collections and later reshuffled anthologies have been huge sellers from the first, in England as well as America. With their slang and perverse tense logic the stories should be all but untranslatable, but they have even gone over in France, in a collection called *Broadway Mon Village*. E. C. Bentley, who edited a *Best of Damon Runyon* in 1938, claimed to have spotted one verb in the past tense in a Runyon story, but he wouldn't say where.

Then there is the unnamed Runyon narrator, not Runyon himself but one of the gambling set, on intimate terms with, it seems, everyone along Broadway. As he is Runyon's point of contact with the reader, he is the instrument by which Runyon tames his people, removes them from the reality of Owney Madden's New York.

Runyon was by profession a reporter: a realist, not a fabulist. Yet we have seen how intricately connected were the worlds of crime and show biz in the concept of "Broadway," and show biz is fabulism. Covering the scandalous Snyder-Gray trial, Runyon reported as if at an entertainment event. Ruth Snyder and her boy friend, Judd Gray, had murdered Mr. Snyder, and both were facing the electric chair. Yet, as Runyon describes it, their court date is a show:

> Dizzy-looking dolls said to represent the social strata of Park Avenue—
> the upper crust, as I understand—were there, not a little proud of their
> heroism in getting out so early. Some were escorted by silly-looking
> "muggs" wearing canes and spats.

Runyon even joked that business was so good that they were thinking of sending a national company out on the road, "and 8,000 different blondes are being considered for the leading female role."

Satire. Yet Runyon is scorning his own system: his art. Right from the start of "Romance in the Roaring Forties," Runyon's first guys-and-dolls story, in 1929, his narrator is soothing the dangerous Broadway scene with "Only a rank sucker will think of taking two peeks at Dave the Dude's doll." The very idea of a Dave the Dude creates a milieu without a Madden. Or try the start of Runyon's fourth story, also in 1929, "Madame La Gimp":

> One night I am passing the corner of Fiftieth Street and Broadway, and
> what do I see but Dave the Dude standing in a doorway talking to a
> busted-down old Spanish doll by the name of Madame La Gimp. . . .
> Now this is a most surprising sight to me, because Madame La Gimp . . .
> is nothing but an old haybag, and generally somewhat ginned up.

The plot is festive, as Dave the Dude directs a harmless scam whereby Madame La Gimp's sheltered daughter can marry the son of a count. Amusingly, Runyon's cheats and moochers show up at a gala "meet the folks" disguised as American royalty. Good Time Charley Bannister is then Mayor Jimmy Walker, the Pale Face Kid is Herbert Bayard Swope, Guinea Mike is Hoover's vice-president, Charles Curtis, and the narrator shows up as O. O. McIntyre. All ends well, and when Hollywood turned it out as *Lady For a Day* (1933), there were four major Oscar nominations. Nobody won, but for little Columbia Pictures—in the year before it shockingly swept the Oscars for *It Happened One Night*— *Lady For a Day* was quite an event.

It even got a remake, in 1961 (as *Pocketful of Miracles*), but the 1930s was the heyday of Runyon-into-film, because that's when Hollywood became fascinated with gangsters in the same way that Winchell's and Runyon's readers did. There had been gangster silents; as with so much else in cinema history, D. W. Griffith gets the invention byline, for *The Musketeers of Pig Alley,* in 1912. Still, the gangster had to wait till sound technology could reveal the all-defining spoken dialect of crime, from James Cagney's triumphant cackle to Edward G. Robinson's "Ehnyah, *see?*"

Walter Winchell did some inventing, too. Before he appeared in Hollywood musicals, he devised the plot for one. They called it *Broadway Thru a Keyhole* (1933), and it told how Ruby Keeler found herself caught between singer Al Jolson and gangster Johnny "Irish" Costello. Not only in the film: in life. (It had happened in 1929.) They changed the names, and Constance Cummings, Russ Columbo, and Paul Kelly, respectively, played the roles,* but Jolson still took a swing at Winchell when next they met. It occurred at the fights in the Hollywood Legion Stadium, with both men's wives present: more Column. *Broadway Thru*

---

* Kelly was a case of authentic casting, as he had done time in San Quentin for manslaughter, beating to death the husband of a woman Kelly later married. Kelly's movie career was insignificant, but when he returned to the stage he got some choice roles, including a hero part in the war play *Command Decision* (1947).

a Keyhole established atmosphere with eye-witnesses such as tavernière Texas Guinan, socialite musical-comedy ingenue Frances Williams, and vaudevillian Blossom Seeley. All that was missing was the kind of gangster who knows what Owney Madden knew.

But Hollywood had already discovered the charisma available in a genuine rufftuff. Clark Gable popularized the type in the earliest talkies, before MGM realized that his good-bad man was more compelling. Yes, he skewed crooked, but he lived in honor by his own strange code. And when copping one of those Oscars for *It Happened One Night,* Gable wasn't even crooked but a newspaperman. Better, a real one—not Walter Winchell but a discoverer of stories: intrepid, resourceful, and, if he likes you, protective. He defeats the foe and not only saves the damsel (Claudette Colbert as the indispensable runaway heiress) but helps her develop her own intrepid side. How marriage survived American womanhood's experience in absorbing the appeal of Gableism is one of the mysteries of the 1930s.

Gable before then—the early-talkie Gable—is rapacious and codeless. He never looked taller or tougher than in *A Free Soul* (1931), as a barbarian in bespoke tailoring, pleasing his fancy and simply killing all who resist. He hasn't even bothered to grow that suave little mustache; for now, the Gable trademark is shoving people. He shoves Leslie Howard, he shoves skinny little James Gleason, he shoves his own Chinese butler even though the butler is carrying a platter of iced champagne, and he even shoves Norma Shearer (into a chair, and not hard). "She's mine," he snarls at Leslie Howard. "She belongs to me." This Gable is so evil that the picture can't end happily unless Howard—creampuff cupbearer to Gable's Zeus—murders him.

However, by mid-Depression the gangster is going legit. This is not only because of the reimposed Motion Picture Code censorship but because trouble abroad forced Hollywood to bring the gangster into the national community—reform him, in effect. So in *Manhattan Melodrama* (1934), Gable is above all affable. He remains dangerous, but doesn't make a point of menacing anything that moves—and he ends in sacrificing himself to judicial execution to save those nice people William Powell and Myrna Loy.

Manhattan Melodrama is another work using the Arnold Rothstein murder. Remember the overcoat found in that hotel room in the Park Central Hotel? The movie builds a murder plot around it, then tries to throw us off when Powell, the District Attorney, calls this killing "as tough as the Rothstein case." No, this *is* the Rothstein case, and we know it because The Column told us. Americans had become aficionados not only of fame and money and Broadway thru a keyhole but of crime and its stars. Yes, they were stars. Al Capone was so celebrated that Hollywood filmed his bio as early as 1932, in *Scarface,* though they changed his name to Tony Camonte. Ruth Snyder was a star—a *Daily News* reporter sneaked a camera into the viewing room at her execution, and she made the front page frying. Then James Cagney, in *Picture Snatcher* (1933), did the same thing in exactly the same way—the camera was hidden in a trouser leg—and his photo came out clearer than the one of Snyder. Later that same year, in *Lady Killer,* Cagney starts as a gangster but ends up as a movie star. He retains some of his lawless field expedients, however, forcing a snide movie critic into the men's room, making him eat one of his reviews, then Gable-shoving him into a toilet stall. Sight gag: we see only the critic's outstretched feet, but the toilet flushes, telling us where his head must have landed. "The public is tired of those handsome, curly-haired leading men," a producer tells his flunkies just before tapping Cagney for membership in the prominence club. "The rough-and-ready type is what women go for nowadays."

Of course, like others of the brotherhood, Cagney would have to channel his energy into confronting bad guys, in *Here Comes the Navy* (1934), *G Men* (1935), and so on. There are occasional reversions to the gangster, but Cagney's makeover is so complete that, at least till the war has come and gone, they seem like acts of nostalgic caprice. True, Gable is still the rogue, but a *good* rogue. He even enlisted in the Air Force and stayed off the screen for the duration.

Runyon, however, maintained his characters without reflecting this switch in tone, because they had been a fantasy from the start. This is the essential difference between what Runyon and Winchell mean today as summoning terms. Winchell operated in a headline *dolce vita* in which all kinds of fame were integrated into one fame and all deeds were morally equal. But Runyon was a minimalist whose characters lived below the fame line. They were what police detectives mean when they say, "Round up the usual suspects."

Winchell and Runyon crossed paths at the Lindbergh kidnaping trial, yet another example of a murder case's being "produced" like a show. They didn't know each other at the time, and Runyon in fact scorned Winchell as man and symbol. Winchell was a kind of sanctioned gangster, a news racketeer. The Column and the craft of good news writing were so far apart that one could call Winchell an artist, as if he was making it up. Even when he told the truth—and, mostly, that is what he told—he still seemed to be creating in an alternate universe.

Later on, when Runyon was facing the methodical destruction of his faculties that cancer likes to visit upon its victims, he changed his mind about Winchell. Something about sharing the command of Table 50 buoyed Runyon's spirit. Taking the Winchellian late-night zoom ride through Manhattan to admire the Roar of the Town as others fly over Alaska to view the Northern Lights, Runyon felt inspired, fulfilled, vital. Anything but doomed—even if he could speak only through a writing pad printed with "Damon Runyon Says." One night, incensed at a remark of producer Mike Todd, Runyon furiously scribbled an answer and thrust it at Todd.

"Will you please stop shouting at me?" Todd replied.

In a way, the friendship of Runyon and Winchell mirrors another union of opposites, that of the new art of scandalmongering and the old fiction interested in characters of family and money. A union, let us say, of *Broadway Thru a Keyhole* and F. Scott Fitzgerald, leaving one unable to distinguish the morals of an Ivy Leaguer from those of a crook. Sometimes the Ivy Leaguer is a crook. It is as if the Astors and their kind had started reading The Column and told some servant, We'll have what they're having. The prophet of this particular art was John O'Hara, arguably our least truly appreciated twentieth-century writer.

O'Hara's flaw lies in his excellence: with the keenest ear in the business, O'Hara could place a character's social background by his argot the way Henry Higgins can by his vowels. Thus, the huge O'Hara oeuvre overflows with language magic, in which people reveal themselves in grammar and usage to such nicety that they become as vivid as exotic birds. It makes his short stories astonishing yet today, but it slows his novels. The stories revel in abrupt enlightenment, over in five or six pages; the novels, doing the same thing but on the grand scale, meander. O'Hara nevertheless felt—as they tried to make Dorothy Parker feel—that a great writer leaves his mark only on the novel. Anyone can write a short piece—or so the wisdom runs. But O'Hara wrote short so well that he became (and remains) the most-published author of fiction in *The New Yorker,* an achievement without rival in American letters.

O'Hara fought continually with the magazine—over money, over a sleazy review of one of O'Hara's books by that lavish nonentity Brendan Gill, over O'Hara's extravagant characters' peculiar verbal tics, even over an O'Hara specialty that was to become the identifying element of "the *New Yorker* story," an ambiguity in authorial omniscience that asks the reader to "solve" the story as if it were a problem in human geometry.

Actually, O'Hara fought with everyone, starting with his father, an upright smalltown Pennsylvania doctor whose death impoverished his large family and left the Yale-bound O'Hara to skip the higher education that, frankly, he didn't need. Still, like F. Scott Fitzgerald, O'Hara wanted to Fit In with the potentates of the Ivy League—of the stag line at debutante balls and the bar at tony men's clubs. Having to skip Yale, a prerequisite to the Fitting In lifestyle, disappointed O'Hara, but he got over it. What he didn't get over was the way his enemies and even some friends acted as though O'Hara nursed an obsession with Yale and kept twitting him about it. O'Hara didn't have an obsession with Yale. He had an obsession about not letting anyone get away with twitting him.

So it's a rowdy profile, made of feuding and even a little fighting, though Brendan Gill's repeated attempts to stick his stupid grin in O'Hara's face ended only in verbal fisticuffs. ("You son-of-a-bitch," O'Hara tells Gill, "I wouldn't go to a dogfight with you.") Then, too, O'Hara was Irish in the first post-Tammany generation, when, like the Scandinavians before them, the Celts were starting to disappear into the American population pool in all but name. So you could twit him about his birth as well, if you felt ornery.

Handsome in youth, O'Hara drank himself into an early florid middle age, then went teetotal. But he was not a practitioner of Irish charm; he barked a lot. And there is this odd note: O'Hara was not only heterosexual but straight to a fault, without a shred of interest in the whimsey, irony, glamor, and camp that gay writers like Noël Coward and Cole Porter were unleashing upon society. Even Walter Winchell had his merry moments—but O'Hara saw a world embittered by missed chances and enlightened by lies. The whole planet is screwy, but not in an entertaining way: in a screwy way. The writer who lives on this perception and, further, can't have a drink will not be an easy date. Besides, O'Hara knew that central human truth that almost nobody wants to admit: in the scramble for a seat at the dinner party of fame, everything is personal.

Aside from his skill in capturing real life in the colloquial, O'Hara was known for his frankness in sexual matters. Such honesty could shock in the 1930s, O'Hara's first decade as an author, when he was moving from his twenties into his thirties. "Infantilism" is what Sinclair Lewis called it. "The erotic visions of a hobbledehoy behind the barn." And O. O. McIntyre's blurb was ready: "Swill." O'Hara had none of the sly "watch this" of James Branch Cabell, no pop + eros = art. O'Hara's people fell in and out of bed with each other because that's what people do. It wasn't a literary device; it was natural. That's what made it so offensive, to those whom honesty offends.

What sets O'Hara apart even more than all this is his observation that human nature obtains evenly throughout the class structure—that those with family and money are no more virtuous, polite, or interesting than those without. On the contrary, family protects one's reputation hypocritically and money gives them freedom to sin. In O'Hara's fiction, as never before in American lit, "honest" people get involved with shady people. The movie producer hires killers; the grande dame in mink beds a drifter. The social order is singing off-key.

This may remind some of *The Great Gatsby*—and Fitzgerald was O'Hara's predecessor (and friend), true enough. But Fitzgerald's world is glamorous, everyone in crisp tennis whites or after-six Dress To Kill. Arnold Rothstein, we know, makes an appearance, and Gatsby himself is his own beautiful invention. Still, the atmosphere is elegant, because everyone who matters aspires to be socially top.

In O'Hara, everyone aspires to slum. His second novel, *BUtterfield 8* (1935),* takes place largely in speakeasies and bedrooms, the most classless places in Manhattan. This facilitates O'Hara's mating of squire and varlet. Bars especially are an O'Hara haunt. In "The King of the Desert," two wisenheimers are baiting a California rancher named Dave in one of those O'Hara somewheres, where he will skip the boilerplate—how they met and sat down together, even who the two jokers are. Stay alert; you'll figure it out, if it matters. What O'Hara cares about is what happens: the two clowns keep pushing it, stretching their tight O'Hara verbal muscles—"Multiply that by forta forta forta forta," says one, "times sibba sibba sibba sabba"—till we get an uneasy feeling about how the rancher is taking it. Sure enough, they finally cross a line, and the rancher, still sitting, punches one of them so hard he's out on the floor. "He did not finish the long smile that he had begun," O'Hara tells us. "His face was not there." Dave grabs the other one, but then he just laughs and lets him go.

"We'll fix you in Hollywood, mister," the guy tells Dave, in a powerless taunt. But now we know who these people are: two screenwriters on holiday, putting up in a hostel on Dave's property. At least Dave's guests end up alive. In the most characteristic O'Hara story, "Everything Satisfactory," a saloon owner tires of a difficult longtime customer, another Hollywood character, and lets him drive off staggering drunk. "We'll read about him in the papers," he says, anticipating an obituary.

---

*The title employs the telephone exchange associated with Manhattan's most affluent quartier, along Park Avenue in the seventies. O'Hara never uses the exchange in the novel, but the movie version (1960) substantiated the title in the number of heroine Elizabeth Taylor's answering service. Thus, the novel's clever metonym for swank becomes the sleazy whisper of a call girl's contact information. Writers often give the novel's setting as the 1920s because of O'Hara's allusions to, for instance, the Algonquin Round Table and, once again, the Rothstein murder. O'Hara himself doesn't state the time of the action, typically expecting the reader to discover it from narrative data. And, finally, it arrives, as someone reading a newspaper remarks that Susan Glaspell's play *Alison's House* just won the Pulitzer Prize. The piece opened at the end of 1930 and won the award on May 4, 1931.

Thus, O'Hara offends the petit bourgeois household gods of seemliness and proportion. Everything's personal because everyone's so hungry, devious, angry. Even the once important concept of class dwindles indistinctly into a pileup of oxymorons: charming thugs, sleazy Ivy Leaguers, talentless artists.

Or how about a Kresge's Romeo working as a nightclub singer and writing letters to a bandleader friend and signing off as "Pal Joey"? His workplace of course provisions that quintessential thirties meeting of glamor and crime, show biz and money, and Joey himself will be uneducated, solipsistic, and little more than a con man. Couching Joey's skinny saga exclusively in his own letters gave O'Hara the chance for a tour de force in his best elliptical style, for much of what we need to know Joey cannot articulate himself: we have to pick up on clues. For instance, why is someone so subliterate and lazy writing at all? O'Hara—Joey, really—never tells us. Eventually we see Joey's angle: the man he's writing to, addressed as "Friend Ted," is making it big, with hit recordings and column inches, and Joey is presumably hoping to cash in on their friendship in some way.

The *Pal Joey* stories appeared in *The New Yorker* from 1938 into 1940,* which gave O'Hara some two years of sparring matches with Harold Ross over how much patois *New Yorker* subscribers could comprehend. As always an enthusiastic reader but a sometimes overly conservative editor, Ross appreciated O'Hara's conjuring up an entire subculture in its vernacular. But he kept trying to water down O'Hara's verbal flash. Joey is almost pre-Adamite in his grammar, and he never uses commas. For example:

> I was out getting my breakfast around 4 one afternoon and right near where I eat is this pet & dog shop. . . . I saw this mouse standing there. . . .

---

* The magazine ran twelve *Joey* stories in all, averaging out to about one every two months. That's a lot of Joey, but *The New Yorker* was at the time in the thrall of series stories, not least because Clarence Day's *Life With Father* tales proved so popular they were thought to account for much of the magazine's subscription security. Adding in the two *Joey* stories that *The New Yorker* had rejected, O'Hara published the set in book form in 1940.

She was about twenty and I didn't care if she had a face out of the Zoo but spring was in the air and this mouse had a shape that you dont see only on the second Tuesday of every week and when you do see a shape like that you have to do something about it.

Besides usages peculiar to show biz—"earning my coffee & cakes" means "making enough to live on"—Joey teaches us a bit about the scene on its lower end. We learn that a "bumper" is a man who arranges little physical accidents in dimly-lit clubs during which he lifts your wallet. We get as well a taste of the hierarchy of the working talent, of who gets "up there" and who hustles for work. Everyone's got an angle or a fatal flaw, a genuine gift or an in with somebody rich. Thus, when Joey sizes up a band that has been working in the same club for fifteen years: "There was one old guy playing cornet that looked as if he was worried for fear the Confederates wd catch him for being a deserter."

Unlike Clarence Day's *Father* stories, the *Joey* pieces have no plot. They functioned as *The New Yorker* equivalent of The Column: data on the interesting lives of people they would never actually meet. And then O'Hara had a really strange idea—wouldn't the *Joey* stories make a dandy musical comedy?

One can only surmise that O'Hara had never seen a musical himself, because the shows of that era lacked the vocabulary to accommodate Joey's milieu. Underworld figures proliferated in musicals of the day, to be sure, but as cartoons fit for that lovable zany Jimmy Durante. There's nothing lovable or zany in O'Hara. Yet when he approached Richard Rodgers and Lorenz Hart about a *Joey* musical, they jumped at it. Hart lived in Joey's world, after all, and Rodgers loved a challenge. Further, the pair had been making history in a series of dance musicals with George Balanchine: *On Your Toes* (1936), *Babes in Arms* (1937), *I Married an Angel* (1938), and *The Boys from Syracuse* (1938). Balanchine led the musical's blending of hoofing and dance into an instrument of character development, so here was an opportunity. A dancing Joey might locate something beyond O'Hara's verbal skill—male sex appeal. Musicals were always coying around the appetitive element of the boy meets girl. This time, a musical could be made of it.

Balanchine, however, might prove too arty for the hammer-and-tongs aesthetic of a cheap nightclub, so another Rodgers and Hart alumnus, Robert Alton (incidentally an expert in the latest hoofing styles) would choreograph. George Abbott was to produce, direct, and edit O'Hara's script if necessary. (It was.) And Rodgers already knew of the actor who could not only dance and sing Joey but had the *non so che* to embody him: Gene Kelly.

Now all they needed was a plot. O'Hara invented a society woman, Vera Simpson, who takes up with Joey in adulterous union, treats him to a club of his own, then drops him. It was all-basic O'Hara, a mating of class and trash. The "mouse" from the pet shop incident quoted above was to serve as the ingenue, a hard-boiled club dancer would provide Leg and a foil to Joey, and a creepy "agent" would enliven the second act with a blackmail scheme.

Vera was a role any number of Broadway women could play. I rather fancy Eve Arden in it, and she was just then commuting between Broadway and Hollywood. Twenty-eight years old when *Pal Joey* opened, on Christmas Day, 1940, Arden might have been a bit young. But she was playing older than her age, and was just about to take on a role similar to Vera, in Cole Porter's *Let's Face It!* (1941). Vera has since become an older woman's part, like the *Rosenkavalier* Marschallin, and, indeed, Vivienne Segal was forty-three when she created Vera. Everyone knew she was going to, because she was Lorenz Hart's official beard when he had to date hetero.

One other piece of *Pal Joey* casting detains us, because this performer eventually became one of the most famous characters in the musical. She didn't play one: she is one. It's Baby June, in *Gypsy,* who was, in the real life of Gypsy Rose Lee, her sister, June Havoc. And Havoc it was who played the club dancer, who rejoices in a name that also functions as an explanatory sentence, Gladys Bumps. Having separated her destiny from that of sister Gypsy, Havoc was arguably about to become a major song-and-dance star in the tough-broad division when Betty Hutton appeared. Hutton did everything Havoc did and did it famous, sidelining Havoc. (The two share a data trifle in that they both took

over the role of Miss Hannigan during the original run of *Annie* [1977].)
Today, the most notable thing about June Havoc is that whoever plays
her in *Gypsy* vanishes midway through Act One and has to wait ninety
minutes to take her call.

The best known thing about *Pal Joey* is that it wasn't a hit till it was
revived in 1952, but this is another of those factoids: everyone's wrong.
It was a hit in 1940 and a bigger hit in 1952—and not because the authors soothed any aspect of O'Hara's inferno of users. The lyrics match
the dialogue—even the music matches the dialogue, with an arched
eyebrow crabbing the lilt of "The Flower Garden of My Heart" and
the gleeful hot of a quickie sweating up "That Terrific Rainbow."
When, at the end of Act One, Joey anticipates the power of headlining
in his own place, "I'll own a night club that's tops" is mated with "And
I'll be in with the cops": pure O'Haraworld, where the underdog sees
success as rising above the law. Isn't that what The Column taught?
The rich and famous—the elite—are licensed outlaws and the poor get
children.

Kelly couldn't turn down his first starring role, but he did worry
about how playing a heel might affect his career. Abbott himself seems
to have suffered a case of second thoughts during the rehearsal period.
When the first-act finale turned from Joey's soliloquy into a full-cast
dream ballet called "Joey Looks into the Future," designer Jo Mielziner
warned Abbott that it would inflate the show's budget by ten percent,
and Abbott wanted to kill the number. Rodgers then demanded that
Abbott step aside in favor of a producer-director with more faith in the
material or get on board, and the chastened Abbott got.

The Philadelphia tryout played to frosty houses, but if ever there was
a New Yorker's show, it's this one. The *Times'* Brooks Atkinson completely missed the point, with "offers everything but a good time." But
the *Herald Tribune*, the *Daily News*, the *Daily Mirror*, the *World-Telegram*,
The New Yorker, *Time*, and *Newsweek* gave *Pal Joey* top ratings. Most often,
the breakthrough musicals are the arty ones—*Show Boat*, *West Side Story*,
Cabaret. *Pal Joey* isn't arty: it's a jest.

Look at its source, after all: letters from an urban rustic who stands somewhere between Lochinvar and loser. Joey apparently has charm, yet for all his cunning he's unworldly. In the only one of the original story episodes to go into the musical at length, Joey is interviewed by a reporter named Melba.* Her dress and demeanor lead him to take her for a lesbian:

> She is wearing this suit that you or I wd turn down because of being too masculine. Her hair is cut crew cut like the college blood. . . . Then the dame came closer to me and I was just about to cover my face with my hands and scream . . .

The musical follows this sequence closely, as Joey tries to create a high-status backstory and keeps getting slapped down:

> JOEY: I was up at Dartmouth University—
> MELBA: What for?
> JOEY: Going there. I was a "soph."
> MELBA: I thought they called it Dartmouth College. . . . However, you were up there.
> JOEY: As a soph. I was living at the Frat House.
> MELBA: Frat?
> JOEY: Sure!
> MELBA: You make it sound like one of those colleges where Betty Grable's always going.

Joey has finally met a mouse he can't con. In fact, Melba is anything but a mouse, and definitely not a lesbian. Because when she poses in a skimpy showgirl outfit with him for the Sunday edition and he hits on her, she laughs him off. As she tells him in the original story:

---

* Throughout the stories, Joey uses full names only when referring to the famous. Those on his own level appear by first name or simply as "the mouse" or "the owner." Not till the musical appeared did we learn everybody's phone-book listing, as in Melba Snyder and, amusingly, Joey Evans, a name fit for the marquee: short, easy to recall, and bearing a friendly sort of "going places" self-importance.

You just saw as much as you will ever see so get rid of such ideas because among other things my husband used to play football at Dartmouth U. as you call it. He is also satisfactory in every other way and I must be running along.

Expanding on this, Rodgers and Hart wrote *their* Melba "Zip," which simultaneously spoofs and emulates the concept of striptease. It's a show-stopper in the right hands.*

If a single moment of *Pal Joey* encapsulates its reinstruction of the mu-sical's worldview, it is the famously cynical ending. In his script, O'Hara originally got uncharacteristically gooey at this point: Joey walked off arm in arm with the pet-shop mouse. In the revised version unveiled on Broadway, Joey let her exit stage left as he eyed a brand-new girl moving right. Starting to follow the mouse, he turned . . . and went off right, after the new challenge. We can imagine the audience's gasps of amused exasperation as the curtain fell: it's a sight gag.

In other words, *Pal Joey* didn't pose as an act of artistic evolution. It was doing what musical comedy always did at this time, incorporating the news of the day, which is now sex, crime, and power and also how their corruption had permeated society. It's the musical turning into The Column, perhaps a Damon Runyon story:

> Of all the flashy young fellows that Chicago ever sees, there is no doubt
> but that the vocalist at the Club Paree has the local monopoly on flash.
> And what with singing his sweet lullabies to the Harvards, and romanc-

---

* The original Melba, Jean Casto, went on to play *Carousel*'s Mrs. Mullin, another tough woman, and the 1952 Melba was Elaine Stritch, just starting the rise to sellout stardom that took her about fifty years to complete. The role has long been thought a spicy cameo, for, among others, Renee Taylor, Kay Medford, Dixie Carter, Jose-phine Premice, and Bebe Neuwirth in her deadpan looks-could-kill Lilith mode. At the City Center in 1961, Eileen Heckart's Melba changed a lyric to "Rosalind Russell will be cast in the part," a reference to Russell's constantly inheriting other stars' stage roles for the movie version, including Heckart's own Rosemary the school-teacher in *Picnic*. Richard Greenberg's wholly new script for a 2008 Roundabout revival eliminated Melba entirely, reassigning "Zip" to Gladys as a nightclub floor number.

ing his many fans who are high-class dolls, and one thing and another, he is very quickly taken up by a wife of one of the Harvards, who is quite some doll herself.

Perhaps it's better as a blind item in the gossip paragraphs, teasing and knowitall:

We hear it's phffft for that oh-so nice-looking emcee at that new Chicago nightclub and his major investor. Or is that investrix?

7

Dorothy Thompson: Man's Work

I t went like this: if you happened to agree with what she said, you called her brilliant. If you disagreed, you called her shrill, self-righteous, a scold: because there had never been a woman like her before, and some people either could not or would not accept her unapologetically de-genderized professionalism. In 1936, when Dorothy Thompson con-tracted with the *Herald Tribune* to write a thrice-weekly column called On the Record—in size and placement an exact complement to the *Tribune*'s star commentator, Walter Lippmann—she invented something remarkable for the era. Dorothy Thompson became The Woman Who Tells Men What To Think.

Born in 1893 and raised in rural New York State, Thompson was college-educated, progressive on women's social issues, and, she soon learned, in love with Europe. She got there as a reporter just when major twentieth-century history was happening, with its explosion of inflam-matory isms, and that was what Thompson wanted to think over, con-verse upon, and write about, now as a pundit. She maintained her status through arguments of force and clarity, eventually making her, with Eleanor Roosevelt, one of the two most influential women in the country and possibly one of the ten or twelve most influential people, period.

Famous women in the late 1930s tended to be movie stars or perhaps Dorothy Parker—the name you pasted on a wisecrack when you were quoting. But movie stars and Dorothy Parker couldn't deconstruct for you the issues at stake in the coming European war, nor justify defensive warmaking in the stabilization of democracy. Dorothy Thompson became a summoning term for her genre of woman when she was its only example. Even today, there is no one quite like her or as big as she was, with a reach so compelling that heads of state took her calls. The closest parallel in recent times might be the late Oriana Fallaci; had Thompson been around later, she would surely have copped an interview with the Ayatollah Khomeini and written a blistering attack on Islamo-fascism after 9/11, both of which Fallaci did. Even so, Fallaci, famous in Europe, never attained high-I.D. status in America, though it was her adopted country. Dorothy Thompson was a household name.

Had she been French, she would have received a state funeral. (She died in 1961, aged sixty-seven.) Instead, as an American, she got a *Time* cover, a *New Yorker* cartoon,* and hate mail. And she led the fight against the primary mid-American uprising of the pre–World War II years, this one against the elite of New York and Washington, D.C. In all, the Thompson saga has so many parts to it that the present chapter must be broken into sections.

Dorothy Thompson's Worldview

Historians date the cult of the foreign correspondent from the career of William Russell, who covered events of local and world interest for the London *Times* in the late middle of the nineteenth century. Russell's dispatches were wordy and lacked verbal tang. Still, he had a knack

---

* It was a Thurber, showing, at left, a man seated at a typewriter with an expression of scowling determination. At right, one woman was explaining to another, "He's giving Dorothy Thompson a piece of his mind." Thompson also got a movie: it was believed that the globetrotting knowitall that Katharine Hepburn played in *Woman of the Year* (1942) is a runoff of Thompson.

for bringing the reader along on his adventures, as here in September of 1870, in a series on the Franco-Prussian War:

> I had a long conversation with a French gentleman today, who told me that . . . the respectable classes . . . were actually afraid of the enemy going, because then the thing they most dreaded—the proclamation of a Red Republic by all the rogues, villains, and dreamers—the poets and the *polloi* of rascality—would be sure to take place in Paris.

Interestingly, Russell's informant has correctly predicted the ghastly interlude of the Commune.

Russell covered all sorts of events, from the first (unsuccessful) attempt to lay a transatlantic telegraph cable to the coronation of Alexander II of Russia. However, like most of the notable foreign correspondents after him he was celebrated for war reporting, preferably from inside the danger zones. We have seen Damon Runyon doing his bit, in Mexico with General Pershing—but the war reporter was expected to leap ahead of generals into peril. The most dashing of the breed, Richard Harding Davis, was very nearly shot as a spy by the Germans during their assault on Belgium in 1914.

Besides nerve, the correspondent had style. During the Spanish-American War, Davis and the novelist Stephen Crane decided to improve on the army and "capture" a piece of the Puerto Rican map themselves. Crane, hot for a scoop, betrayed his buddy and marched alone into a place called Juana Diaz. There he declared Carnival. The next morning, when Davis and the American forces arrived, Crane told the commanding officer, "I'm really very sorry, Colonel, but I took this town myself before breakfast yesterday morning."

Foreign correspondents were the rock stars of their day, and even though their work was reporting rather than opinion making, they had great power. Russell's exposure of the British military leadership's incompetent handling of the Crimean War brought down a government.

"Intrepid" goes with "foreign correspondent" just as "brazen" goes with "hussy": the position was for men only. True, Nellie Bly went around the world in less than eighty days for the *New York World* in 1889–90, a momentous undertaking, given the prejudice from both genders against the Achieving Woman. Still, Bly's feat turned out to be a one-off; the junketing reporter in dangerous places remained a job for those who could bluff, finagle, and intimidate: men.

And along came Dorothy Thompson. Central Europe was her beat, especially Vienna and Berlin in the 1920s and early 1930s. She spoke fluent German and knew how to get around impedient bureaucrats—not by feminine charm but through the application of common sense and, when that failed, by pulling off a con. Thompson *could* have charmed her way around, for she was attractive with especially fetching coloring and, to boot, she ran on a high-energy but not aggressive presence that men found intriguing. They liked as well Thompson's ability to function under fire, her habit of taking her own valor for granted. If there was a story to be scooped two towns away—say, a popular insurgence that could spark outright rebellion—and if there was a single automobile at service and the boys were piling in to break the scoop, Thompson would get right in with them. This was not the adventurism of the twenties flapper, with her "Daddy will simply *die* when he hears!" This was a writer like them, in love with the recording of history in real time.

In Thompson's day, the Republican party had not become enmeshed in identity hating, as now, and many liberals were Republican, though they emphasized cultural tolerance rather than social safety programs. Thompson was one such. Further, she belonged to the last American generation raised with a solid religious background. It's astonishing how many famous people of her time were the offspring of clergymen—or, really, how many clergymen there were, period. Thompson was the daughter of a Methodist preacher, and it was, quietly, a Methodist age: the confession was in that day the largest Protestant sect in the country.

Today, one might say that nobody famous is religious except for those who are. America's spiritual life, among its public figures, is either-or: blithe agnosticism or gung-ho belief. However, growing up, as Thompson did, in the very early twentieth century meant being so to say unnoticingly aware of the church in its many forms and social structures. Folks could actually tell one Protestant from another; your Methodist, so the wisdom ran, was something of a Calvinist Quaker. There were jokes at the parishioners' love of austerity, at least in Methodism's pure form. In Gilbert and Sullivan's *Ruddigore,* one character "combines the manners of a Marquis with the morals of a Methodist." It's praise—though the Wesleyans did not maintain testimony against religious prejudice that typified the Quaker. When Al Smith ran for president, the *Wesleyan Christian Advocate* noted Smith's constitutional right to the nomination, concluding, "And we [Methodists] have a constitutional right to vote against him because he is Catholic." Yet Methodists spoke of "a light" as the spark of God in Man, much as Quakers speak of "the inner light."

If one might fairly caption Methodist exhortation as "Set forth the facts, persuade belief, and thus convert," that might well describe Thompson's approach to political discourse. On at least one occasion, as an adolescent, Thompson actually preached for her indisposed father, and the Thompsons were not simply a professionally religious family but a family living more or less in grace. "God was everywhere," her sister, Peggy, later recalled. "Jesus was father's personal friend." The piety—or simply the belief in God's will—never deserted Dorothy, and in the last few days before September 1, 1939, when Hitler plunged the world into war, she cabled Liberal Parliament member Harold Nicolson with a suggestion that even she knew would sound odd. She urged Nicolson to organize a worldwide day of prayer and meditation, accompanied by readings from the Bible on radio. "England's strength," she declared, "is not appeasement with the enemy of peace, nor war, but a glorious Christian resistance." In closing, she added, "I am not at all crazy."

In a way, Thompson's newspaper columns and radio speeches made declaration, though not in such spiritual terms. Thompson would set forth the facts to convert her audience to her side on questions of the day. She would inform you of what you didn't know, remind you of what you did know, then warn that ignoring evil is condoning evil. Her columns had the quality of sermons. In 1937, on Nazi infiltration into Northwest Africa, Thompson wrote:

> Reports from Morocco indicated that industrial exploitation was being combined with political propaganda among the Arabs; anti-Semitic

literature was being distributed—incidentally with the assistance of French Fascists, for the Fascists have their own International, their own Faschintern, a fact which the world persistently refuses to see and believe, thinking that only Communists are revolutionists and all Fascists are loyal and conservative patriots. Distributing Hitler's *Mein Kampf* and agitating the Arabs against the Jews is not immediately related to mining ore.

Thompson seemed aware that most people tolerate the aggressor simply because it's easier than fighting. Identifying an enemy brings one into the dangerous territory of moral clarity: the place in which one comprehends what the word "freedom" really means. Or, to quote a line generally attributed to Leon Trotsky, "You may not be interested in war,* but war is interested in you." Indeed, Thompson was one of the very few writers who, early on, saw the Nazis as a menace to the entire world. Oddly, one other of this exclusive crew was that squawking Ulysses in Nighttown Walter Winchell, much to the distaste of his publisher, William Randolph Hearst. The freest man in the republic, Hearst believed what most businessmen believe: moral clarity bankrupts the counting house.

Thompson was more a national figure than a New Yorker, but she maintained various Manhattan domiciles, along with a Vermont "farm" that she favored in summer. A red plaque on the facade of 237 East 48th Street commemmorates Thompson's residence there: a most indigenous New York address, an elite one, as a brownstone in Turtle Bay. This rectangle uniquely encloses one huge backyard that communicates with every house's back door as if a transplanted London green. Many a celeb has dwelled here; Katharine Hepburn's house was the next over from Stephen Sondheim's.†

---

* An alternate version gives the noun not as "war" but as "revolution."
† Now it can be told. In the summer of 1969, a colorful story ran through New York's gossip circuits. It seems that, one night, Hepburn bearded Sondheim in his lair because his piano playing was bothering her. Each teller of the tale relayed it in different words, but the action itself was unvarying. Thus: Hepburn: "You're disturbing my work on *Coco*!" Sondheim: *Coco*? I pronounce it with cedillas: *Soso*. And my

Thompson had a celeb dwelling not next to but with her, for her second husband (of three) was one of the best-known men in the country. Before he went into the customary American second-act eclipse he was not only a bestselling author but an Important one, the first American to win the Nobel Prize for Literature. Thompson and he were in mid-divorce when she moved into Turtle Bay, in 1941, but he was a major part of her life all the same and their influence on each other is essential to the narrative.

Sinclair Lewis

Some of the famous are easy—Robert Benchley. Some are difficult—Edna Ferber. Some are both at once—Dorothy Parker, always in her mildest humor when being most impossible. Some are obnoxious, megalomaniacal, vicious backbiters. But Sinclair Lewis was everything at once: charming, irascible, thoughtful, reckless, arriving at a party in a hail of enthusiastic greetings only to try to persuade everyone immediately to join him on a road trip to somewhere far away. Or he would tear off on his own, because he loved you but he needed to get away from you. He was a great misser of people.

And he was brilliant, with what appears to be a photographic memory for everything he'd ever read. His party turn was to improvise on

---

show, which you hear me composing, is *Company,* which will change the history of musical theatre." Hepburn: "How dare you? As I practice my Lerner and Loewe!" Sondheim: "It's Lerner and Previn, actually, but so what since you can't sing in the first place." Hepburn: "Well, everyone knows you're an evil drunk in these gay times." Sondheim: "I hear Spencer Tracy was an evil drunk. And about as straight as a three-dollar watch." Hepburn then huffed away, speechless at being defied for perhaps the first time in her life. Sondheim intimates longed to hear the authentic version, but he was disappointingly succinct. Sondheim: "Katharine Hepburn came to the back door and asked me to stop playing the piano." It's barely gossip at all. More recently, Sondheim gave a fuller version to the London *Times*. It was three A.M. and Hepburn appeared in a babushka and no shoes. Hepburn: "Young man, I cannot sleep with the noise you're making." No doubt that is what happened, but the folk version does give an arresting view of two of New York's elite fighting over who gets to make the next bit of theatre history. Sondheim won.

any old theme in the style of five or six celebrated poets, one after the other, metre, rhyme, and all. He was also a wild drinker, the kind that smashes furniture. Tall and ungainly in ruddy, freckled coloring, he was known as Red, though his wives called him Hal, short for Harry: Harry Sinclair Lewis, born in Minnesota in 1885, graduated from Yale, and a citizen of the world of the Big Idea novel.* When he met (and immediately and repeatedly proposed to) Dorothy Thompson, Lewis was about to complete his Big Five: *Main Street* (1920) and *Babbitt* (1922), on the vapidity of bourgeois life; *Arrowsmith* (1925), on medicine; *Elmer Gantry* (1927), on the religion hustle; and *Dodsworth* (1929), on Americans enlightened by Europe. *Main Street* and *Arrowsmith* were once staples of the high-school reading list, but now that Lewis and his Importance have receded somewhat, we must reinvestigate the writing itself.

It is at once thick and precise, a stampede of words and images chewing each other up till you almost hear the author gleefully shouting his book at you. Try this piece of *Elmer Gantry,* on Dr. Bruno Zechlin, one of Elmer's seminary professors:

> He was one of the dozen authentic scholars in all the theological institutions of America, and incidentally he was a thorough failure. He lectured haltingly, he wrote obscurely, he could not talk to God as though he knew him personally . . . Elmer despised him, because . . . he was

---

* Lewis not only wrote but reviewed fiction. He savaged John O'Hara's first novel, *Appointment in Samarra,* in the *Saturday Review,* and O'Hara retaliated in his second. One of *BUtterfield 8*'s most memorable bits is a kind of camera pan through the interior of what we take to be "21," speakeasy of the elect. (O'Hara begs to differ, explaining that most habitués' fame "did not extend more than twenty blocks to the north, forty blocks to the south, seven blocks to the east, and four blocks to the west": the midtown of Walter Winchell, the Lunts, and *The New Yorker.* O'Hara never was entirely comfortable with the notion that the cultural elite surveyed in these pages was all that important outside of central Manhattan.) Interestingly, one of the notables on hand in O'Hara's "21" is a notorious lush called to the telephone up at the club's entrance—"the first move, although he did not know it, in the house technique of getting rid of a drunk." O'Hara identified the man as a writer named Harry S. Lewis. Luckily, O'Hara's publisher, Harcourt Brace, had formerly been Lewis' publisher, and O'Hara was persuaded to change the character's name, to Henry White.

enthusiastic about Hebrew syntax, because he had no useful tips for ambitious young professional prophets, and because he had seemed singu-
larly to enjoy flunking Elmer in Greek.

Lewis and Thompson had been married for two years when he won
the Nobel Prize, setting off a tumult in the American lit community.
Everyone knew that the Swedes were bound to award "one of ours"
right about then; everyone knew it was going to be Lewis or Theodore
Dreiser (or, less likely, Willa Cather). Partisans of the last two and other
arguably imposing authors were outraged, not least because Lewis had
already refused the Pulitzer Prize (for *Arrowsmith*), and with a rather
high-minded statement at that.

Most limited their objections to Lewis' winning—and, note,
accepting—the Nobel to viva voce harangues among themselves, for in
those days it was thought ungainly to complain in public. Besides, Dreiser won attention more for his humanist perspective than for his talent.
He lacked humor and color, and his paragraphs piled up like the data of
a street-corner orator. Dreiser was the nag as graven image, and in fact
he never did win the Nobel.*

The union of Lewis and Thompson is great storymaking, for they
created a variation on the stereotyped bad marriage: the patient, rational
man and the emotionally driven helter-skelter woman. Thompson lived
her life the way she wrote her columns, using reason rather than personality as a magnet, adducing facts to reach an irresistible conclusion. Lewis
lived frantically, always ready to retire to an alternate universe when the
population in this one thwarted his will. He was a terrible parent, one of
those who doesn't get and, worse, doesn't even try to get children, including his two sons—Thompson had to step in and mother the older,
Wells, born of Lewis' first wife, Grace.

Thompson truly loved Lewis and Lewis truly loved Thompson, but
at his best he was difficult and at his worst intolerable, so the marriage

---

* After Lewis, American recipients in lit were Eugene O'Neill, Pearl Buck, William
Faulkner, Ernest Hemingway, and John Steinbeck, the last in 1962, at the close of the
present volume's chronology.

could not have succeeded in the long run. If Thompson herself had any flaw, it was her ceaseless interest in politics, especially in events in Europe during the 1930s—what Lewis referred to sarcastically as "It" or, in the voice of one of his hayseed characters, "The Sityashun." "It" dominated conversation at the Lewis-Thompson at-homes, thoroughly exasperating Lewis, who wanted to talk about literally anything else. Himself, for instance. So this marriage consisted of a very long war between his restless thousand phobias and her wish for stability at home while she flashed the light of comprehension at her public. Both were ambitious, he to enlighten the world, she to convert it—not as a preacher but as a general. "If I ever divorce Dorothy," Red Lewis would say, "I'll name Adolf Hitler as co-respondent." He began to hate their marriage, their love. One night, she returned home to find that he had broken up the place in a drunken rampage.

Marriages like this are enough to turn women lesbian. In her memoirs, Ethel Waters openly admitted to Going Over simply because women were emotionally available and she couldn't trust men—this in a book published in 1951! Thompson, too, loved in this way, as entries in her journal attest:

So it has happened to me again, after all these years. . . . There's something weak in it. . . . To love a woman is somehow ridiculous. *Mir auch passt es nicht. Ich bin doch heterosexuel.* [It also doesn't suit me. I'm still heterosexual.] . . . Well, then, how account for this which has happened again. The soft, quite natural kiss on my throat, the quite unconscious (seemingly) even open kiss on my breast. . . . Her name suddenly had a magic quality. *C.* I wanted to say it. To use it. I talked about her to others, to hear her name. Like holding an amulet in your hand, that was what saying her name is like. I love this woman.

It does sometimes happen that women with a lot of content become too challenging for men in sexual relationships. They can maintain close *friendships* with men—as Thompson did with the writer Vincent Sheean. Still, George Eliot reminds us of the obvious in *Middlemarch*: "a husband likes to be master." Besides, Lewis was going into his decline just as

Thompson was on her ascent, in the mid-1930s. Their letters to each other drip endearments like syrup, but life in Thompson's household, with its cook, secretaries, children (for Red and Dorothy's child, Michael, needed playmates), and nurse was unbearably stable for the likes of Lewis. He was a Quixote, a gusher, a splurger. The word he greatly anticipated was "adventure" and the word he couldn't fathom was "home."

The movie version: *She Couldn't Tame Her Man.* Yet Thompson influenced Lewis in one all-important way. Indeed, she changed him, albeit without meaning to. Lewis' worldview was cultural rather than political: how Americans live instead of what "America" means. True, he had long planned a novel around the labor movement. He never wrote it—but he did publish a novel that derived, surely, from all those discussions about The Sityashun. Remember, he was married to a woman who knew the Declaration of Independence and the Constitution of the United States by heart, and that marriage coincided with democracy's time of greatest peril. It was Dorothy and civilization; Versailles and fascism; and her friends and the endless gabble about it all, hour after hour into the night. Perhaps against his will, Lewis conceived a book in which democracy came under attack in the U.S. itself. In fact, as the novel begins, the American republic has ceased to be: because an American Hitler named Buzz Windrip has taken over.

It Can't Happen Here

When did the foreign correspondent evolve into the pundit? Just as Ethel Waters never gets credit for laying out the expressive grammar of the American songbook, Dorothy Thompson seldom is cited as the transitional figure between the journalist and the advocate. Yet it is hard to imagine her fascinated reporting on European events not leading directly to her columns of opinion, and hard to imagine how she could have leaped into the men's world of editorializing without having first earned her entitlement on the street.

Or: every correspondent needs his scoop. Thompson's was an interview with Hitler, published in *Cosmopolitan* in April of 1932, when the

Nazis were enjoying a new spike in popularity during the ramp up to their accession to state power. Few reporters got this close to the Führer. Apparently, his foreign press director, Ernst Hanfstaengl (the one always identified by his nickname, Putzi), wanted to create some sort of understanding with the American press.

"The oddest imaginable press chief for a dictator," Thompson thought, of Hanfstaengl. An "immense, high-strung, incoherent clown." And Hitler, who showed up an hour late for the meeting, in Berlin's Kaiserhof Hotel, seemed the oddest imaginable dictator: "inconsequent and voluble, ill-poised, insecure. He is the very prototype of the Little Man."

Hitler gave his usual performance: lecturing rather than conversing, now dainty—"I'll bet he crooks his little finger," Thompson wrote, "when he drinks his tea"—and now screaming and pounding the table. He was unremarkable in all but his eyes: "They have the peculiar shine which often distinguishes geniuses, alcoholics, and hysterics." Thompson predicted that Hitler was no more than a passing fancy, a leader not of Germany but of the worst element that one finds in every demographic.

This error in judgment followed Thompson for the rest of the decade, and not just among *Cosmopolitan* readers, for the interview appeared in book form, as *I Saw Hitler!*. But then, everybody who counted got the Nazis wrong at this time in particular, because they were so improbable. Thompson's view was correct by the standards of bourgeois-liberal civilization: she was unprepared for the sheer anachronism of Hitler, springing out of a primitive epoch to actualize apocalyptic fantasies. Further confusing her was "the startling insignificance of this man who has set the whole world agog." As the modern German historian Joachim Fest puts it, Hitler's "unmistakable vulgar characteristics give his image a cast of repugnant ordinariness that simply will not square with the traditional concept of greatness."

But if Thompson's view of Hitler was clouded, Hitler saw Thompson clearly. She was dangerous. In August of 1934, she became the first journalist ordered out of Germany. It seemed logical—what the Nazis don't like they get rid of—but to Thompson it only emphasized how unGerman the Nazis were, a nationless barbaric calamity imposed on one of her favorite cultures. Nazism was a global, not a local, phenomenon: "National Socialism was designed for export," she later wrote, "with the object of taking over the world-revolutionary role once assumed by the Comintern." We have heard from Thompson a few pages ago on this very theme; it was to become her obsession. Free peoples must conquer Nazism or lose their freedom. "It is," she said, "a complete break with Reason, with Humanity, and with the Christian ethics that are at the base of liberalism and democracy."

Her fellow reporters assigned to Germany, used to gathering information without analyzing it, were irritating enough to the state in a land where the native press was controlled. But Thompson was an outrage, because she alone appeared to understand what was meant by what the Nazis termed *Gleichschaltung*—the "coordination" of culture, an enforced alignment with no differences of opinion. "One people, one nation, one Führer" was the explanatory cry: a land with no exceptions or minorities of any kind. And yet, in her journal, Thompson defined "elite" as a condition obtaining only "in a society where minorities can exist. The *characteristic* of an elite is that it has standards other than [that of] the mass. Ortega [y Gasset, the Spanish humanist writer] says: If ten or twelve men died the whole of modern physics would vanish." So: "Are we for freedom," Thompson asked, "or are we for the totalitarian state?"

Some of us were not for freedom; this was one of Thompson's unique revelations. In the *Saturday Evening Post,* in 1933, she wrote that civilized people believe that Western culture, humanitarian and idealistic after thousands of years of development, was "greatly cherished by all men." Unfortunately, the civilized were wrong:

> This culture is, actually, to the vast masses . . . a burden, which can be borne only under exceptionally favorable circumstances. [If] by reason of economic malfunctioning masses of people are, for years, hungry and idle, they will grow to look upon civilization as a restraining, impeding force, and to identify revolt against it with freedom.

More specifically, "Germany has gone to war already," she said, in 1934, "and the rest of the world does not believe it."

And so, because the Lewis household so rang with everyone's opinion of The Sityashun that Red had to chime in in *his* way, as a novelist, he told how Nazis take over the U.S. almost exactly as they had done in Germany. Published in 1935, *It Can't Happen Here* spells out the American equivalents of Nazism, complete with iconic insigne (a five-pointed star instead of the swastika), shorthand title (Corpo for Nazi), lawless S.S.-like militia (the Minute Men), the wholesale murder of political enemies, an Enabling Act, book burnings of such dangerous tracts as *A Farewell to Arms, Alice in Wonderland,* and the works of Dickens, and famous names carried off to concentration camps, including two exquisites of the Algonquin Round Table, Franklin P. Adams and Heywood Broun.

Thus, *It Can't Happen Here* expressed a central fear of the age: that mass-movement politics would overwhelm democracy with thinking at once crude and irrational, and with "leaders" driving nationalist mobs into acts of revenge against imaginary enemies in hidden power centers. International bankers, liberals, New Yorkists. The Corpos of *It Can't Happen Here* are, in effect, what the small-town "booboisie"—Fundamentalist America—turns into when roused.

Ironically, Lewis had heretofore viewed Main Street as drab rather than dangerous. The heroine of Lewis' position paper, the novel *Main Street* itself, senses "a forbidding spirit" in the conformism and lack of intellectual curiosity in Gopher Prairie, Minnesota. Yet when Lewis specifies the town's failings, he cites "the stink of stale beer," or, hanging on the wall, "carbon prints of bad and famous pictures," or, in the local sports' hangout, "young men shaking dice for cigarettes." Yes, the place lacks an opera house and a lunching Round Table, but on the whole it's banal: not evil.

Still, in the fifteen years between *Main Street* and *It Can't Happen Here,* a leader took one of the most civilized European countries into barbarism—and there had been more than a touch of homicidal rage in the Prohibition movement, already noted. To the passionate ranting of Hitler's public presentation, Lewis opposed a tyrant better suited to American behavior: his villain, the aforementioned Berzelius "Buzz" Windrip, strikes the American tone we call "folksy." Lewis sometimes did so himself, when imitating rural manners—"The Sityashun," for instance.

So Windrip isn't anything like Hitler in his personality, despite the correspondence between the Nazis and the Corpos. There was another major innovation, for Windrip could not enter government the way Hitler did. Contrary to a factoid popular in America at the millennium, even among the educated, Hitler *lost* his presidential election, in 1932. He was later appointed Chancellor—a position with no American counterpart—by the election's winner, President Paul von Hindenburg. Buzz wins his election and becomes President Windrip.

Another break with history lay in Lewis' anticipation that Nazi power structures would make it relatively easy for one of Windrip's henchmen to effect a coup, and his Secretary of State, one Lee Sarason, does just that, albeit very late in the action. But Lewis brings in the homosexual element made notorious by Hitler's "old comrade" Ernst Röhm, giving Sarason a flavor quite radical for a novel of 1935. Lewis contrasts Windrip's residence, a "plumber's dream of paradise," with Sarason's "gold-and-black and apricot-silk bower in Georgetown, which he shared with several handsome young [Minute Men] officers." Sarason likes it rough: "He was either angry with his young friends, and then he whipped them, or he was in a paroxysm of apology to them, and caressed their wounds."

To humanize the narrative, Lewis chose an unlikely hero, a peaceful New England newspaper editor named Doremus Jessup.* Jessup's personal nemesis is his handyman, Shad Ledue, who essentializes the vindictive stupidity of the low- and mid-level Nazi placeman, a scandal even among the more intelligent Nazis themselves. Shad Ledue is the ultimate

---

* Lewis' erratic gift for naming his characters runs from inspiration (George F. Babbitt) to implausibility (Bradd Criley). Often, his people sound less like real-life beings and more like characters in a Sinclair Lewis novel. Doremus Jessup is perhaps too peaceful, almost physically lame. He's not exactly heroic, but he does have sand. We should note that Tennessee Williams, with a far more illuminating catalogue of names (Maggie the Cat, Chance Wayne, Hannah Jelkes and her moribund "nonno," Jonathan Coffin), created for *Summer and Smoke* a woebegone little gay . . . and called him Roger Doremus.

loser, blessed with the power to avenge his grievances against the world. So despicable does Lewis make him that *It Can't Happen Here*'s suspense lies less in whether or not the Corpos will be overthrown than in whether Ledue will be. The reader is appalled at the Windrip regime and its collaborators, but it is Ledue who arouses visceral disgust. In the American tradition of dispatching bad guys in arcane ways, Lewis keeps us eager and frustrated till quite near the novel's end. Mark Twain left Injun Joe to wander through miles of cavern maze till he dropped forever; Frank Norris handcuffed McTeague to a corpse in the Death Valley desert, after first making sure that his mule was dead and his water bag flattened.

Lewis rises to the challenge. Arrested for cheating another Corpo of his share of extortion money, Ledue is placed in a concentration camp. There his fellow prisoners stage an altercation in front of his cell and, in the fake confusion, throw a lighted ball of waste through the bars. "The whole room looked presently like the fire box of a furnace," Lewis comments, as "Doremus remembered the scream of a horse clawed by wolves in the Far North. When they got Shad out, he was dead. He had no face at all."

Though intended as a political study, *It Can't Happen Here* is instead a dystopian thriller. It was a success, yet Lewis came to feel that it wasn't any good, most likely because it was more a plot-and-character work than a Big Idea work. Further, it ends inconclusively. Jessup has fled to Canada, and, on the novel's last page, he is roughly awakened by a confidant who warns him to get moving: "Corpo posse after you." And off Jessup goes, for, Lewis tells us in his final line, "a Doremus Jessup can never die."

On the contrary, Lewis has invented too pure a pacifist, impotent and imbued with every principle except that of killing the bad guy before he kills you. It is worth noting that, when the concentration camp inmates plan their vengeance on Shad Ledue, Jessup pipes up with idiotic excuses for him. This hero is that twentieth-century invention the professional appeaser, always looking for an aggressor to surrender to. Is this the hope of democracy when Nazis steal power?

It Can't Happen Here at least changed Lewis' life, if no one else's, because the Federal Theatre—FDR's employment program for thespians—

mounted a stage version to premiere simultaneously in twenty-one cities: and Lewis was instantly stagestruck. He took up acting and became deeply involved with a very young actress named Marcella Powers. Yes, it's the Don Pasquale syndrome—but why do folks discredit an older man's infatuation with youth if his girl friend's having fun, too?

Dorothy Thompson was having different fun, because we are now in 1936, when her column, On the Record, started its run, on March 17. As the *Herald Tribune*'s new star, Thompson was writing for a conservative outlet and addressing conservative readers. This was to get her into trouble with her boss, Ogden Reid, when it turned out that Thompson was something of a liberal conservative. Still, for her five years with the paper she served more and more as a loyal opposition in her own church. Instead of preaching to the choir, she was attempting to convert it to heresy. Such was the response from readers, both convinced and outraged, that a special truck had to be hired to deliver Thompson her mail. Reid himself was so angered when she abandoned the Republican candidate in 1940, Wendell Willkie, to support FDR in his of course unprecedented (and now unconstitutional) third-term run that Reid refused to renew Thompson's contract. She was fired.

Many of the *Tribune*'s readers were delighted at this end to five years of having their core beliefs rebutted, three breakfasts a week. Two weeks before Thompson's last *Tribune* column, the paper ran an editorial denouncing its own "Brunhilde of the Bronx"* as being in league with the Roosevelt regime to drive the U.S. into war with Germany, "risking a million American lives. . . . These are not Roosevelt, or at any rate not Franklin Roosevelt lives. The boys of that family are in positions of relative safety. They appear to be no more exposed than is Miss Dorothy Thompson's son, [currently] aged twelve."† In short, "She is no Nathan Hale in skirts," the editorial observed: others would die, not she. The parallel is poorly drawn, for while, unlike Hale, Thompson did not give

---

* From 1934 till the divorce, in 1942, the Lewises spent the cold half of the year in a villa in Bronxville, given up when Thompson bought the brownstone in Turtle Bay.
† Michael Lewis, Thomas' biological son, was indeed twelve. As I've said, however, Thompson was just as close (and possibly even closer) to her step-son, Wells Lewis, who died in uniform of a sniper bullet in 1944.

her life for her country, she proved, like Hale, one of its outstanding patriots in a time of peril. From the very start, On the Record rang the tocsin, as in this rendition of the German plebescite on Hitler's policies in March of 1936, which reported 98.79 percent in favor:

> Flags out! screamed the radio, and the hooked cross blazed in a million windows. Silence! cried the radio, and every man . . . stood still. Vote! cried the radio, the press, the Storm Troopers, the Nazi commissars in every city block. An entire people poured to the polls. . . . There was no provision for voting No. . . . One Yes, one mob, one mass, one voice. The voice of a single man.

More usually, Thompson's tone was icy, as in this command from the office of reason, after Chamberlain's frantic toadying over Hitler's demand for the Sudetenland at Munich in 1938:

> Hitler will [now] raise his demands. . . . [E]very single concession ever made to Hitler has been the basis, not on which to achieve stability and peace, but from which [Hitler can] move forward.

Yes, it seems so obvious—to us. The overwhelming view at that time saw Hitler as a statesman, unconventional in style but reasonable in the long run. A week later, after the democracies appeased once again, Thompson wrote:

> What happened on Friday is called "Peace." Actually it is an international Fascist *coup d'etat*.

Thompson's most conclusive piece on the imminent danger came in 1939, on the publication (in Zurich and New York, in German only) of Hermann Rauschning's *Die Revolution des Nihilismus*. A former Nazi, Rauschning had fled to the democracies to write *The Revolution of Nihilism* as a warning, and, as the English translation would not appear till 1940, Thompson devoted her column to rendering an abstract of

Rauschning's analysis. Nazism, he revealed, was like the Devil in Goethe's *Faust*—"the spirit of no" and an endlessly expanding barbarism in which the unthinkable becomes routine. In Thompson's words:

> It is not even the "totalitarian state"—nor a state at all, but it is that apocalyptic thing "the Total Revolution"; the Permanent Revolution. [Rauschning] warns that it cannot come to rest, that it cannot construct and that it cannot be appeased.

With this revolution comes a wholly new notion of the elite:

> The elite are biologically selected. They are . . . consistently trained to be free of any inhibitions imposed by . . . Christianity or intellectual tradition . . . to take consummate joy in the liberation of their most primitive instincts. . . . The concept of "noblesse oblige" is transformed into . . . a leadership of super-bandits, who will plunder the world; to whom organized murder . . . will seem the natural, even the organic way of life.

Thompson took to referring to herself as "Cassandra," because at times it seemed she was the only one who knew what was coming. She famously dared to laugh at a rally of the German-American Bund in Madison Square Garden in 1939, and had to be escorted to safety by a phalanx of solicitous New York City cops. "Oh, boys, come *on*," she told them. Yet it was Berlin all over again—"*Mein Kampf*," she called it, "word for word."

And here we have arrived at the twentieth century's central battle between New York's elite and the rest of the nation. True, for all Dorothy Thompson's prominence, she represented New York—symbolized it—without typifying it. It was too dense a concept to be typed, whether by the Algonquinites, Jimmy Walker, or any other single organism.

And yet conservative America had a take on New York: everything intellectual, sophisticated, or artistic—the identifying modes of the new American elite—was hostile to the values of the heartland. And it was not only New York. Now it was Washington, D.C., as well, as if everyone had heard Frances Perkins' dating of the New Deal from the Triangle Shirtwaist Fire, as if everyone "knew" that Franklin Delano Rosenfelt's regime had in some uncanny way brought the attitudes of New York-ism into the federal government.

The heartland, as we have seen, often resists what it sees as encroachments upon its culture. But the resistance may be somewhat disguised, whether under the cover of Prohibition or, today, in a circling of the wagons against gay marriage.

Here, in the late 1930s, the resistance will find expression in a complacency about Nazism—in some minds, even an enthusiasm for it. As a longtime Germanophile, Dorothy Thompson knew the difference between admiration for the place of Goethe and Beethoven and admiration for the place of Hitler.

America First

Isolationism per se was not pro-Nazi. To put it informally, the isolationist held that we had only recently intervened in a vast and pointless European war which ended only in provoking another. This time we ought to stay out.

However, as the interventionist saw it, this next war wasn't pointless. It concerned the survival of democracy in a totalitarian age—the survival, even, of the United States: because the Revolution of Nihilism, forever growing, would eventually come after us. Isolationists insisted that the Atlantic and Pacific created Fortress America. Interventionists feared that air warfare and aviation technology, in ceaseless development, could make oceans into trivia.

From the late 1930s right to the moment you heard about the attack on Pearl Harbor, the isolationist-interventionist debate was an inescapable part of daily life in America, an intense and bitter one. Isolationists routinely accused interventionists of inflammatory behavior and occult plotting—so much so that the picture of the interventionist as villain slipped into common "knowledge," even into popular art. The very first Superman adventure, published in *Action Comics* Number One, in 1938, found the hero foiling a shady lobbyist and a corrupt senator, bribed to ensure passage of an interventionist bill. "Before any remedial steps can be taken," the senator promises, "our country will be embroiled with Europe."

In 1940, isolationists formed the America First Committee, devoted more to the occasional big-media event than to the grassroots mobilization that busied the Prohibition movement. America First concentrated on holding rallies featuring speakers on a national radio hookup, and the dais of Distinguished Guests attracted a few genuine celebrities and politicians along with crackpots and haters. Dorothy Thompson had been advocating defensive action against Nazism, as we know. But the emergence of America First as the isolationist's communications organ focused her argument even more, because she realized that Nazism wasn't the only enemy: America First was as well. As Roosevelt's most exhaustive biographer, Kenneth S. Davis, put it:

> From its inception, America First was attractive to people who sympathized with Hitler's "solution" to the "Jewish problem"—people who believed or professed to believe that Jews, dominating the financial community, had inveigled this country into World War I for profit-making reasons and were now engaged in the same nefarious purpose during World War II. They constituted a growingly significant portion of America First's membership; anti-Semitism was a part of their motivation as they pressed for a negotiated peace, knowing full well that such a peace must be on Hitler's terms.

We see this clearly now; few seemed to see it at the time. Even those not involved in America First in any way—some of the sanest and most intelligent people one knew—appeared to be as hypnotized by Hitler as a portion of the German people was.* Your attorney, your old college

---

* In the aforementioned German presidential election, in March and April of 1932, the incumbent, von Hindenburg, received 49.6 per cent of the vote. This necessitated a runoff election, in which von Hindenburg got a decisive 53 percent. Hitler got only 37 percent and the Communist Ernst Thälmann 10 per cent.

buddy . . . your banker friends, no less! "God damn it," Thompson wrote to fellow columnist Philip Wylie, "they've discovered that Hitler is a good Republican!"

And from America First's agitation came the old European cry *The Jews! The Jews!*: in poison-pen letters sent to leading interventionists, in front-parlor conversations along Main Street, or on the job, where co-workers would share conspiracy theories, the candy of the insane. To which Thompson replied, "There is no such thing as 'the' Jews." She cited "the gangster Arnold Rothstein" on one hand and Supreme Court "Justice Brandeis" on the other—"just as the Anglo-Saxons . . . include John Dillinger and Dr. Harvey Cushing."

America First's leadership was aware of how many of Hitler's admirers and even idolaters were swelling their membership yet did nothing to dissociate the movement from them. Then came The Photograph, a now-famous shot taken of key speakers and those Distinguished Guests at an America First rally, in which they all seem to be giving the Hitler salute. It was later explained that they were simply waving to the crowd. That may well be—but behind those in the foreground are others, unmistakably caught in mid-*heil*.

One of the figures in this shot, right up at the front, became the protagonist of isolationism, just as Dorothy Thompson was the protagonist of interventionism. Never before had a national controversy been so personified. Prohibition had no comparable outstanding "face" on either wet or dry side. Similarly, the battle over gay marriage does not conduce to any single pair of symbolic antagonists. But the Great Debate of the years ramping up to December 7, 1941, very nearly comes down to a He Said, She Said.

Charles Lindbergh

In January of 1941, when President Roosevelt asked Congress for his lend-lease legislation, Lindbergh testified before the House Committee on Foreign Affairs. An able speaker who worked without a trot, Lindbergh demonstrated what "neutrality" toward the opposing forces in the European war really meant. A few of the interventionist congress-men wanted Lindbergh to state what he thought of the possibility that Germany might conquer all of Europe—that is, most imminently, Great Britain.

No doubt realizing that they wanted to hear him declare unequivo-cally whether or not he favored fascism over democracy, Lindbergh danced. He was a champ at hurdling verbal traps, and at each attempt to get him to admit which side he was on, he insisted he wasn't on a side. He was neutral.

Neutral in a survival contest between destroyers and victims? Rep-resentative Luther A. Johnson, Democrat of Texas, edged the question into the matter of American security. Perhaps then they'd get a straight answer:

JOHNSON: [Between Great Britain and Germany,] which side would it be to our interest to win?
LINDBERGH: Neither.

Thus, Lindbergh refused to declare that he wanted Nazism to win. He just didn't want Nazism to lose.

And when W. Wirt Courtney, Democrat of Tennessee, asked, "Do you think either Germany or England is more to blame for the present conflict?," Lindbergh, incredibly, answered, "Over a period of years, no."

Lindbergh had famously accepted a Nazi decoration, the Order of the German Eagle.* His defenders pointed out that it was presented to him (by Hermann Göring) without warning, at a reception with the American ambassador looking on. However, Lindbergh really had turned from the Lone Eagle of The Flight to a German Eagle. As Roosevelt's Secretary of the Interior, Harold Ickes, put it, "I have never heard [Lindbergh]

---

* The medal comprised four tiny eagles, each holding a swastika in its talons, between each limb of a white Maltese cross, the whole suspended from a red ribbon. It was awarded at Hitler's personal nomination to foreign friends of the Nazis. Recipients included Benito Mussolini; his Minister of Foreign Affairs and son-in-law, Count Galeazzo Ciano; Admiral Horthy of Hungary; Henry Ford; and Thomas J. Watson, the president of I.B.M. (who returned it two years later, in 1940).

express a word of pity for Belgium or Holland or Norway or England [or] for the Poles or the Jews who have been slaughtered by the hundreds of thousands by Hitler's savages."

The medal became an embarrassment to Lindbergh's supporters and a lightning rod for his enemies, yet Lindbergh never gave it back. On the contrary, Lindbergh supported the Nazi side in every single matter without exception. Even after Kristallnacht, the nationwide pogrom of November 1938, Lindbergh wrote in his diary not to deplore the murderous violence but to note simply that it contradicted the Germans' "sense of order and their intelligence." After all, he went on, "They have undoubtedly had a difficult Jewish problem."

Note that Lindbergh uses a Nazi idiom. Germany didn't have a Jewish problem any more than it had a Wiener Schnitzel problem or an operetta problem or a Lederhosen problem. Worst of all, immediately after the war, as part of an official state mission in Germany, Lindbergh saw for himself the slave-labor camp at Nordhausen, in north-central Thuringia, where the young from all over occupied Europe were starved and worked to death in Sauron's war factory. Amid the furnaces and pits of bone chips and ash, all that Lindbergh could say of it was that the Allies had committed "atrocities," too: "What is barbaric on one side of the earth is still barbaric on the other," he said.

Most of those who write about Lindbergh prefer to think of him as "naive." Viewing the evidence of Nazi barbarism, from the Nuremberg Laws and Kristallnacht through the brutal subjugation of Belgium, the Netherlands, Norway, and other lands, on to the Blitz and Auschwitz, Lindbergh somehow Doesn't Get It. And this even while uttering bizarre encomiums of Hitler's Germany—a "stabilizing factor" in Europe is one such.

Let's sample a typical rationalization of the "naive" Lindbergh from a modern historian: "Lindbergh's tolerance for moral ambiguities was nil at the best of times, and the enormity of the horror of Nazism was too much for him to grasp." Here's another: "Certain political and social implications of what was going on in Germany seem to have escaped [Lindbergh]."

Implications? Franklin Roosevelt put it more precisely, in a now much-quoted remark to his Treasury secretary, Henry Morgenthau, on May 20, 1940: "If I should die tomorrow, I want you to know this: I am absolutely convinced that Lindbergh is a Nazi."

Roosevelt biographer Conrad Black sees the America First Lindbergh as pioneering a type all too common today—"entertainers or sports personalities or cultural figures trying to translate their talent or celebrity in their own fields into positions of political influence, more often than not for the propagation of sophomoric, fatuous, or even seditious views."

Perhaps Lindbergh might be seen as neither sophomoric nor naive nor even a Nazi, but rather as a Nazi fellow traveler, operating not from within Nazi doctrine but in a line running parallel to it. As another historian, Albert Fried, points out, speaking specifically about Lindbergh's role in the isolationist/interventionist debate, "The ideal fellow traveler is himself one of us . . . and is in addition universally respected for his achievements or status." He "persuades us—and through us our neighbors, friends, community, government—to support a country or party whose views we may not share and whose behavior we may not even approve of."

Strengthening Lindbergh's position as the Nazis' ambassador was his pleasant vocal tone and smooth delivery. If one didn't listen to what he was actually saying, the performance was absolutely reasonable, without the bombast and cranky infatuations of the fanatic. Hearing Lindbergh's radio addresses today, it is easy to see why so many isolationists wanted him to run against Roosevelt in 1940. It was in fact a pet terror of some on the left that Lindbergh might become not the next president but the first American Führer. It would happen here.*

Some of you might be wondering what Anne Morrow Lindbergh

---

* In 2004, Philip Roth published his own version of Sinclair Lewis' counter-factual, *The Plot Against America,* in which Lindbergh leads the nation into fascism. Unlike Lewis' uninspiring, middle-aged protagonist, Roth's is a charmingly awkward youngster bearing the author's own name. Lewis' narrative is filled with public figures and the political sityashun; Roth's focuses on a single Jewish family and its reaction to events in the great world outside. To them, America's leader is no more than "a goyisch idiot flying a stupid plane."

was up to during all this, especially because she was a published writer herself. In 1940, she provoked the wrath of what seemed like the entire American left with *The Wave of the Future.* Just forty-one pages long and subtitled *A Confession of Faith,* the book purported to explain why democracy was facing a mortal challenge from Communism, Italian fascism, and Nazism. They were not Mrs. Lindbergh's "wave of the future," she explained, but rather "the scum on the wave." Still, as every historian has pointed out, she never stated what the wave itself *was.*

Why, then, were so many enraged by her book? It may be because her temporizing attitude seemed to accommodate totalitarianism; one passage appeared to accept and even welcome the forces ranged against democracy. On page fifteen, Mrs. Lindbergh asked, "Is some new, and perhaps even ultimately good, conception of humanity trying to come to birth, often through evil and horrible forms and abortive attempts?"

A good conception of humanity is trying to come to birth through Nazism? On page nineteen, we read "that it has happened before," and the analogy offered is the French Revolution, with "the Dantons and the Robespierres." They were guilty of "atrocities," yet today "few seriously question the fundamental necessity or 'rightness' of the movement."

There is no mistaking her intent now: just as the French Revolution eventually implanted the concept of the rights of man, Hitler and his dream of murdering millions will eventually implant some noble concept, too. And that is so beyond the meaning of the word *stupid* that many who had known and liked the Lindberghs now thought them appalling: a marriage of the century was revealed as the idyll of a pair of suburban Macbeths. An instant bestseller, *The Wave of the Future* became possibly the most hated book in publishing history—"The Bible," Harold Ickes called it, "of every American Nazi, Fascist, Bundist, and appeaser."

By then, Dorothy Thompson had engaged Mr. Lindbergh in mortal combat on the cultural level, using On the Record and her radio time to attack his America First speeches (from October of 1939 up to a few days before the Japanese bombed Pearl Harbor). "This somber cretin," she said, was "America's number one problem child," a creature "without human feeling" who "has a notion to be the American Fuehrer." As I've said,

Thompson had been here before: "I recognize the manner, the attitude, the behavior of the crowds." It was Hitler's Germany that she recognized in Lindberghism, and a mild-mannered Hitler in Lindbergh himself.

Oddly, Vincent Sheean believed that Thompson was motivated in part by anger at Lindbergh for one of his practical jokes: he had cut a rare Burgundy with mouthwash at a dinner party way back when Prohibition was still law of land and Burgundy unobtainable. "I do not believe that Dorothy could have been so thunderous on this subject," he later observed, "if she had not retained a vivid personal distaste based upon the experience of that practical joke."

That cannot be right. As Thompson saw it, at stake was the fate of democracy, not of a bottle of wine. Further, Lindbergh's speeches were intensely provocative to Thompson precisely because they were so "sensibly" presented that some might fail to see the cajoling sophistry at their foundation, as here:

> These wars in Europe are not wars in which our civilization is defending itself against some Asiatic intruder. There is no Genghis Khan or Xerxes marching against our Western nations. This is simply one more of those age-old struggles within our own family of nations.

There most certainly was a Genghis Khan on the march, and this was very different from any previous struggle—but Lindbergh drew no moral distinction between Nazism and democracy. Try this one, for instance:

> If the Jewish international financiers succeed in involving the nations in another war, the result will be the liquidation of the Jews in Europe.

That wasn't Lindbergh. That was Hitler, readying his war in a speech to the Reichstag on January 30, 1939, the sixth anniversary of the Nazi takeover. Now here's the Lindbergh version:

> Instead of agitating for war, the Jewish groups in this country should be opposing it in every possible way, for they will be among the first to feel its consequences.

Lindbergh's singling out of a Jewish influence in warmongering—along, he said, with the British and the Roosevelt administration—outraged even many isolationists, for he had finally tipped what had been an argument over foreign policy into the freak's playground of conspiracy theory. Thus, Dorothy Thompson became the spokesperson for liberty and humanism while Lindbergh became the spokesperson for psychopathic despotism. "What she told us," wrote Vincent Sheean, "was that we were doomed unless we woke up in time to fight the appalling danger of Hitler's conquest." Sheean didn't see Thompson as Cassandra: "I always thought a better name for her, if we had to have one, was Boadicea, the warrior queen of ancient Britain."

While defending the greater concept of democracy and its survival, Thompson inevitably also defended the New York arts culture invented to a large degree by the children of immigrants in the early-middle twentieth century. As I've said, their parents had been the assimilating generation; the youngsters were the achieving generation. However, only in a democracy that monitors its bigots can a liberal elite protect itself from the power elite, using a tolerance that is nourished by love of art and a curiosity about the now reassuring and now challenging positions in which art operates.

The bombing of Pearl Harbor terminated the debate between isolationists and interventionists; America First simply evaporated. About a year earlier, on November 10, 1938, Kate Smith told her radio listeners, "And now, it's going to be my very great privilege to sing for you a song that's never been sung before." She was about to introduce a number that had been written during World War I yet never readied for performance till now. "It's something more than a song," Smith went on. "I feel it's one of the most beautiful compositions ever written—a song that will never die. The author—Mr. Irving Berlin. The song—'God Bless America.' "

A Sentimental Ending

Dorothy Thompson's columns and speeches were dialectical in nature, far removed from what used to be called "creative writing" (though she did co-author a play about German refugees, *Another Sun,* that failed miserably, in 1940). Every so often, however, Thompson would cut loose with what, again, used to be called a "human interest" piece. After the Nazi invasion of the Low Countries, when France was still fighting, Thompson wrote of her experience watching French soldiers departing for the front. The piece was called "On a Paris Railway Station":

> First the men from Mars, and then the masses. Breed them, mothers! Prizes for the most fertile! Equality for the illegitimate! Born in love or lust or for a bonus, all are equal, all alike, one folk, one Reich, one Fuehrer.

But the French soldiers she sees are not alike. One has "ascetic bones" and "cynical eyes," another "the gleeful mouth of a peasant epicurean":

> You, lover of books and you, lover of your girl, and you with the nervous lips—you have to get to meet the man of tomorrow, No. 1135, type B.

The soldiers' train arrives and, silently, they board as their girls and wives weep on the platform. The train starts off, and Thompson says:

> There goes France.

8

Culture For Free

Early in the MGM movie *Babes in Arms* (1939), just before Mickey Rooney gets the idea of putting on a show "right here in Seaport," two of the babes entertain the others with a kind of song contest. Betty Jaynes, a trained soprano, gives "You Are My Lucky Star" the opera treatment, complete with coloratura and cadenza. Then Judy Garland offers the tale of a certain barber of Seville in hi-de-ho format, riffing on the name Figaro in the vocal equivalent of jitterbug. The pair concludes with a sing-off, Jaynes flying high on a Hollywood version of the Sextet from *Lucia di Lammermoor* while Garland swings. And as if MGM hadn't yet made its point about the dichotomy between classical and pop, an early outline of the characters in the studio's *Wizard of Oz* movie proposed Jaynes once more, as "The Princess of Oz who sings opera," to Garland's "An Orphan in Kansas who sings jazz."

It was an obsession of the day, especially at MGM: sweet or hot? Art or . . . American? Yet it was the peculiarly American notion that an alchemy of the artistic and the popular creates something special, something perhaps related to Katharine Hepburn's assessment of the magnetism between Fred Astaire and Ginger Rogers. You already know this, but

I'll give it, anyway: "He gives her class, and she gives him sex." Or even: he gives her style and she gives him democracy.

Classical began dating pop in the 1920s, when highbrow composers in America and, especially, Germany brought jazz (in its widest meaning) under the jurisdiction of the conservatory. This offered a breakaway option to composers looking for something beyond nineteenth-century romanticism besides neo-classicism or Arnold Schönberg's tone row. "Classical jazz" fascinated when it worked. When it didn't, it was Paul Hindemith's piano suite *1922:* Marsch, Shimmy, Nachtstück (that is, "Nocturne"), Boston, and Ragtime. The Boston—the proper name of the "hesitation waltz"—hesitates appropriately, but by the time Hindemith finished applying the scientific method to American dance rhythms, he was left with the physics of the music rather than the music.

A more vital entry in this line was Wilhelm Grosz's *Africa-Songs* (1930), a cycle for mezzo, baritone, and chamber group sparked by a little jazz band in their midst, complete with banjo. Here was Germany embracing New Yorkism,* for the texts were translations of poets of the Harlem Renaissance—terrible translations, unfortunately, for German has no equivalent for Langston Hughes' southern ear in "Ballad of Gin Mary." Implacable Judge Pierce gives the defendant eighteen months "so licker'll let you be," but the impeccable German that Grosz had to set might be telling of a court date in Stuttgart.

The high point of all this was reached in the most New Yorkist work yet, Ernst Křenek's opera *Jonny Spielt Auf* ("Johnny Starts the Music," 1927), a flash hit the way Puccini had flash hits, though it's seldom heard today. In its first year alone, it was booked in Leipzig (where it debuted),

---

* Grosz was Austrian, but *Afrika-Songs* was commissioned by German Radio. While we've paused: Grosz's later years offer an intriguing tale on how to turn adversity into a career enhancement. Fetching up in England as a refugee from Nazism, Grosz realized that the conservative British public had no use for the experimental modernism he had worked in back home. So Grosz applied his gifts to the composition of easy-go pop tunes, sometimes as Will Grosz but also as Hugh Williams—"Red Sails in the Sunset," "Harbour Lights," "Along the Santa Fe Trail," the daintily tangoing "Isle of Capri." Irresistibly vapid as only the most appealing pop can be, the songs counted among the smash hits of their era all over the world—including Nazi Germany.

Berlin, Hamburg, Dresden, Cologne, Nuremberg, Frankfurt, Weimar, Zurich, Antwerp, Prague, Budapest, Leningrad, and some twenty other cities. Oddly, when it reached New York itself, at the Met in 1929, the piece did not go over. Even more oddly, the Met presented the title character (sung first by Michael Bohnen, then by Lawrence Tibbett) as a white man who performs in blackface, like Al Jolson. But Jonny is no minstrel man. A black American jazz player on the loose in Europe, Jonny is aggressive and lawless, the embodiment of the attitudes of jazz, at least as the authorities saw it: playful but dangerous.

We have seen how many meanings "jazz" contains; here, it is America itself. *"Schnelles 'Grammophon' Tempo"* Křenek directs at one point: not your continental *allegro* or *animato* but *"Fast as a record side,"* sizzling hot. Fast as the sex and crime of Broadway, as fascinating to Europeans as to Hollywood. First there was imperial Rome, then the Renaissance in Italy, then the banks of London and the fairs of Paris. Now history showed off on Forty-second Street. Jonny steals a priceless violin, to reorder the sound of Western Civilization in his way. As all intone in the opera's final chorale, "The New World crosses the sea like lightning to conquer old Europe with dance." The new music is not *Paradise Lost,* but *Star Wars.*

George Gershwin was of course the exemplar of the symphonic jazz movement. His *Rhapsody in Blue* starts and ends in B Flat Major, with important episodes in the harmonically relevant supertonic and submediant. Still, the *Rhapsody*'s most famous tune, the *Andantino Moderato,* arrives in an "incorrect" E Major, from the "blue" world of sexy syncopation and lopsided harmonic relationships. As *Jonny*'s choristers warned us, the new music doesn't tolerate the old: it conquers and absorbs it. It was as if art was turning into fun and fun into art.

Perhaps the great moment in this mésalliance occurred in 1937, when Walt Disney's *Snow White and the Seven Dwarfs* started its unheard-of five-week run at Radio City Music Hall. Like *The Birth of a Nation* and the combination of the first two Al Jolson features, *The Jazz Singer* and *The Singing Fool, Snow White* was not just a huge hit but a corrective event: it changed the way people comprehend film.

The first full-length cartoon, *Snow White* combined the two forms that the Disney studio had developed in its cartoon short, the Silly Symphony: the fairy tale and the animals farce. Along with the newsreel, the short subject, and the coming-attraction preview, the cartoon was an essential element in American moviegoing, so *Snow White* was, in effect, familiar material. Yet the film hit with tremendous impact as novelty and masterpiece at once. It was that rare event in art: universally appealing yet indescribable.

Why? Disney's storytelling excels above all in details, embellishing the basic action with a curiosity shop of arresting bits—introducing the merrymaking in the dwarfs' cottage by a long view of the forest animals sedately assembled at the windows like the spectators at a show; Grumpy accompanying the number on a piano-ized organ with elaborately carved humanoid pipes; Dopey "exiting" screen right after his solo in an eerie dumdum pose.

There is as well the way Disney animation internalizes the soundtrack, matching music to action. One thinks, for instance, of the most famous of the Disney shorts, *The Band Concert* (1935). The premise, in the funny-animals line, is simple: Mickey Mouse conducts his orchestra in Rossini's *William Tell* Overture, despite heckling from Donald Duck and a devastating tornado. But the synchronization of music and incident is intense, as when two flirty reed players finger scales on each other's instruments, or when ice cream slides down Mickey's back under his uniform and his band hoochy-kooches Rossini as he wiggles. Best of all is the way Donald's interference draws the players from classical to pop: producing countless flutes from his idiotic little sailor suit, he plays a "Turkey in the Straw" that actually *folds into* while taking over the overture's *Allegro Vivace* (the "Lone Ranger theme," if you will).

One might say that the Disney atelier consisted of artists working in a commercial medium, which oxymoron might explain why *Snow White* became for a time the highest-grossing film in Hollywood history. Not surprisingly, this keen integration of action and music demanded a keenly integrated vocal score, to dramatize Snow White (in the appealingly infantile voice of eighteen-year-old Adriana Caselotti) and the dwarfs with artless rightness. The songwriters, Frank Churchill and Larry Morey, were strictly Hollywood journeymen, and Disney sought number after number from them, to be certain that their storytelling matched his. He finally accepted nine, but "Music In Your Soup," accompanying the dwarfs' dinner, too closely followed their "washing up" song, "Bluddle-Uddle-Um-Dum." Completed through final animation and scoring, the number was cut at the last minute to survive as a bonus curiosity on the DVD release.*

Snow White's phenomenal success inspired Paramount to commission a cartoon feature from the Max Fleischer outfit, home of the studio's *Popeye* shorts. But *Gulliver's Travels* (1939) demonstrates how much Disney achieved, for it fails with his materials. Like *Snow White,* it is an integrated story musical. The Lilliputians are simply dwarfs multiplied. There's a prince to romance a princess, and some menace, from the Lilliputians' neighbors on Blefescu, and while there's no sorcery, Gulliver's size provides a kind of magic. Yet the film lacks everything: a good score, sharp comedy, pacing (the sequence in which the hero is bound on the beach is interminable), and, quite simply, beauty. Worst of all is Gulliver himself, a giant bore and not even fully animated. Apparently, the Fleischers "rotoscoped" him, tracing his movements upon those of a real-life model. Disney's critics complain that *Snow White*'s prince, too, is an android, generally stiff but at times almost molten in his movements.†

Disney's definitive union of the elite and demotic was *Fantasia* (1940), a monumental Silly Symphony. Those who loved it were amazed at its spendthrift imagination—again, precisely synchronized to the music. Just one example: the appearance in Beethoven's *Pastoral Symphony* of a cherub playing Pan pipes when the oboe turns the work's opening theme into a freakish little prance.

But there were those who hated it: for besmirching Tchaikofsky, Stravinsky, even Schubert's "Ave Maria." Worse, one of the nation's very

---

* A sappy title song was published at the time, but it was intended for promotional use and is not heard in the film even in underscoring.

† Some rotoscoping was required in *Snow White,* to Disney's regret, to speed up the animation process and complete the film in time for its first engagements. The studio claimed that live models were used only for study—a false statement, but a necessary one, to keep the complex technical issue of animating humans from distracting the lay public.

few household-name conductors put his imprimatur on it—Leopold Stokowski, leading the Philadelphia Orchestra on the soundtrack and even . . . *even* appearing in the film's live-action intervals!

But "You can dismiss the complaints of the little hierarchy of music men," said Pare Lorentz, in *McCall's,* "who try to make music a sacrosanct, mysterious, and obscure art. Disney has brought it out of the temple." Yes, but "I left the theatre in a condition bordering on nervous breakdown," Dorothy Thompson wrote in her *Herald Tribune* column. "I felt as though I had been subjected to [a] brutalization of sensibility in this remarkable nightmare." Noting that "the chief characteristic of this decade of the twentieth century is the collapse of the civilized world," Thompson declared that *Fantasia* was "a social symptom" of that collapse.

Because its stereophonic sound system was too expensive for general theatrical release, *Fantasia* was seen in its proper form only in road-show bookings. In a reserved-seat, two-shows-a-day run at New York's huge Broadway Theatre, the film stayed for a year. Small-town audiences, however, saw it trimmed in length and in standard mono sound on double bills with a western. So the initial release lost money, though *Fantasia* subsequently made the list of top earners, and its bizarrely confident mixture of frolic, horror, and kitsch, which may have mystified when new, is now a treasure of unique American art. Simply setting Mickey Mouse into a cartoon version of Goethe's poem *Der Zauberlehrling*—literally, *The Sorcerer's Apprentice*—is beyond audacious. It merges not only pop and art but the bourgeois and the noble, true revolution.

With Hollywood, we bring in Coastal Culture, not New York alone—but Hollywood, too, could arouse Main Street reactionaries with its erotic pioneering, not only in movies themselves but in stars' offscreen behavior. Many think of Walt Disney as the heartland's artist, an elaborated greeting-card salesman and anything but an exponent of New Yorkism. However, that view of Disney dates from later in his career: from the theme parks and canned television and Mickey Mouse the Corporation. Disney's work around the time of *Snow White* and *Fantasia,* despite its national appeal, is radically artistic and at times disturbing.

Moving back to New York, we find another instance of pop's wish to "improve" itself in a form even lower than the cartoon: the comic book. The Disney of this operation was Albert Kanter, who in 1941 launched Classic Comics. His firm was the Gilberton Company of, mainly, 101 Fifth Avenue, and his line was to sell over a billion copies worldwide in its thirty-year history. "Complete. Entertaining. Educational" read lettering on the spine of the first three entries, *The Three Musketeers, Ivanhoe,* and *The Count of Monte Cristo,* at sixty-four pages (with no ads) for ten cents. Because only boys read comics, Kanter favored action—*Moby-Dick, Robin Hood, Lorna Doone, Tom Sawyer, Lord Jim,* all five of James Fenimore Cooper's *Leatherstocking* series, and even *Crime and Punishment.* True, *Alice in Wonderland* and *Black Beauty* were included, and at one point *Heidi* was promised, though it never appeared. To emphasize the educational aspect, Kanter included back-of-the-book articles on the author's life, sagas of heroic dogs, "Pioneers of Science," "Famous Operas" ("It is recess time at a cigarette factory in Seville, Spain . . ."). *Les Miserables* offered virtually a French-American republican kit, with Hugo's life, our Bill of Rights, a page on how "La Marseillaise" came to be written, with the words and a translation, and "The Statue of Liberty: A Gift From the French." (In fact, all the end-of-book essays may have been inspired by postal regulations that offered lower shipping rates to comics bearing at least one full page of text.) In 1947, rightly sensing that comic books were about to suffer another of those uprisings from bluenoses, Kanter changed the name of the series to Classics Illustrated.*

The output eventually comprised 167 titles, along with special publications and a separate line of seventy-six Classics Illustrated Juniors, and unlike the superhero and humor comics Kanter's books were not meant as ephemera. Even as the page count for successive releases dropped to fifty-six and then to forty-eight, even as some titles fell out of print or were readapted with new art, the output as a whole survived till 1971.

---

* Kanter also sought to disarm the Mrs. Grundys by revising or replacing borderline objectionable cover art—a vast, slobby Quasimodo grasping Notre-Dame as if a toy, boatmen finding a hideous corpse in the water for the *Musketeers* sequel *Twenty Years After,* and, amusingly, an *Arabian Nights* genie showing pubic hair above his cache-sex.

New Yorkism: A Photo Essay

Hotel Astor "*At The Crossroads of the World*"

It All Starts in the Astors' Hotels

Left, the little Waldorf (left side of the edifice) and the much grander Astoria, joined on the site of today's Empire State Building, in Little Old New York. *Right,* the Hotel Astor commands Times Square in a later, livelier Manhattan.

I ♥ New Yorkism

But Charles Lindbergh didn't. *Left,* Lindbergh the hero, in 1927, just after The Flight, with New York's favorite wag, playboy, and even mayor, Jimmy Walker. *Right,* Lindbergh the professional Aryan, in Germany in 1938, jesting with Hermann Göring. Mrs. Lindbergh, in white jacket, tries not to notice.

Top, the heartland hates New Yorkism: tea-partying Prohibitionists exploit their children. *Bottom,* the heartland loves New Yorkism, as boy scouts of Camp Kanohwahke (now Bear Mountain State Park) hail Governor Al Smith as "Grand Sachem" (in Tammany Hall parlance) of their preserve.

Broadway

Opposite, top left, Ethel Waters was the only lead left off *As Thousand Cheer*'s playbill cover, in 1933. (Note Marilyn Miller, Clifton Webb, and Helen Broderick, dressed for "Easter Parade.") But two years later, Waters broke into *At Home Abroad*'s Peter Arno logo art, *top right.* Then, *bottom,* Waters (*center right*) pursued her emergence, in a straight role in *Mamba's Daughters.*

Above, more of *As Thousands Cheer*, as England's Prime Minister (Hal Forde), Queen Mary (Helen Broderick), and King George (Leslie Adams) interrogate the Prince of Wales (Thomas Hamilton) about That Mrs. Simpson. New Yorkist art loved gossip; topical revues and their celebrity imitations kept the heady names of the Guest List in rotation.

My Cozy Little Corner in the Ritz

Top left, Grace Church was the face of Society in Mrs. Astor's day, when the elite was seldom glimpsed by the public. Later, Café and Divorce Society's face was, to many, Barbara Hutton *(top right),* the heiress of the world. Still later, Publiciety reigned at the Stork Club, especially the Hollywood contingent, such as *(bottom)* Susan Hayward and Mr. Hayward, Jess Barker—soon to be, as Walter Winchell would say, *phffft!* Note the distinctive Stork bud vase, matches, ashtray warning

"For Fatima [Cigarette] Ashes Only," and, in Hayward's hands, the house perfume, Sortilege.

Above, a maximum leader of New Yorkism was Cole Porter, at his early height in *Anything Goes*, in 1934: Ethel Merman leads the corps in "Blow, Gabriel, Blow," as Gabriel toots at the upper right. By the early 1940s (*overleaf*), however . . .

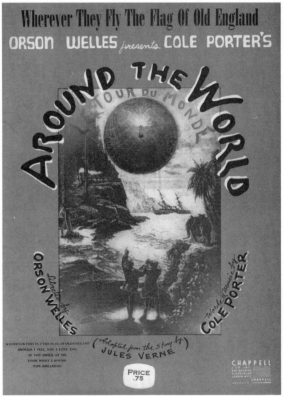

Porter was in a slump, signaled here by the louche gags-and-gals fest *Mexican Hayride* (*top,* with Bobby Clark) and an Orson Welles spectacle that was barely a musical, *Around the World*. In 1948, Porter made his comeback with *Kiss Me, Kate*, adding a new name to the Guest List: Shakespeare.

There have even been attempts to resuscitate the line, albeit without lasting success.

This was a transnational phenomenon, too, with translations and even local titles not issued in the U.S.—*The Canterville Ghost* in England, for instance, or *König Rolf und Seine Krieger* in Germany.* Nevertheless, critics in this terrain deplore Classics Illustrated as ersatz classics and lame illustration. Except in Shakespeare, Longfellow, and Scott's *The Lady of the Lake,* the original writing is scanted or missing, and the page layouts are pedestrian. *The Three Musketeers* is amateurish, a crawl of stick figures posing in finery from the costume closet. *Ivanhoe* leaves out too much of Scott's view of, so to say, the unfairness of everything in a Saxon land oppressed by France's arrogant Normans, and *Monte Cristo* navigates through Dumas' subplots so doggedly that even the occasional outsized panel cannot relieve the tedium of talking-head rectangles. Of the earliest issues, only number eleven, *Don Quixote,* re-creates the atmosphere of the original, in playful art and a fond look at the imperious grandeur of the unreachably demented. For all its impact on American life—it provisioned three decades of high-school book reports, for starters—Classics Illustrated may have had no influence on American art. Even so, like the Disney films, these comics recall a time when the notion of an elite in art was breaking down.

Or perhaps the word "art" was compiling meanings—as in the "musical play" introduced on Broadway in the 1940s, with its renewed development of the interpretive dance narrations introduced in the 1930s and a new emphasis on community, politics, and the transformation of social structures. The essential thirties musical was Cole Porter's *Anything Goes,* a shipboard farce in which everyone who is interesting runs around in disguise and the only virtue is to be famous. Essential forties musicals include *Oklahoma!,* on tribal customs; *Carousel,* on the class system; *Bloomer Girl,* on the oppression of women and blacks; *Brigadoon,*

---

* Rolf Kraki, who appears in a number of ancient sagas, including *Beowulf,* outwits the King of Sweden in battle by tempting him with a golden ring, then slicing him in the buttocks while he's distracted. "Hell sang der Stahl" ("Brightly rang the steel") is the caption's dry comment in the Illustrierte Klassiker version.

on an urban sophisticate's search for spirituality. "You're Ovaltine!" chortles someone in *Anything Goes:* it's the top. In *Carousel,* the heroine sings, "Common sense may tell you that the ending will be sad": and that's what happens. *Snow White* ends sadly, too, in a way, because the dwarfs, having discovered the redemption of beauty, lose access to it forever. But then, the musical, heretofore essentially a capricious medium, was developing an emotional reality, low art learning from high just as high was absorbing elements of low.

At the same time, the endless American quest for heroes took an interesting turn. Besides looking in the usual places—the film and sports worlds, where Errol Flynn won World War II and Joe DiMaggio would have beaten Babe Ruth's home run record but for Yankee Stadium's extra long left field—the public took up a highbrow hero. He was a symphony and opera conductor who by some odd alchemy made the performing of Mozart, Beethoven, and Verdi an act of anti-fascism, a war effort, though all three belonged to enemy nations. He was a general of culture, an artist of politics. He became sacrosanct, till criticizing his musicianship was almost an act of treachery—of treason, even. His very looks, though by the early 1940s he was in his seventies, were thought politically definitive: as grave as the bust of a philosopher-king leading his people to certain victory.

Arturo Toscanini's political background was better known than that of, literally, any other major conductor: he defied Italian fascists and refused to work in Hitler's Germany. Other musicians had defied and refused, but Toscanini's headlines gave him the patent. Further, his partisans in the media so publicized his superiority that it became an article of faith among not only music lovers but the population generally: Toscanini was the greatest conductor in the world.

Arguably, he was. Many of the other important conductors said as much, or nearly, and his minutely detailed command of the scores he played was unrivaled. Toscanini was a perfectionist not only in the sense of "striving for perfection" but in achieving it: he could play difficult passages exactly as the composer demanded where other maestros approximated.

I'll offer one example, in five measures of the first act of *Aida.* Everyone except Aida's father (who hasn't come into the story yet) is on stage as the King of Egypt announces who will lead the army in its coming campaign. It will be Radames, the love object of both soprano Aida and the usual tempestuous mezzo, Amneris. At the announcement, Radames breaks into a long line of descending quarter notes, easy to sing in tempo. The two women have very short eighth-note lines to place against his, alternating with each other. That part is not easy to sing in tempo—and the chorus men have brief interjections as well. Verdi was without question the most experienced theatre man in opera history. He knew that this passage would never come off with the needed surgical precision in live performance, and the plastic-bubble security of studio recordings under virtuoso conductors lay in the future when Verdi died, in 1901. Why did he ask for the impossible, then? Because when he wrote *Aida* he was aging, permanently exasperated with everything, and reckless of the odds. *Buona fortuna!*

And, indeed, though virtually every great conductor of the Italian repertory in the postwar era—from Serafin, Solti, and von Karajan to Muti, Abbado, and Mehta—has recorded *Aida* in the studio, no one gets this passage exactly as it's written. A few come close. But only Toscanini plays precisely what Verdi asked for—at that in a live concert, without the security guarantee of studio retakes.

As a human being, however, Toscanini was a great artist, which is to say jealous, devious, intransigent, and monomaniacal. Obsessed with music, he was uninterested in anything else and maintained a lifestyle consistent to the point of monotony. He wanted everything the same at all times: to wear the same clothes and eat the same foods, even to conduct the same classic nineteenth-century maestros over and over, with an occasional airing of, for example, Elgar, Debussy, Gershwin, obscure Italians . . . and the American premiere of Shostakovich's Seventh Symphony.*

---

* This was the "Leningrad" Symphony, composed during and about that city's sixteen-month siege during the Nazi invasion of Russia and therefore prime Toscanini material despite his aversion to what little he knew of Shostakovich's music. (He did also conduct Shostakovich's First.) Toscanini presented the Seventh on a radio broadcast, on July 19, 1942, when Leningrad was still resisting the Nazi blockade and one day before Shostakovich made the cover of *Time* in his Leningrad fire brigade

What most people knew of Toscanini, besides his anti-fascist identifi-cation, was his temper. He could forgive almost nothing, but particu-larly titanic rages would break out when he felt the orchestra was treating a rehearsal as . . . well, a rehearsal. To Toscanini, there was no difference between rehearsal and performance: music is to be made, at all times, with commitment at its absolute. He was just as hard with singers in his days at La Scala and the Metropolitan Opera, much earlier in the century—or when, before the Anschluss, he led celebrated productions of opera at the Salzburg Festival. One of the works was Beethoven's *Fidelio*, a piece about a freedom fighter, a woman who dons men's clothes and gets work in a prison to save her incarcerated, outspoken-liberal hus-band. It's the perfect Toscanini opera; it's virtually about him. The hero-ine of the Salzburg *Fidelio*s was Lotte Lehmann, incidentally another foe of fascism.

Fearful of Toscanini's eruptions, Lehmann had no choice but to ac-cept his invitation to certify her Beethoven with him; dedicated artists cannot subcontract such opportunities. Then, during an orchestra re-hearsal, Toscanini stopped the music and looked sternly at Lehmann. "My God," she was thinking, "what happens now?"

"You," Toscanini thundered, "are an *artist!*"

All too often, however, what one got from the maestro was not praise but the smashing of the baton, the breaking of a watch, the throw-ing over of chairs and podiums, the bellowing and screaming, which resounded through the building as he stormed off to his dressing room.

Then why attempt to make music with him? For the same reason that drove Lehmann to Salzburg: he really was the great conductor of great music that everyone believed him to be. And he blessed his collaborators with that sense of power and self-belief that the greatest art gives to those who cultivate it. Samuel Antek, a violinist with the orchestra espe-cially formed to play for Toscanini in America, the NBC Symphony, has

uniform. The Seventh had already been heard in Russia, but the microfilmed score was exported to the U.S. (and to England) by way of Tehran, where it was handed over to Allied security operatives and thus sneaked out around the war front. When the work was given in Leningrad itself, the city's Radio Orchestra had to be re-formed because so many of its players had died of starvation.

left a famous set of impressions of what it was like to play for Toscanini for the first time. The work at hand is Brahms' First Symphony:

> In a rough, hoarse voice, he called out "Brahms!" He looked at us pierc-ingly for the briefest moment, then raised his arms. In one smashing stroke, the baton came down. A vibrant sound suddenly hushed forth from the tense players like blood from a severed artery. . . . Was this the same music we had been practicing so assiduously for days? Like ships torn from their mooring in a stormy ocean, we bobbed and tossed, re-sponding to those earnest, importuning gestures. With what a new fierce joy we played!

So all that longhair temperament was in fact centered on an artistic mission, the making of music under ideal conditions: the marriage of technique and spirit in pop-eyed concentration.

Were no others working on this exalted level? There were plenty. Serge Koussevitsky, the Russian émigré who led the Boston Symphony, was not only a gifted and versatile conductor but one with an angle: he insistently programmed modern American compositions, which gave his concerts an adventurous quality. And we've already encountered Leopold Stokowski, leader of the Philadelphia Orchestra; his angle was conducting without a baton. ("Stokowski's hands" was a buzz term.)

Above all, there was Wilhelm Furtwängler. Because he worked almost entirely in Europe at this time, he never became famous in America. Today, however, Furtwängler is regarded as Toscanini's chief rival in the post of Great Conductor of the Twentieth Century.* The two have certain things in common; both excelled in Wagnerian opera, for in-stance. Still, Furtwängler's every concert was unique. Even works he was close to, such as Schumann's Fourth or Schubert's Ninth Sympho-nies, might sound merely valid last season and unspeakably brilliant now. Toscanini, too, could be unpredictable—in his youth. In 1924, Kurt

---

*Though he resented having to say so, Toscanini thought Furtwängler his only equal as a conductor. Furtwängler was not a Toscanini admirer, finding the Italian's literal-ism "discipline" without "inspiration."

Weill heard him at La Scala "playing" the orchestra with "capricious *rubati*": taking liberties. However, by the time we speak of, Toscanini had morphed into a *historical* conductor, tyrannical about playing the printed notes as if after consultation with the composer himself. Furtwängler was always an *existential* conductor, each performance a contrasting tour through the mysteries that lay inside music.

Then, too, Furtwängler was a composer himself, with a Brahmsian Second Symphony still played today; Toscanini composed only a few salon vocal pieces, in his youth. But Toscanini excels everyone in volume of lore and legend, an anecdote collector's Santa Claus with his turmoils here and adulterous knowledge of sopranos there. He even had a sense of humor. His son Walter, who as manager, go-between, and pep master worked for what we might call Toscanini Inc., was one of those who somehow cannot manage to show up for anything on time. Had he been anyone else he would have been fired, but Toscanini was family-centered and forgave. Speaking of it to a music critic, Toscanini said, in the English that he never perfected after many years in the U.S., "Is good, but not punctual. Only once was punctual. I was married June 21. He was born March 21."

Furtwängler doesn't seem to appear in anecdotes at all—and he could not challenge Toscanini's power to create synonyms out of "Beethoven" and "liberty" in his importance as a political symbol. After all, Toscanini's era of greatest American fame coincided with the era in which the first notes of Beethoven's Fifth Symphony served as a musical code for "Allied Victory." In truth, Toscanini had agitated against fascism all his life. Back in 1922, an audience at La Scala demanded that Toscanini start the last act of Verdi's *Falstaff* by conducting the fascist hymn, "Giovinezza" ("Youth"), and Maestro smashed his baton and stormed out of the pit. *Conduct it yourselves!* As the house roared in fury, a Scala official appeared to promise "Giovinezza" at the end of the work, and Toscanini returned to finish *Falstaff*. The curtain of this particular opera comes down with the entire cast on stage, so the house staff simply told them to remain standing for the singing of "Giovinezza." And then Toscanini appeared.

"The Scala artists aren't vaudeville singers!" he shouted. "Go to your dressing rooms, all of you!"

Everybody ran away, and "Giovinezza" was not sung that night. But there is no question that only Toscanini's international renown protected him from the vicious castor-oil treatment favored by Mussolini's thugs.

Furtwängler's defiance of regime was far less momentous. He hated the Nazis and put himself in danger to protect musicians from the regime's evil cleansings. Still, what folks remember first of all is that Toscanini refused to conduct in Nazi territory and left Italy in disgust while Furtwängler stayed in Germany and made music there. This alone has branded Furtwängler with a false calumny, because none of the other major German and Austrian conductors who pursued their careers under Nazi rule is ever blamed for doing so the way Furtwängler is—including a few who were Nazi Party members or even outright enthusiasts of the regime.[*]

One has the feeling that some writers penalize Furtwängler the better to worship Toscanini. The Italian's record label, Victor, contributed to the Toscanini cult with press releases that had everything but the halo. Indeed, Toscanini's being a Victor artist in the first place is significant, for Victor's much-publicized "Red Seal" discs—its high-priced "celebrity" line—had long been a guarantee of not only technical leadership in the recording industry but of almost all of the first-call names in classical music. When people found a cache of Caruso 78s dozing in the attic of a newly-bought old house, they were Red Seals, because from 1904 on Caruso was a Victor exclusive, to a total of some 215 sides. Then, too,

---

[*] Rudolf Bing was one of the few with blame at the ready when he was the general manager of the Metropolitan Opera, starting in 1950. Bing tried to lure conductor Erich Kleiber to the Met, but Kleiber (who had left Germany for Argentina in 1934) had prohibitive commitments, and when Frau Kleiber suggested another musician, Bing replied that he was willing to consider "an outstanding conductor who was a mediocre Nazi, but not an outstanding Nazi who was a mediocre conductor." Bing did not name the subject in his retellings. Many assume it was Herbert von Karajan, but von Karajan did eventually conduct at Bing's Met.

Victor had long been the label of choice for the status conscious, a badge of bella figura but also of prosperity. In 1907, a one-sided Victor 78 of the Quartet from *Rigoletto* was priced—right on the label where one's neighbors might see—at $6.00. This represented $2.00 per star for tenor Caruso, mezzo Louise Homer, and baritone Antonio Scotti. (The soprano, Victor stringer Bessie Abbott, was thrown in for free.) At today's prices, that is something like $200.00 for four minutes of music.

Like virtually everyone else profiled in this book, Toscanini got his *Time* cover, but, among the few, he made the cover of *Life* as well, sitting with his granddaughter at the piano. Toscanini the god of music, the freedom fighter, and now . . . the family man! He's like you and me! That is, if we ran around in striped pants and a cutaway and gave Fearless Leader stomachaches.

And had our very own orchestra with which to hold a nation spellbound every Saturday night starting in December of 1937 with a program of Vivaldi, Mozart, and the Brahms that we just heard Toscanini rehearsing. The concert was broadcast from NBC's Studio 8H in Radio City, which seated 1,200; some fifty thousand had requested tickets. The reviews might well be the single greatest set put together for anybody, anywhere—and everyone, it seemed, wanted to get into the act to tell of "the maestro's hypnotic power . . ." and "the number one interpreter . . ." Or try this one: "He has the grace and agility of a boy, the temperament of a man of thirty, and the working power of a perfect machine. . . . Watch the left hand. It is one of the most beautiful and eloquent hands in the world."

That was Dorothy Thompson. What on earth does she know about music? And were there no Toscanini detractors of note?

There was one. Virgil Thomson, the music critic of Dorothy Thompson's home paper, the *New York Herald Tribune,* composed as well, in the nationalist, folkloric American school that competed with the jazz symphonism noted earlier in this chapter. Thomson's music sounded like an old maid tatting lace. Attaching his relentlessly diatonic harmony to Gertrude Stein in *Four Saints in Three Acts* (1934), he enjoyed a minor vogue, mainly out of support for the advantages its "Negro" casting gave to black opera singers. Still, Thomson's art was prim and picky at a time when American music had come into its young manhood.

Thus overwhelmed, Thomson continued to compose but sought to reestablish himself as opinion maker more than creator. He had already written criticism, including a grandly synoptic book entitled *The State of Music* (1939), but his *Tribune* columns, from 1940 to 1954, gave him prominence as he compiled his impressions into an aesthetic. Whether or not one agreed with it, Thomson was at least a better writer than music critics tend to be. As with George Bernard Shaw's comparable work, the verbal confidence mitigated the effect of the often shabby positions. Thomson's dismissals of new or newish work that have since become classics typifies him, as in his report on Sibelius' Second Symphony: "vulgar, self-indulgent, and provincial beyond all description." Topping this is the accompanying "if you like this music you're an idiot" review of the public as well: "I realize that there are sincere Sibelius-lovers in the world, though I must say I've never met one among educated professional musicians."

The ideal self-advertisement is an assault on a titan, thus to borrow majesty. Here's Thomson on Verdi: "He never learned how to build a melodic line that would be at the same time monumental and penetratingly expressive of the text." That sentence is so deaf to words as well as music that it's virtually inspired. And Thomson fooled many of his readers: because surely only the most intellectual sensibility would dare attack the canon.

To shock more truly, however, this sort of critic needs, like the spider, to feed on the living, and when Toscanini turned eighty, in 1947, Thomson capped a series of offensives with an essay explaining why Toscanini "will not loom large, I imagine, in the history books of the future." No, he'll be as forgot as Sibelius. The maestro's daughter Wanda caught Thomson snoozing during her father's concert of—once again—*Falstaff.* Approaching Thomson at the end, she told him who she was and what she saw, smacked him with her program, and then called one of the keepers of those Columns to be sure that incident became public lest Thomson retaliate.

Yet by the late 1940s Toscanini was beyond the reach of music critics. This was a man, after all, who represented the Triumph of Civilization Over Barbarians. New Yorkism dealt mainly in midcult—Jerome Kern and Oscar Hammerstein turning Edna Ferber's *Show Boat* into a musical produced by Florenz Ziegfeld, say, with its plea for racial tolerance, its Tin Pan Alley folk anthem in "Ol' Man River," and even the melting-pot demographics of its cast, with virtually every minority from black to Jewish. Toscanini's day job put him on the highest cultural level, but his participation in NBC's "art is good for you" symphony franchise made him something of a New Yorkist—elite in both the old and new sense, and above all demotically available.

Still, there had to be a tradeback: because America will take its Toscanini like medicine as long as it can turn to a bit of riffraff as a chaser. That is—recalling the original plan for MGM's *The Wizard of Oz*—if someone's going to sing opera, someone else has to sing jazz. Along with the Toscaninis, then, one looked for figures a little more local and a lot less holy—names from The Columns, perhaps. But not in the way that Toscanini was in The Columns. Someone who *read* The Columns. Someone like Billy Rose.

The neighborhood Ziegfeld, Billy Rose was, in chronological order: a shorthand whiz (in the Gregg method, at the time in competition with more established systems), a sort-of songwriter, a husband of Fanny Brice, and, mainly, a producer of spectacle. He was also, at five feet three inches, a classic instance of the aggressive short guy and, according to Brice, "the most evil man I know." In fact, he was more correctly a devious finagler. A bluffer and a cheat. He liked to tell the story that when he was born, in 1899, his mother announced, as mothers will, "Some day he'll be President!" To which his father replied, "He's all right, I guess. But what we really needed was an ice box."

Like Al Smith, Rose was smart and a good listener, sponging up the wisdom of the great and near-great to be rich in borrowed experience. He really was a shorthand ace, which surely denotes a skill of some kind, but he did not start to impress himself till he got into songwriting, as the business partner of composers and lyricists. They would supply the art, Rose would add in a line or phrase, sign his name with theirs, and partake of the royalties: because he was the one who made the deal with the publisher. Ever on the rise, Rose married Brice after she divorced her real love, Nick Arnstein, a character straight out of Runyonland who couldn't stay out of jail. Rose was never even arrested. His interest in Brice was social-professional, social because she hobnobbed with the show-biz high-hats Rose wanted access to and professional because as his wife she was bound to appear in the shows he intended to produce. Rose had it, as they say, all figured out: he was going to be the next Florenz Ziegfeld.

Keep in mind that, after the stars, the producers were the best-known element in show biz at this time. The general public knew nothing of directors because "directing" as a profession had only just been invented. Before something like 1920, blocking stage traffic and coaching characterization were undertaken by stars (the troupe-heading "actor-manager"), by the author of the play, and by the producers themselves.*

Besides listening to sages, we can learn from those who have done what we're about to do. One thinks of Ronald Reagan's advice to Bill Clinton before he moved into the White House: one, learn how to salute properly; and, two, use Camp David. (Because the commander-in-chief needs to cut a dashing figure and because vacations are essential in keeping the head clear.) The lessons that Billy Rose took from the example of Florenz Ziegfeld (whom Rose apparently never met before the older man's death, in 1932) were, one, do everything in public, for maximum PR collection; two, leave your name on your work; and, three, those who produce cheap never leave the midway: spend the money and know millionaires.

So Rose took over the biggest theatre in New York to produce the most expensive show imaginable, getting the bulk of his $340,000 capitalization from that most social of millionaires, John Hay Whitney. Known as "Jock" to about ten thousand intimate friends, Whitney was more than well off: he was class in every particular. Yet Mrs. Astor wouldn't have known what to say to a man whose idea of opening night

---

* There were a very few men who staged musicals without being stars, authors, or producers—Edward Royce and Julian Mitchell, for example, director-choreographers of note in the business but unknown outside it.

was not top hats at the Met but "ducats" for Cole's new show. Whitney's wife even took mention in a Porter list song. (It was *Let's Face It!*'s "Farming," in a sly jest in which "Liz Whitney has, on her bin of manure, a" runs into "clip designed by the Duke of Verdura.")

Further, Rose hired the biggest names in the business for this superproduction, and he set his own name into its title. Then he outdid Ziegfeld by rehearsing the piece for six months, postponing the premiere over and over—here for a few days, there for weeks—thus to keep reminding the public what marvels awaited. And, yes, the show became famous long before it finally admitted a single audience, a smash that hadn't opened. Rose stoked the PR fires yet more, for instance offering a private showing of one of the countless dress rehearsals to anyone who'd pay $10,000. When the piece—though that noun is modest in this context—finally started its run, the usual celebs dropped by the radio announcer's microphone on opening night to offer pleasantries. George Burns and Gracie Allen were among them, and Gracie predicted great things for the show. Why? "Well," she explained, "if it stays open as long as it stayed closed . . ."

The show was *Billy Rose's Jumbo* (1935), so entitled, and it played the 5,200-seat Hippodrome because it was less a musical than a circus punctuated by plot. The action centered on a *Romeo and Juliet* couple whose fathers run rival tents. Jimmy Durante and an elephant named Big Rosie headed the cast, Paul Whiteman led his band, Rodgers and Hart wrote the score, and John Murray Anderson—a specialist in spectacle and the unconventional—supervised the staging. To top it off, Rose pulled out the center orchestra seats to create an amphitheatre's horseshoe seating with a big-top feeling. He even outfitted the main street entrance with a billowing canvas marquee, as if one were actually attending a circus.

Historians view *Jumbo* as a curiosity shop of landmarks. It marked Rodgers and Hart's return to Broadway after four years in Hollywood and introduced them to George Abbott, who directed *Jumbo*'s book scenes and was to make major history with the team in four later shows. *Jumbo*'s score included three standards, "My Romance," "Little Girl Blue," and "The Most Beautiful Girl in the World," along with one of the loveliest in the line of the patented "Rodgers waltz," scored to accompany a trapeze act, "Over and Over Again." (A fourth standard, "There's a Small Hotel," was written for *Jumbo* but dropped, to resurface in *On Your Toes*.)

Jumbo was also the last Hippodrome booking involving Broadway people (as opposed to the operas and concerts that also played there). This is worth noting because the Hippodrome had been in the first two decades of the century one of New York's proudest tourist sites. It was not only *Jumbo* itself that bore Rose's name: he erected a huge sign running down the southwest corner of the Hippodrome structure with nothing on it but the words "Billy Rose." Passersby saw it, of course—but so did riders on the Sixth Avenue subway line, elevated in that stretch of midtown. The theatre had been the boast of the city; now this producer was.

Ziegfeld never did anything like that. His monuments were his shows and his theatre and his PR escapades, such as the milk baths that star Anna Held supposedly took. One might be showy but one must be suave. One will be known, above all, for one's taste. Rose was known for nightclubs and for aquacades, in which the "stage" was a swimming pool for mermaids stroking in precision, high divers and a diving clown in a funny suit, and two Olympic stars, Johnny Weissmuller (later Buster Crabbe) and Eleanor Holm. Rose made a fortune—and divorced Brice to marry Holm—but this was not the production calendar of a Ziegfeld.

And Rose knew it. Once again applying his learning expertise, Rose noticed that the elite of the world he admired didn't press so hard. Life was not art. They pushed when they worked, because they had theatres to fill, right up to the second balcony. But when Fanny Brice got offstage, she set aside the Lower East Side patterning—the accent, the loony posture, the "gookie" (Harpo Marx's term for a blowfish "face").

Of course, there were exceptions. Dorothy Parker's life was an art—but Dorothy Parker was nuts. For most of her days, especially at the end, she was chronically broke, yet when royalty checks arrived she slipped them into drawers, never to be banked.

Rose never lost track of checks. He lived to bargain, no matter how low the asking price. And he swindled. Almost nobody liked him, especially in the 1930s, when he was yet on the rise. They told a joke on The Street:

Q: Who has the biggest prick on Broadway?
A: Fanny Brice.

However, by the 1940s, Rose had arrived and was in need of mellowing; the arrived are supposed to seem content. *Satisfied.* Remember, this was a time when Americans took celebrity more or less respectfully. The frothy turmoil of today's names—usually a criminal act followed by a disappearance into "rehab"—was all but unknown in the 1940s.

Rose's need to make public a new, improved Billy Rose—an intelligent and responsible Billy Rose—may explain Rose's telegram to Charles Lindbergh at the height of the aviator's America First adventure, urging him (as many of Lindbergh's associates also did, to no avail) to denounce Nazism: I WILL ENGAGE MADISON SQUARE GARDEN AT MY EXPENSE," Rose promised. "MY ONLY CONDITION IS THAT THE PUBLIC MELTING DOWN OR HAMMERING OUT OF SHAPE OF YOUR NAZI MEDAL BE MADE A FEATURE OF THE RALLY." Lindbergh never responded; it is unlikely that he even knew who Billy Rose was.

As we have seen, membership in the new elite meant taking in one's culture, so Rose suddenly stopped gluing his name to aquacades to become what he himself might have called "a Broadway producer of class." A straight play: *Clash by Night* (1941), written by Clifford Odets and directed by Lee Strasberg. As alumni of the Group Theatre, this pair were continuing the Group's experiment in aligning social-problem playmaking with ensemble acting; you couldn't buy such class, even if Rose hired Tallulah Bankhead to star, for old-fashioned show-biz excitement.

That's the straight play. Now the opera: *Carmen Jones* (1943), Oscar Hammerstein's English translation of Bizet's *Carmen,* reset among blacks in wartime. This was the stage equivalent of *Fantasia,* perhaps, bringing music out of the temple, as Pare Lorentz phrased it. It was a labor of love for Hammerstein, for, as already stated, there was so little opportunity for black opera singers that there almost weren't any. Yet Rose leaped at the project and hired the best in the business—Hassard Short—to stage it. Rose even sent the show off on its tryout without a Broadway booking, and at a time when the theatre was enjoying an attendance surge. Even terrible shows weren't closing the way they used to. *Carmen Jones* played Philadelphia and then Boston—at the Boston Opera House, as the city's playhouses were full—hoping that a Broadway stop would open up.

The problem was the wartime audience, especially servicemen and their dates, who would enjoy anything. It was they who made a smash out of *Star and Garter* (1942), a revue drawn largely from the burlesque that Mayor La Guardia had finally managed to shut down. Gypsy Rose Lee and Broadway's lowest comic, Bobby Clark, headed the cast. Actually, a great many others took in the show along with the men in uniform, for while the middle class never dared try burlesque in its seedy venues, a Broadway run excited curiosity. Others saw an opportunity to put on their own *Star and Garter*—and here Rose got lucky. Utilizing the title of a series of twenties Shubert revues, *Artists and Models* crashed into the Broadway Theatre with Jackie Gleason, Jane Froman, and an act in which a woman pianist was accompanied by four women harpists, "all of whom," George Jean Nathan observed, "apparently took xylophone lessons." Despite the strangely lavish capitalization of $225,000, *Artists and Models* seemed shoddy, and it closed in four weeks. The following Friday night, *Carmen Jones* replaced *Artists and Models* at the Broadway, to critics' startled raves. "Going to the theatre," wrote Lewis Nichols in *The New York Times*, "seems again one of the necessities of life."

Rose made his hirelings pester the press into drumming up business. And when business slowed, the box office of the Broadway Theatre somehow sold two sets of tickets for a theatre-party benefit, so that some 3,500 people showed up to occupy 1,750 seats. The police and fire departments had to be called, and when the story made the papers Rose didn't even bother denying having set it up. It was an instance of "All publicity is good publicity," even if the bad kind of bad publicity compromises one's membership in the great world. Rose didn't care. He was willing to change his format from spectacle to art, but a lack of ethics was hardwired into his self-belief.

The straight play, the opera. Now comes the theatre: Rose bought the showplace of Florenz Ziegfeld himself. Erected on the northwest corner of Sixth Avenue and Fifty-fourth Street, the Ziegfeld Theatre had suffered from the location, off in the marches of the theatre district. The walk-in business that still supplied much of the nightly trade (matinees, the haunt of women and families, tended to sell in advance) habitually arrived at Broadway and Forty-second Street and peeled off from there. By Forty-eighth Street or so, customers had purchased their tickets and were looking into dinner, so the Ziegfeld was packed only when theatregoers had a reason to make a pilgrimage. They did so when the house opened, in 1927, with *Rio Rita.* They came again for the second offering, *Show Boat,* later that year. After that, however, the theatre's occupants couldn't sustain a worthy run. On Ziegfeld's death, in 1932, the theatre's real owner, William Randolph Hearst, leased it as a cinema to MGM, with whom he had a business relationship for the making of movies starring his life's love, Marion Davies.

Then, in 1943, the Ziegfeld was put on offer, and Rose, a cash millionaire because of *Carmen Jones* and his two nightclubs, the Casa Manana and the Diamond Horseshoe, outbid MGM for a total of $630,000. As he refurbished the interior and considered what reopening attraction would make the biggest noise, Rose must have realized that he had reached a culmination. He had purchased the place of Ziegfeld, the name of Ziegfeld, the magic of Ziegfeld. The play, the opera, the theatre . . . and now a *Follies:* the greatest revue ever assembled.

With Hassard Short again in charge, there would be Stravinskyan ballet with Alicia Markova, musical-comedy sketches by Kaufman and Hart, Salvador Dalì paintings in the lobby, Benny Goodman jamming on stage, Bert Lahr and Beatrice Lillie. Ziegfeld tended to create headliners, graduating unknowns to lifelong stardom on opening night, but Rose wanted the luminescence prefabricated. As *Seven Lively Arts,* his show was perhaps literally bulging with talent, and Rose piled Ossa on Tin Pan Alley by hiring Cole Porter to write the score. Knowing Rose, one might guess that he in fact approached Rodgers and Hammerstein first, biggest of the lot ever since *Oklahoma!* the year before. But they were busy writing both *Carousel* and the film *State Fair* while producing the straight play *I Remember Mama*.

Broadway opening nights were the new hotels, where the elite celebrated their Mass, and Rose had so ballyhooed *Seven Lively Arts* as the ultimate event in the, so to say, prestiging of pop that *Life* magazine did a layout on not the show but the audience, in the Ziegfeld at the premiere. BILLY ROSE HAS BIG FIRST NIGHT ran the head. GLITTERING AUDIENCE SEES "SEVEN LIVELY ARTS." A photograph overlaying a double-page spread showed conductor Maurice Abravanel in tails with mounted carnation, with le tout New York behind him. Thoughtfully including a blueprint so one could pick out Alfred Hitchcock, Oscar Hammerstein, George S. Kaufman, Elsa Maxwell, and others—leaders of sets, like Maxwell, or visiting dignitaries, like Hitchcock—*Life* plopped in shots of the party that Maxwell threw after the performance, at the Waldorf-Astoria (the second and present one, on Park Avenue between Forty-eighth and Forty-ninth Streets).*

Rose charged a $24.00 top—vast at the time—and served champagne in the Ziegfeld that night; but the show itself fizzled. To start with, there was too much of it—eighteen minutes of classical ballet, for instance, in what many people mistook as a "Cole Porter musical." Along with Lahr and Lillie, Rose hired seven performers to embody the arts as youngsters ready to launch their careers. "Big town, what's before me?" they caroled in the first number: William Tabbert, twenty-three years old, as a budding playwright; the just-out-of-her-teens Dolores Gray as an actress; and so on. Just in case the evening wasn't full enough, Ben Hecht was asked to write scene-change commentary for dreary comic Doc Rockwell, enervating the seven arts at his every appearance. Topping all this off, the two stars, who saw the show as, respectively, a Bert

---

* Note that, unlike the original Waldorf and Astoria buildings, which we saw rise separately on adjacent lots down on Thirty-fourth Street, this new hotel, conceived as a single entity, has no practical reason to be called by the old agglutinated name. Fame, egged on by tradition, demanded it.

Lahr musical and a Beatrice Lillie musical, were irritated at every thing else that was going on and at each other. The show ran 183 performances and lost a lot of Billy Rose's money.

Incredibly, Rose promptly put on a sequel—this time more modestly—as *Concert Varieties* (1945), again at the Ziegfeld. Promising to add "sock to the sacrosanct," he let *Fantasia*'s Deems Taylor again play emcee. In Act One, dancers interpreted Rimsky-Korsakof's *Capriccio Espagnol* and the "Ritual Fire Dance" from de Falla's *El Amor Brujo*. The Katherine Dunham troupe and a group choreographed and led by Jerome Robbins occupied Act Two. Interspersed among these were Zero Mostel, Imogene Coca, a distinguished Italian marionette outfit, and probably the most disliked comedian who ever lived who wasn't El Brendel, Eddie Mayehoff. This one lasted 36 performances.

Then Rose began to dissociate himself from producing. He did take over a second theatre, the National, in 1959, renaming it after himself. (Today it is the Nederlander.) For the house's reopening, Rose once again went "class," with an all-star and largely English revival of Shaw's *Heartbreak House,* starring Maurice Evans as Captain Shotover, made up as Shaw himself. A year later, Rose put on his own show, his last and a very odd item for him, *The Wall,* Millard Lampell's adaptation of John Hersey's novel about the Warsaw ghetto. Reviewers generally praised the large cast for getting a lot out of writing unworthy of the subject. *The Wall* ran for 167 performances, a decent showing but for the small houses: because it turned out that not a single Jewish theatre party had booked the piece at a time when theatre parties had become the method by which most suburbanites did their Broadway. It was a case of New Yorkers neglecting New Yorkism—as if the cause was over, the battle won. "Instead," wrote playwright Morton Wishengrad in a letter to *Commentary* magazine, the Jewish charities "were patronizing *Irma la Douce* and *Under the Yum Yum Tree*." Wishengrad noted how well this affirmed humorist Harry Hershfield's* jest that "If it's a

---

* Hershfield is not to be confused with Al Hirschfeld, though both were cartoonists. For many years, Hirschfeld decorated *The New York Times*' Arts and Leisure section with impressions of the latest big opening, hiding in the artwork renditions of the

play about Jews, the Christians won't come and the Jews will want passes."

The Wall was a notable understatement as a Billy Rose production. After all, this was the man whose idea of theatre was something like three thousand people enjoying Rodgers and Hart during a trapeze act. But then, the later Billy Rose was known less as a producer than as the husband of Eleanor Holm. Theirs was a showy lifestyle, with a town house in Beekman Place just like Auntie Mame and a country home in Mt. Kisco filled with antique furniture and expensive art. In a Madison Avenue shop, the Roses were looking at a dilapidated chair with an asking price of seven hundred dollars. It seemed steep. "But it's genuine Louis the Fourteenth," the clerk told them. Rose thought the chair not only broken down but too small. "Show me a Louis the Sixteenth," he said.

It was pretend dumb; remember, Rose had done his listening. He liked to tell these stories on himself and had his press agents send them around for publication. Here's another: as a country squire, Rose had to learn to drive, and Holm elected to teach him. A nervous student, Rose asked what to do if the brakes fail.

"Hit something cheap," she suggested.

She was as tough as he was, and when their marriage fell apart in the mid-1950s she hired Louis Nizer, the most taking divorce lawyer of his day, one of the first to be Attorney To the Stars. By 1966, when Rose died, he was the opposite of what Toscanini had become by *his* death, in 1957. Rose was a kind of famous has-been. Toscanini departed the earth with his reputation intact and his music echoing on countless recordings. If anything, Toscanini died more celebrated—and beloved—than ever.

The two men's funeral services are instructive. Toscanini's was held in St. Patrick's Cathedral, and the body was then flown to Italy for burial after a state funeral. Milan's Piazza della Scala was filled to the utmost, and the many thousands then trailed after a cortège of uniformed guards,

name of his daughter, Nina. The Martin Beck Theatre, on Forty-fifth Street, was renamed for him. Harry Hershfield was best known for the comic strip *Abie the Agent,* about businessman Abe Kabibble. Sample jest: Abe assembles a fancy library of classics, *Ivanhoe* among them. When found reading a library copy, he explains, "Why should I ruin my fine editions?"

officers, and family surrounding the hearse on its way to the cemetary. There everyone stood at attention as a huge chorus drawn from the opera, Italian radio, and the Conservatory of Music sang "Va, pensiero," from Verdi's *Nabucco,* possibly the most famous chorus in Italian culture. In 1901, at Verdi's funeral, Toscanini had led the singing of this number. Now they sang it to him.

Billy Rose's funeral takes us back to New York. It was held at his "other" theatre, partly because a smallish crowd was expected and partly because Rose had destined the Ziegfeld for the wrecking ball. Buying up the smallholders' properties adjacent to the theatre, Rose had assembled a lot for commercial development in the rebuilding of Sixth Avenue with office towers from Forty-second to Fifty-seventh Streets. He had, in fact, doomed one of New York's most cherished possessions, even if it always had been, in its own way, forty-five minutes from Broadway.* It would have been blasphemy to eulogize Rose in the house that he chose to destroy.

So they gathered in the Billy Rose. The deceased drew a decent congregation, although wags borrowed an old Hollywood joke to observe that everyone showed up to be certain Rose was dead. It was an uneventful event. A rabbi spoke, giving of course no voice at all to what was on the minds of those assembled. Most of them truly did hate Rose— for his arrogance, rudeness, underhanded dealings, and his belief that (in his own words) a man should be judged "by the size of the check he can write."

And yet. As a citizen of the New York entertainment world of that time, Rose couldn't help but see the higher culture as a partner of the lower culture. It wasn't the size of a man's check but the size of his

---

* One problem that dogged the Ziegfeld's location that is seldom if ever mentioned today was the difficulty in finding an empty taxicab when the shows broke, at 11:30. (Curtain time in those days was 8:30, not 8:00.) That section of Sixth Avenue was almost completely deserted after hours, and few hack drivers bothered to cruise it for fares. Usually, parties had to fight one another for the cabs that dropped riders at the Warwick Hotel, across the street, or walk up to Seventh Avenue. One wonders how that "glittering audience" found its way to the Waldorf-Astoria for *Seven Lively Arts'* first-night jamboree.

ambitions. The popular had become venturesome and flexible, attractive to artists. It was still sexy and vital, but it dared its practitioners to idealize it. Rose may be a poor example of the aspiring popmaster, true. His sometime PR agent Richard Maney thought he had "neither the taste nor the talent to triumph in the theatre," adding a crushing epitaph, in the light of Rose's inspiration: "Ziegfeld's crown never fit him." Why, then, was Rose so successful? "He [had] a skill," Maney admitted, "at selling his product."

We often hear this said of achievers who bestrew their way with enemies freshly made—David Merrick, for instance. Yet how can you sell what folks won't buy? Maybe Rose had no skill but rather an instinct about this moment in the history of Western Civilization, when its highest art became embedded in the daily life of the American people and when some of its most gifted artists flattered the creative potential of its lowest art. Or when an Italian symphony conductor became a rock star by fusing the concepts of art and liberty at a time when the two were under mortal assault by totalitarian wreckers. Billy Rose, with his dealing and lying and Tinkertoy media proclamations, never got out of the neighborhood, but Toscanini never really had a neighborhood: he was as big as music.

9

Who Killed Society?

Looking for a name with which to center the meaning of Society in the years between the world wars, rather as "Mrs. Astor" centered it in the late nineteenth century, we find none. There is no queen of the realm and not even a few scuffling duchesses in contention for the title. We recall Frederick Townsend Martin's "After Mrs. Astor there was chaos," but, really, after Mrs. Astor there was nothing. Society vanished.

That is, it went on functioning in its unseen world of clubs and balls, observing etiquette's intricate tick-tock, intermarrying, and deploring the lowering of standards. But the balls got much less press now, and Social folk seemed less colorful than their grandparents.

Then, too, from the Algonquinites on, the new elite of arts and letters appropriated Society's coverage with their bons mots and their very public presence on the stage and radio and in film. They even replaced Society as Public Millionaires Number One, though we know from Dorothy Parker's example alone that fame isn't necessarily congruent with financial security. The general public assumes that creative people who become prominent must be highly paid, as if every writer got Bill Clinton's book deal, as if all actors were movie stars. In fact, it was the great irony of the new elite that it drew its pay primarily in new coin: visibility. Old-school

Society was well off but physically unavailable, a list of names. The new elite was not just names but faces.

Even some of Society—at least its new-school members—took part. We must draw back to a famous moment in 1919, when Maury Paul—professionally the gossip writer Cholly Knickerbocker of the *New York Journal-American*—was dining in the Ritz Hotel. This is the Ritz mentioned in the Cole Porter song quoted earlier, and from Paul's own cozy little corner he caught sight of grandees heretofore veiled from the public's gaze—"a Widener," Paul noted, "a Goelet, a Corrigan, and a Warren all together" at a single table. These Society leaders had been graduated from At Homes on the family plate: they were eating out! In the next day's piece, Paul reported on this close encounter of the third kind, dubbing it "café society."

This returns us to Ellin Mackay Berlin's *New Yorker* piece, "Why We Go To Cafés." But now, from our contemporary vantage, we finally learn why: it was easier. Punctilio was suddenly so corny. Worse: unfashionable, and what was the elite without fashion? Planning elaborate dinner parties as if they were state dinners had become pre-modern. Employing hordes of servants was pre-modern. Having hard-on contests over whose ancestors were bigger was pre-modern. Rules against enjoying yourself were pre-modern. And regarding yourself as elite though you were nothing more than a descendant with money while it was others who were quizzed by and quoted in the press was incorrect. You weren't elite. You were a has-been.

This chapter's title echoes that of Cleveland Amory's book of 1960, a history of and tour through Society while asking what became of it. Most of those interviewed in *Who Killed Society?* didn't know, though one respondent—Florence Nightingale Graham, the cosmetics empress known as Elizabeth Arden—had an arresting reply. "I don't think Society means a thing any more," she said. "I've even noticed it with the horses."

Others were less elliptical. One accused Elsa Maxwell of the fatal deed. Right you are, if Maxwell be taken by synecdoche for the urge toward not only café society but "publiciety": the system by which heretofore exclusive social loops condoned seeing their names in the papers and their privacy compromised—or even actively commissioned deputies to arrange it. Maxwell always had some couple in tow who paid her to "launch" them in this very way, packing them into her entourage at parties and cajoling her press contacts to paragraph them.

Maxwell once did this for a couple that didn't exist. With Cole Porter's connivance, she launched Mr. and Mrs. S. Beech Fitch, newly rich on Oklahoma oil and filling the tattle columns with their exploits in Europe. One read of their charitable donations, their travel plans, a papal audience. Porter even sent to the press letters signed by Mr. Fitch and other members of the clan, all of whom were an invention. Then a death notice was mailed out, and Maury Paul and Walter Winchell exposed the hoax, having been apprised by Porter in time for a musical-comedy funeral. His show *Gay Divorce* (1932) was about to open, and *Gay Divorce*'s tunestack included "Mister and Missus Fitch," a specialty number for Luella Gear. Coming forward after a plot scene, Gear simply started in on the saga of the couple enthusiastically adopted by "the crowd they call 'elite'" till the Crash despoils the Fitches of their only attraction, their spending power. So it was all a dream—or, really, a fantasy about something real: readers' hunger to learn about those who have what the rest of us don't. Whether it was money, fame, looks, or talent, it redefined the elite: they were news now.

Who was Elsa Maxwell? After a start playing piano in vaudeville and in movie theatres during the silent era, Maxwell earned her income by no profession known to the dictionary: promoting and hustling in the world of the rich and famous. Party thrower to the stars might be a modern-day description, though it doesn't quite cover it. With Maxwell's help, the unknown—like Mister and Missus Fitch—became prominent and the prominent became Names of the Day. Maxwell also produced celebrations on behalf of individuals and organizations, usually with her trademark scavenger hunts, centered on a list so dodgy that gamers could attract the curiosity of the police. Further, Maxwell performed favors of a delicate social nature, with the unspoken understanding that she would be tipped with a jeweled trinket suitable for resale; and that's how Elsa Maxwell earned her living.

Everyone liked her, because she was too unattractive to threaten and had a keen sense of fun. Her enthusiasm filled ballrooms, as she flattered and agreed and called anyone you named "an angel" and "my most intimate friend." Moss Hart (and Cole Porter again) based a character on her in *Jubilee* (1935) that is as close to the original as skin. Note how blithely Maxwell—here called Eva Standing—imposes on a friend and how fiercely she edits her favorites list:

EVA: Laura, my sweet, this is Mr. and Mrs. Watkins of Kansas City—I'm showing them the town. They're *angels*—you'll *adore* them. . . . Darling— what are you doing tonight? You *must* come to my party. *Everyone* is coming . . . Laura, *do* be a dear and lend me your house for the party— mine's being decorated for the party *tomorrow* night! *Do* be an angel!

LAURA: Of course.

EVA: Isn't she *wonderful!* My favorite person of the *world!* . . . Have you enough champagne? There'll be about three hundred! . . . Heifetz wanted to play for me, but I wouldn't let him. I've *turned* on violinists.

MRS. WATKINS: Jascha Heifetz?

EVA: My most *intimate* friend! I discovered him, you know—gave him his first violin. He didn't have a G string to his name.

One cannot blame Maxwell alone for the murder of Society, because she was simply riding the wave of history more noticeably than the rest of her pack. It was The Column that killed Society, for it solemnized the transition from an aristocracy of families and manners to one of notoriety and talent. And that aristocracy held court in the most famous place in America that was not a landmark or a theatre or sports arena. It opened as a brownstone basement speakeasy on West Fifty-eighth Street in 1929, moved once and then again, in 1935, to its permanent location, on Fifty-third Street just east of Fifth Avenue. It closed in 1965, but its era had ended before then—the era of Winchell and Runyon at Table 50, because of course it is the Stork Club we speak of. This was where The Column came to be seen.

Seen, that is, not only by each other but by the entire nation, because the Stork had its own press corps snapping pictures of the Names at the Tables to send copies to the media for publicietization. European movie stars—so Tyrone Power knows Rex Harrison! Plutocrats with their as a rule Beautiful Wives. Broadway figures winding down after a show. People thought social, people thought outlaw, and people thought influential. Who went to the Stork? Anyone who could get in, except the disapproving Mayor La Guardia.

As for how the place got its name: no one knows, including Sherman Billingsley, its owner, manager, and passionate lover. To run the Stork Club was to control the celebration of the most powerful folk in the land. Paraphrasing Ben Kingsley in the movie *Schindler's List,* the Stork is life. When Billingsley opened the first Stork Club, the one on Fifty-eighth Street, the logo visual showed a red stork standing in water against a light-blue background with a swaddled infant hanging from its beak. By the time Billingsley reached Fifty-third Street, the stork was sleek and simple—confident, as befits a place destined to become The Place. The infant was gone and, against a black background, the animal now bore a top hat and stood on one leg, the other rakishly bent. He seemed to be winking at the viewer.

It was one of the most iconic sights in the theatre of the elite—along with the checkroom, the bar, the main room, and the Cub Room (for the elite's elite, where Table 50 stood); the little bands for dancing; the courtesy gifts of Sulka ties, Tiffany cigarette lighters, and perfume (the house brand, Sortilege), all on Billingsley's personal whim; and the famous black ashtrays with white "Stork Club" lettering on the sides and a slit for the color-coordinated Stork Club matchbook, more or less expected to be slipped into your date's purse as a souvenir.* Less immediately visual was the flashy smog of big money that went along with the big fame and big power. The Stork was where tippers of legendary extravagance came to effect the gesture of their careers; one night, the maitre d' got twenty thousand dollars.

It was quite a jump in the life of Billingsley, who was born in Okla-

---

* Also on the tables were the less celebrated bud vases, in the form of the logo stork holding a clear plastic tube in which a single flower sat. They were too bulky to steal, though some found a way. Like the ashtrays and matchbooks, the bud vases do a snappy business on eBay.

homa before statehood, when it was still a territory, and who got into rumrunning during Prohibition. He even did time in Leavenworth, and those who knew him in his Stork years noted the nasty edge of the desperado under the tailoring. At that, Billingsley's first Stork opened when the mob was running Jimmy Walker's New York, and Billingsley had to operate under the "protection" of Owney Madden's crew. Not till the late 1930s was Billingsley finally free of their hold, after Dutch Schultz's assassination and the retreat of Madden and his associate Frenchy De Mange to Hot Springs, Arkansas. It must have helped, too, that J. Edgar Hoover and *his* Beautiful Wife, Clyde Tolson, were Stork enthusiasts; continued gangland harassment of Billingsley would have been not a Manhattan secret but a national scandal. Quite simply, the Stork Club had become essential to the culture's romance with "Broadway."

Billingsley thus became as necessary to the maintenance of Manhattan lore and legend as Winchell and Runyon, or as Dorothy Parker and Dorothy Thompson. Securing a top-okay adulterous girl friend in Ethel Merman, Billingsley owned as well the fealty of the entire celebrity calendar, out of fear of being banned from the Stork. (This occasionally happened, especially when someone showed up drunk and irritable.) Today we speak of "micro-management"; Billingsley might have invented it. He patrolled his domain obsessively, demanding not only the usual loyalty but vigilance and concentration from his subordinates. To bestow upon favorite guests a gift, the freedom of the bar, or an on-the-house tab, Billingsley employed a signal code. He even had one—cupping his ear—for "Save me from these squares by calling me to the phone."

When he launched the Fifty-third Street location, Billingsley tried touting the place as a Society nightspot, where the younger blades and damsels might relax. He even featured a Society orchestra, with a bandleader and singer drawn from the *Social Register*. However, that wasn't where the power resided by 1935. Social names meant nothing unless they belonged to the grandest families, and those people cannot be lured. They aren't in the business of making places chic; the place must achieve chic first.

Besides, Billingsley was feeling his way into a success story like that of Irving Berlin or Ethel Waters. He had nothing in common with them save his origin in poverty—but each in his different way was part of this new meaning of Broadway in its broadest sense. It was nationalized show biz, America's most apparent industry, the jobs everybody in the country wanted. Berlin wrote America's national anthem. Waters crystallized the national singing style. And Billingsley opened the national "hotel" favored by the grandees of Western Civilization, from Shakespearean actors to the leisure-class parasites attendant upon the Duke and Duchess of Windsor.

So the Stork Club was indeed the "Mecca for celebrities all over the world," just as Billingsley said it was. Well, not Billingsley himself: actor Bill Goodwin *playing* Billingsley in Paramount's 1945 film *The Stork Club*. The studio paid Billingsley one hundred thousand dollars to exploit the name and premises, building sound-stage replicas of the bar, checkroom, kitchen, main room, Cub Room, and even Billingsley's office, the only spot that isn't crammed to blazes. As befits the subject matter, an in-crowd mentality informs the doings, as when the maitre d' warns Goodwin's Billingsley that "Lieutenant and Mrs. Robert Taylor" have arrived. "Oh," comes the reply, "that would be Ruby Stevens."*

The Stork Club told of the romance between hat-check girl Betty Hutton and bandleader-in-marine-uniform Don De Fore, but the movie was made specifically to let the nation "visit" the shrine, to see where the famous went to stay famous. The script was the work of B. G. De Sylva (who also produced) and John McGowan, veterans of the Broadway musical at the start of its Golden Age, in the 1920s and 1930s. Yet there is little of the saucy charm we associate with that timeplace; the film is Hollywood product to its toes. It does give us one musical-comedy highlight in a number for Hutton and a men's quartet, "Doctor, Lawyer, Indian Chief," by Hoagy Carmichael and Paul Francis Webster. Hutton is known for her "enter pursuing a bear" energy, but here she judges perfectly the balance between hot swing and nonchalance that the song needs. Adding zany dance steps to her vocal and gaming with the vocal-backup

---

* Devotees of Column life of course knew that "Ruby Stevens" was Barbara Stanwyck, Taylor's then wife, before she went on the stage.

boys, Hutton created a deathless cameo that remains an article of faith among Hollywood fans to this day.

Of special interest to us is *The Stork Club*'s supporting cast, for our old drinking buddy Robert Benchley plays an attorney in his appealingly unacted acting that tells us why his friends genuinely liked him. Benchley's comic gifts consist of not getting his own jokes. When De Fore, mistakenly thinking that Benchley is making a play for Hutton, beefily confronts him, De Fore says, "There's only one thing I want from you!" And Benchley, without a hint of irony, replies, "Well, I hope I've got it."

If you were wondering how the Algonquin corps were getting on by 1945, the answer is: poorly. Heywood Broun had died six years before, at the age of fifty-one. He got a funeral on the grand scale, a rare event attended by both Walter Winchell and Mayor La Guardia. Alexander Woollcott followed Broun in 1943, aged fifty-six, stricken with a heart attack while on the air. George S. Kaufman had just embarked on a five-year losing streak; then he collided with Damon Runyon as director of *Guys and Dolls* (1950), not only an eventual classic but seen at the time as an outstanding experience. Kaufman's career was spotty after that. Still, he died more or less on top, in 1961, a year after Franklin P. Adams died senile and penniless. In 1945, however, Adams was a panelist on a popular radio show, *Information Please*.

Dorothy Parker's 1945 was less happy: of course. She had more or less ordered her hearse, though the Last Ride wouldn't occur till 1967. For now, Parker was just hitching. She spent the mid-1940s doing very little work, selling or optioning stories to the movie studios and divorcing Alan Campbell, whom she would remarry. It was Parker who started the rumor that Campbell was gay, partly because she liked mixing everybody up about the facts of her life but also because Campbell was a sweetheart, eager to please, and Parker thought of men as edgy and ungiving. A nice one had to be queer. But she outlived them all, the last of the Round Table to leave us. Her beloved Robert Benchley died the year he shot *The Stork Club*, at fifty-six.

One interesting aspect of Manhattan's new elite was its lack of leadership. The Round Table did function with Policy Authority in a limited way, but the diners had dispersed by 1930. Walter Winchell could be regarded as a monarch of a certain kind, but his vassals were unruly in their hearts and, as we'll shortly see, seized their first chance to dethrone him. Others had leadership quality in the influence of their art—Cole Porter comes to mind, as the essence of mid-century sophistication. But the elites of Broadway comprised a set of interconnected autonomies without a centralizing figure. So, indeed, after Mrs. Astor there was chaos.

Or: after Mrs. Astor there was Barbara Hutton. Here is a twice-told tale, to put it mildly—the unloved and lonely child who takes a lifetime to realize what none of us wants to believe: that money really can't buy happiness. Early on, Barbara discovered that people seemed to like her when she gave them cash or expensive gifts—a fur coat to the sales girl who helped her pick out a half-dozen of them, a Rolls-Royce to some guy who got her a drink at a party. She was an impossible combination of eccentric and stubborn, impervious to good advice—and, right to the end of her days, she impulsively distributed her wealth with a generosity that could be called thrilling if it hadn't been so pointless. Because in fact people didn't like her because of her money. They liked her money.

Born in New York in 1912, Barbara Hutton lost her mother at the age of four and was raised here and there by relatives other than her uninterested father. So Barbara became a citizen of the world. She eventually built or bought palatial homes in London (twice), Cuernavaca, Pacific Palisades, Tangier, and Palm Beach, and often lived in hotels: because no matter where she was or what she was doing, she kept jumping up and darting off to somewhere else. Coming into forty-two million dollars on her twenty-first birthday, in 1933, she was of course a magnet for fortune-hunters, and she was a pushover for a hunk with a line. That's when you *know* you're loved—not by sales girls or that obliging guy at a party, but a Suave Handsome Man, the kind who can have anyone he wants: and he wants you.

Barbara's Suave Handsome Men were mostly Europeans. It's a classic plotline, from Henry James to Danielle Steel: the titled ladykiller, the sympathetic cousin (Barbara's was Dina Merrill), the continental confidante who favors the match yet spills all the secrets to Mercedes de Acosta, and of course the disapproving father, thundering about these truffle hounds sniffing out their next American fortune. In James' day, only the communicants and the servants would know what was happening, but Barbara inherited her fortune in Walter Winchell's day, so everybody knew. It was a fable of the time: Irving Berlin's aforementioned "newspaper" revue, *As Thousands Cheer*, devoted one bit to Barbara and her transatlantic popinjays. Headlined as BARBARA HUTTON TO WED PRINCE MDIVANI, the scene presented the heiress herself (Marilyn Miller) being wooed by four princes of the blood, French, Italian, German, and Austrian. Crowded out of access is Mdivani (Clifton Webb), a Russian. "How's Chances?" is the number, and in real life Mdivani's chances were good, even if the press kept linking Barbara to other men. In fact, she had already married Mdivani by the time *As Thousands Cheer* opened, and she would marry again and again, seven times in all:

Alexis Mdivani	notorious opportunist
Court (also spelled Kurt) von Haugwitz-Reventlow	abusive bully and snob
Cary Grant	movie star
Igor Troubetskoy	penniless prince and cyclist
Porfirio Rubirosa	reckless international playboy
Gottfried von Cramm	longtime friend and baron
Raymond Doan Vinh Na Champassak	Vietnamese painter

If Barbara thought nothing of giving fabulous presents to strangers, imagine what she gave to each husband before the nuptials, during the marriage, and as a go-away fee at the divorce. Millions, every time, with one exception. Worse, these consorts-for-hire did not even trouble to keep up the act once the conjugal papers were signed, becoming generally unavailable or offensively controlling. The exception was Cary Grant. Though he was famously stingy with his own money, he had no designs on Barbara's. Indeed, he seems to have been the one husband who genuinely loved her, tried to make a marriage with her, and, when it failed, took no financial settlement from her. The union, though, was strained from the start by Barbara's insistence on filling her household with servants, a court of sycophants, and plenty of drop-ins. Grant valued privacy. Like all his ex-wives, she never spoke ill of him and eventually came to think of him as My Favorite Husband. Reporters liked him, too, because they could call the pair "Cash and Cary."

Some Column readers saw in Barbara the successor to Mrs. Astor and what she had represented, simply because of all that money. In fact, Barbara and Mrs. Astor were separated by more than their two generations in age. For one thing, no one of Mrs. Astor's era would have indulged in serial divorce. Anyway, the Woolworths and Huttons weren't Family the way Caroline Schermerhorn Astor's Knickerbocker derivation was; and the Woolworth fortune, after all, came from trade, and recently at that.

Edna Ferber catches a paradox of Society in *Saratoga Trunk:* money mattered, but if you had enough family, you didn't need the money. The novel is set mainly in the world of the hotel resort of the Gilded Age, and while the ferocious sixty-seven-year-old Clarissa Van Steed appears to rule that world, she is deathly afraid of the impoverished Sophie Bellop. Bellop is true Society, virtually a princess of the blood. Next to her, "The Goulds, the Vanderbilts, the Astors, the Belmonts" are "upstarts." And Mrs. Bellop gets around: "Every hotel register was an open book to her. She knew how much the faro dealers were paid; which actually were secretaries and which were not in the cottages of the lonely millionaires whose wives were in Europe; had the most terrific inside political information about the doings . . . of the late Boss Tweed. . . . She boasted that she was helping General Ulysses S. Grant with his memoirs; she gossiped with Mark Twain."

The problem with the upstart Society patrolled by Goulds and Vanderbilts is that, once they get in, they insist that the entry be barred to all who follow, sealing their world from the dynamic and contemporary. This encourages parvenus to create their own social system: by spending. True, the ceremonies attendant upon Barbara's debut, in 1930, were supported by Astors, Belmonts, and Biddles, among others. The series of parties took in a tea dance at home and dinner at the Central Park Casino, topped by a ball hosted by Maurice Chevalier and featuring party favors of tiny gold jewelry boxes containing a free-range assortment of precious stones from sapphires to diamonds. It was the debutante rite to outdo all others; it was meant to be. But that was a problem, too. Society liked luxury but not ostentation. Barbara's coming-out ball was reminiscent of the Bradley-Martin fiasco at the old Waldorf—which, remember, was similarly held during a major slowdown in the economy.

Such concerns amounted to fine print to most Column readers, because Barbara was the Woolworth heiress and everybody went to Woolworth's. This chain of "five and dimes," as they were commonly known, began when Frank Winfield Woolworth, Barbara's grandfather, expanded from a few outlets on various Main Streets to an international empire of, in effect, department stores for the masses. Woolworth bought in volume to sell at discount, and he constantly added new features to the standard inventory of ladies' notions, dry goods, and household gadgets, tweaking one's shopping from a chore into an adventure. The Woolworth's toy departments virtually invented the inexpensive-toy industry by creating a demand for it, and Woolworth's lunch counter became a cultural staple—so much so that, years later, pioneers in racial integration blitzed a segregated southern Woolworth's dinette: because the name "Woolworth's" resonated. Then, too, the chain supplied American youth with a social sphere because of the outlets' central locations; and browsing provided entertainment while you waited for your gang to assemble.

It was a dream of a business, and F. W. Woolworth was thus enabled to raise his own skyscraper, the Woolworth Building, down on Broadway opposite City Hall Park. At 729 feet and one inch, it was the tallest building in the world for seventeen years, and Woolworth paid for its cost—$15,500,000.00—in cash. So Barbara's taking possession of that forty-two million on her legal seniority—however immature she proved to be in character—bore an undeniable logic, even at the depth of the Depression. After all, *someone* had to be rich and carefree, and who better than than the granddaughter of a man who pays in cash—and buys retail!

The reason why Barbara's millions were a talking point among everyone in the country was that chaos that followed Mrs. Astor, because it wasn't Society that had been killed. It was honor: the pride in being known about only by those one knew. Your name was no longer entirely yours; anyone could finger it, play catch with it, use it in vain. And nobody minded till he or she got caught in some act—or, in Barbara's case, spending vast amounts on trinkets and the international laughing-stocks she married. The underpaid clerks in the family stores kept demanding that Barbara alleviate their hard lot, but she had no say in the business. Nor did she take an interest in it. She may never even have set foot in a Woolworth's in her life.

Barbara Hutton and the Stork Club do not properly come as a set—she was too seldom in New York to be a Stork Club regular. Still, together they bring us up to speed on where the concept of the elite stood by the end of the 1940s. The ascendance of "Barbara Hutton" as a summoning term for Society proves that "Society" no longer denoted—as in our old definition—a ruling class leading dramatic lives and setting fashion. Barbara's life was less dramatic than pathetic, even ludicrous. She had no relationship whatsoever with those who ruled, unlike the understanding that bonded—though secretly—Knickerbocker aristos and Tammany Hall. And she set no fashion.* If Barbara was Social, then all that the word meant now was "rich and exposed."

This could be said of the Stork Club as well. Like Barbara, Sherman Billingsley popularized a new angle on who the elite were, and it had little to do with the writers, composers, performers, and thinkers we have dealt with in earlier chapters. As one looked around the Stork, one saw "the crust," le tout New York. Even the *Encyclopédie des très connus du monde*. However, one saw little of the intelligentsia, which is really what a true crust includes: the artists and essayists who mix with the nobility in the great salons. Dorothy Thompson might have visited the Stork once, to collect the experience, but the more discreet "21" would have been more comfortable for her—if she had a night place at all. Like most politicals, she preferred her own dining table, where one

---

*One of her rivals did. During Barbara's brief entanglement with Porfirio Rubirosa—the marriage itself lasted nine weeks—the playboy was still playing on and off with his primary light of love, Zsa Zsa Gabor. When "Rubi" supposedly slugged her, Zsa Zsa appeared in public with a Captain Kidd eyepatch that became the rage. Television comics did routines in them, showgirl lines were issued them, and bold hostesses from San Diego to Worcester received in them, to the envy of all.

could wrangle over the Sityashun for hours without being harassed by table-hoppers or forced to endure the owner's great-world badinage.

There was something else missing from a general lookaround of the Stork Club on any given night: black people. They had made tremendous gains in the 1930s and 1940s in show biz, and, as I've said, this tends to precede the making of gains in the social structure of the nation. One might state it as Ethel Waters + *Porgy and Bess* = Jackie Robinson and *Brown v. the Board of Education of Topeka*. Billingsley, however, was an unredeemed product of his poor-white Oklahoma background, hostile to racial integration. Further, he was neither a theatregoer nor a reader of books nor a music buff. He lived entirely in his club, and was quite as unaware of how the arts had changed American life as Barbara Hutton was of the day-to-day workings of the Woolworth stores.

So blacks were not welcome at the Stork Club, even, in the main, those of prominence. One day, a black performer decided to do something about that, and the idea of who the elite were got redefined once again.

The 1950s

10

The War On the Column

In 1951, when Josephine Baker embarked on a nationwide American tour in her cabaret act, she was very different from the kid who energized the *Shuffle Along* tour, lit up Paris, and suffered failure back home in *Ziegfeld Follies of 1936*. She was now forty-five, in splendid physique yet too arrived and grand to play the gamine. She still danced a bit and hadn't lost her sense of fun, but the zany pleasure baby was gone, replaced by a glamor diva *en grande toilette*. Her French had greatly improved despite a thick American accent, and she acquired smatterings of other languages in order to address her public intimately no matter where she performed.

Above all, Baker had distilled her vocal style into the true art of the diseuse ("speaker of lyrics": in effect, "one who uses the music to get to the *words*"). She used her head voice (the soprano range) much less than before, slipping down into the compass of an Édith Piaf, lowering the keys of her signature numbers just enough to darken the timbre. The repertory, too, had become more intriguing, in a broad miscellany ranging from novelties in South American rhythm to deeply-felt ballads. In fact, Baker had transformed herself, from goofy dancer to mistress of song, alternating a velvety legato with a stabbing attack that made every selection a surprise. In the flowing waltz "La Seine," in the calypso "Don't Touch Me Tomatoes," in a medley binding Charles Trenet's "En Avril à Paris" with Vernon Duke's "April in Paris," Baker glided from mood to mood, form to form. She was *réaliste* and *fantaisiste* at once, incorporating the polar opposites of French cabaret as if she was bigger than song itself.

Unfortunately, her mercurial personality had got more mercurial than ever, more paradoxical and maddeningly fixed on her needs alone. Here was a woman of the world who had never outgrown a narrow cultural background: the kid from St. Louis thrust into Western Civilization without having read last night's assignment. Her lack of education and even common knowledge led her to dabble in unworthy issues or try to cross impassable gulfs. She wore the badge of a hater of tyranny and served the French Resistance with courage, yet she befriended the fascist regime of Juan and Eva Perón. A practicing Catholic, she pursued an interest in the Freemasons, not realizing that the Masons and the church are mortal enemies. When she decided to try motherhood, she adopted—twelve children, close in age—and made a point of securing her charges from different races and nations to create her (as she termed it) Rainbow Tribe. She took over a château in the Dordogne, Les Mirandes, renaming it Les Milandes because she never did master that tiny gargle of the French "r," and there she set about raising her family. But was this real life or an experiment? And what happens when all twelve siblings reach the usual mischievous adolescence and Maman is off earning their living? Baker was one of those outstanding beings who were wildly loved and wildly hated: by the same people. Because she was fascinating but drove you nuts. Because she was as ungrateful as she was generous, so ignorant yet so talented. The closest parallel to her I can name is Greta Garbo, similarly unique in a crowded profession, comparably heedless of others' feelings, and, like Baker, the one everybody wanted to know.

The 1951 tour was going very, very well. Baker had always had the gods' blessing; now she had that of the land of her birth. And then, one night, she happened to go to the Stork Club.

Or that's one way of putting it. You might instead say that, having conquered American audiences, she now intended to conquer American racial mores. You might even imagine that, given her intensely political nature and her habit of heading avidly toward confrontation of any kind, she had arrived in the U.S. to get uppity.

Certainly, the Stork Club escapade seems to have been far less accidental than it was popularly thought to be. And of course there are contradicting versions of what took place that night. Still, the core content is indisputable: Baker's party got extremely slow service, and because she needed to put a name on the issue of the Stork Club's racial bigotry, she blamed the genius of the place, Walter Winchell. In fact, he was innocent of involvement in Baker's humiliation, but not of promoting a system of exclusion that—like Winchell himself—was headquartered at the Stork. Once Baker launched the hostilities, she went back to France while others, many others, took up the battle for her. It lasted some ten years, and when it was over both Winchell and the Stork Club were terminated.

The hard data—on the historic night of October 16, 1951—tell of a party of four seated in the Cub Room. They were Roger and Solange Rico, Bessie Buchanan, and Baker. Buchanan was one of Baker's old show-biz pals, by then nursing political ambitions. (She in fact became the first black woman elected to the New York State legislature.) Rico was playing Emile de Becque in *South Pacific,* having taken over the role from Ezio Pinza's replacement, Ray Middleton. Even if we count as well the fourth de Becque, George Britton, Rico was the only one with a natural affinity for the part, as he was French with a colonial (Algerian) background; de Becque is a Frenchman who has become a planter in a foreign clime. Rico's usual day job was at the Paris Opéra, where he maintained a distinguished if not brilliant presence. His Méphistophèles in Gounod's *Faust,* for instance, was stylish and elegant but lacked the tear-up-the-stage charisma that Pinza brought to the role at the Met.

Rico and his wife were Stork Club regulars, and he was aware of the club's racial policy, which was no different from that of the city's other high-end nightspots. As the story goes, Rico troubled to ask others if there might be a problem, and he was told that, as Baker was doing top business at a club called the Roxy, her fame would be more interesting to Billingsley than her race.

Winchell was at the Stork that night, too, but not for long. Given the 8:30 curtain prevalent at the time, *South Pacific* broke just before 11:30, and Winchell was heading for a midnight press screening. So Baker's opportunity to say hello and thank him for his effusive support of her American comeback lasted a few minutes at most.

Meanwhile, the Rico party got its drink order but not its food. Service at the Stork was generally slow, especially during the after-theatre shift. However, the waiters seemed to be pointedly ignoring Rico's attempts to get their attention. Nothing happened in the Stork unless Billingsley wanted it to, so the obvious conclusion was that Baker was being deliberately humiliated. Turning the foursome away at the door might have provoked a scene; frustrating Baker at the table veiled the bigotry.

Billingsley must have assumed that Baker would simply leave and never come back. He didn't realize how intensely she took up her causes, or that the visit was, in effect, a raid—though it was not Baker who had targeted the Stork but Bessie Buchanan. Her intimates felt that her political aspirations needed an incident with maximum publicity value; the Stork was ideal, not least because Billingsley had so many enemies. Ironically, Buchanan was too light-skinned to count on discriminatory aggression, and in any case she needed a celebrity to center the news coverage. Baker, at the height of her American fame, made a tasty victim, and the Stork Club was the perfect storm.

With her characteristic impulsiveness, Baker placed a call to Walter White, the chief functionary of the NAACP. Not the next day: that very night. Baker didn't even wait to get out of the Stork Club first, using the pay phone up front. She then proceeded to White's apartment at what must have been something like two o'clock in the morning, following that up by trying to crash Barry Gray's late-night radio show at Chandler's Restaurant. Gray, too, had an affinity for causes, but Gray's airtime ended at 3:00 A.M., and Baker arrived after signoff. She would appear with Gray two months later, but in the meantime Baker consulted with various sages while considering an interesting option. Why spend energy going after the Stork and Billingsley? The club was an abstraction, really, and Billingsley's name didn't mean anything outside of New York. Instead, why not cut through the wrapping to get to the content: Walter Winchell himself?

The scheme had traps to play past, however. The third one was that no one ever took on Winchell because of his absolute power. Warring with Winchell meant alienating supporters and losing bookings. The second trap was Winchell's outstanding record on race relations. But the first trap was that Winchell was innocent of any involvement in the incident at hand, as he left soon after the Baker party arrived.

None of this mattered to Baker. She felt that, even if Winchell wasn't to blame, The Column was. The case was bigger than the Stork, bigger than the Jim Crow attitudes that permeated society. This was a matter of that unfairness of everything, as if Baker were a Saxon in Norman England. Winchell's Broadway condoned a ceiling on the acceptance of blacks, like an aristocratic elite closed to penetration by new talents that ultimately provokes a revolution. Baker was the revolution.

As the press coverage of the story developed legs, the French embassy in Washington, D.C. sent an official to parley with Baker, to no avail. "She did not know the difference," he said, "between what could be done and what could not be done." For her part, Baker made her customary declaration: "I didn't choose this moment," she would insist when forging ahead on the latest quest. "Moments always choose me." And yet all her life, choosing moments was Baker's survival strategy. Whether jumping the line in *Shuffle Along,* walking her cheetah along the Paris boulevards, or, here, passing historical remark on the nature of Stork Club "aristocracy," Baker made sure that everybody knew she was there. And if there is any quality that New Yorkists share, it is a willingness to wage war against the forces that wish to set limits on culture. These are not quiet lives. Prohibition, Charles Lindbergh, bad reviews, the Stork Club . . . it's always something.

Billingsley no doubt expected the whole thing to vanish by the end of the week, and his denials of wrongdoing were unpersuasive in the extreme. He claimed it was Stork Club policy "to cater to clientele made up of peoples of the world, naturally giving preference to those who have been our constant patrons through the years." No. What Billingsley gave preference to was the acknowledged leadership class, and, as for the peoples of the world, everyone in town knew stories about visitors from other cultures who couldn't get past the gold chain. Billingsley should have apologized, called it "one of those things," and made restitution in some way agreeable to the aggrieved. Granted, Baker was probably unappeasable by then. But it was Winchell who blew the ruckus into a riot. He did not defend himself with the facts of the matter. Instead, he did as always when criticized: he attacked.

And thus he affirmed Baker's demonizing of him, fulfilled it. He became what she said he was, a functionary of the status quo and a stooge for Stork Club bigotry. No, he became something worse: a stooge for the scattershot slander of personal enemies that is one of the several meanings of "McCarthyism." Winchell even hobnobbed with McCarthy and his unspeakable devil-on-the-shoulder Roy Cohn.

So the war began, war on the Stork Club in title but war on Winchell in driveline. Winchell fought back with defamation, aided by a few writers exasperated by Baker's various assaults on America. "White men prate of democracy," Baker observed, "and send the Negro to die in Korea." Novelist Robert Ruark responded with "I could have sworn a few white boys were listed in the casualty reports." One of the few singer-dancers in history to maintain a foreign policy, Baker was especially vulnerable for her championing of the Peróns. Even the *New York Post* called Baker "the pin-up girl of Argentine fascism," though the *Post* was no friend to Winchell.

On the contrary. As Baker filed suit against Winchell for libel, then returned to France and dropped the suit to cascade into her next cause, the war on Winchell heated up drastically. Far worse than Baker on Barry Gray's radio show was Ed Sullivan on Barry Gray's radio show, stating his hatred for Winchell and openly calling on Winchell's countless victims to come forth and denounce him.* Nothing like this had

---

*Because Winchell was so identified with Red-baiting, it is forgot that Sullivan, that beloved creator of America's family-hour variety show, was vicious to show-biz figures who got Named. A Sullivan piece in the *Philadelphia Inquirer* headlined TIP TO

ever happened before, for all the anger Winchell had provoked. Even those who had taken notice of Winchell as little as possible found themselves drawn into battle formation: Roger Rico was hustled out of *South Pacific* before his contract was up—shortly after Baker's appearance with Barry Gray. This was presumably because he had involved the show in bad publicity, although, ironically, *South Pacific* deals very strongly with racism and the Stork Club incident was racism dramatized. Wasn't it?

The *New York Post* thought not. The Stork Club incident was about Walter Winchell's abuse of power, his degradation of the English language, his refusal to print retractions even when an item was wrong and had damaged its subject, and his hypocrisy, particularly regarding his longtime use of a ghost named Herman Klurfeld. The overworked and underpaid Klurfeld is well known to today's aficionados of the Winchell saga, but he was a genuine secret at the time the *Post* ran its exposé on Winchell. Everyone thought of Winchell as, among other things, a writer. Indeed, he had been, once. But, long before the 1950s, Winchell had become the inventor of the format in which Herman Klurfeld wrote. Winchell was the architect, but Klurfeld was the builder.

Unveiling Klurfeld was a small part of the *Post*'s assault on Winchell. Not content with a piece or two, *Post* editor James A. Wechsler kept a team of seven reporters on Winchell for two months, digging and revealing. From the start of 1952 until, it seemed, forever, installment followed installment—Winchell and his feuds, Winchell and his ghost, Winchell and Hollywood, Winchell and Miami (his favorite vacation spot). It was there that Wechsler's men actually approached Winchell himself, if only for the time-honored Denial of Charges that newspapers print along with the charges.

Nothing in all that the *Post* said would be news to us, but back then it was revelation: this grandee of grandees was a vindictive little schoolyard

---

RED PROBERS: SUPENA [sic] JEROME ROBBINS warned that Robbins "has a wide familiarity with Commies of all hues." It is an urban legend that Sullivan forced the reluctant Robbins to testify by threatening to out him as gay, though this cannot be documented and may refer to the fear that all gay men had in that age rather than an explicitly stated menace.

bully, as vulnerable as his prey. The spymaster had finally got Columned himself, Winchell Thru a Keyhole. And Winchell reacted like Superman on Kryptonite, suffering a breakdown of some mysterious kind.

What had happened that night at the Stork Club? Why wasn't the *Post* doing a series on the racism problem instead of on the Winchell problem? No doubt for the same reason that Josephine Baker went after Winchell in the first place: a crusade needs a big target, even if he happens to be uninvolved in the casus belli.

What one hears in all this is sheer impatience. A generation after Ethel Waters had broken Broadway's color barrier to a more lasting effect than Bert Williams had, the culture itself was lagging behind. Of course, the culture generally absorbs show biz's lessons in tolerance slowly. Still, Broadway (and to a lesser extent Hollywood) had been racing ahead while society, symbolized by the Stork Club and its Table 50, held the line on color. And enough, Baker must have thought, is enough. If the French don't care, what's America's problem?

In fact, some of Broadway's casting in these years could be looked on as the project of a civics class. In the 1940s, after *Cabin in the Sky,* the smash 1942 revival of *Porgy and Bess,* and *Carmen Jones,* there was a series of nearly or entirely black musicals, from the jiving *Memphis Bound!* (1945) and *St. Louis Woman* (1946) to the tragic *Lost in the Stars* (1949). There were white shows with major black support, from the period *Bloomer Girl* (1944) to the contemporary *Call Me Mister* (1946), a demobilization revue. *Finian's Rainbow* demolished for all time the ancient tradition of keeping the black and white ensembles physically separated on stage— and *Beggar's Holiday* (1946), an updating of *The Beggar's Opera,* treated mixed-race romance.

None of these shows offered black talent a star role in a major production. *Memphis Bound!* gave leads to Bill Robinson and Avon Long, but not in the kind of work that commands media attention. And while *St. Louis Woman* boasted a Harold Arlen–Johnny Mercer score and such performers as the Nicholas Brothers and Pearl Bailey, a lengthy yet strangely eventless book doomed it.

Now, in the 1950s, black players were graduated to Big Broadway, given tailored roles in major productions. Pearl Bailey, with sole–star billing, got *House of Flowers* (1954), Sammy Davis Jr. *Mr. Wonderful* (1956), and Lena Horne *Jamaica* (1957). These were not all-black shows, for *Mr. Wonderful*'s cast was in fact mostly white and the other two employed one or two white non-singing leads. Anyway, more notable history was made a few blocks south on Broadway at the Met, where Marian Anderson became its first black singer, in Verdi's *Un Ballo in Maschera* in 1955: notable because the Met was even more intransigent than the Stork Club. If Mrs. Astor had a ghost, the Met was where she would have taken her opera. It really was more Marian Anderson than Josephine Baker who should have said, "Moments always choose me"—especially the moment when, in 1939, the Daughters of the American Revolution refused their Washington, D.C., concert hall to Anderson and, through Mrs. Roosevelt's intercession, she sang instead on the steps of the Lincoln Memorial.

Then came Anderson's Met debut, right in the middle of Broadway's black star vehicles, as if giving us more of that interplay of classical and pop we remarked in the 1930s. These three musicals unfortunately lacked the *Oklahoma!* or *West Side Story* impact that keeps titles in repertory, and *Mr. Wonderful* was the least imposing of the trio, on a smalltime singer who somewhat reluctantly crashes into stardom. Sammy, of course, was the singer; Chita Rivera was in it, too, though their paths virtually never crossed. Starting at the Bandbox in Union City, New Jersey, Sammy finished in Miami at a gala place called the Palm Club—but, Sammy being Sammy, everyone assumed it was the Fontainebleau Hotel.

We think of the 1950s as a time of quirky shows—*The King and I,* with its two prima donnas in their closeted romance; the semi-classical *Candide* and *The Most Happy Fella*; the Sprechstimme operetta *My Fair Lady;* and that ecstatically depressing *West Side Story;* not to mention those two great mother shows *Gypsy* and *The Sound of Music.* But *Mr. Wonderful* is so conventional it launched both acts with the venerable scene-setting opening chorus: a pride of Times Square nobodies in "1617 Broadway" and then, in Florida, "(It's yours and it's his and it's) Miami." The evening's sole surprise was Sammy's entrance, onstage at the Bandbox. Sammy's uncle and dad (the rest of the family act, the Will Mastin Trio) slithered on in fezzes to "Arabian" music, attached at the hip. They parted . . . and little Sammy jumped out, to break into "Jacques d'Iraq."

Jamaica was less conventional, but only because it was put together in chaos. It started as a showcase for the breaking Harry Belafonte, but went into rehearsals with Lena Horne in the central role, as a Caribbean who dreams of achieving the higher glamor in Manhattan. She didn't get there, and then there was a hurricane. That was the entire storyline, leaving the Harold Arlen–E. Y. Harburg score sounding like a club act for forty-five people. There was one arresting note in that Horne played her romance with Ricardo Montalban, a violation of Big Broadway's etiquette on race relations: hit musicals do not cross color lines. The afore-mentioned *Beggar's Holiday* had permission because it was a screwy no-tion in the first place—a mixed-up cast of Zero Mostel, Alfred Drake, and Avon Long as a kind of Sporting Life called Careless Love; in a mixed-up updating of an eighteenth-century piece with music by Duke Ellington; with mixed-up direction in that John Houseman and Nicho-las Ray shared the work till an unbilled George Abbott was slipped in for last-minute doctoring. It was seat-of-the-pants play production, excused from the regulations. But *Jamaica* was a David Merrick production—early David Merrick, true, before he earned his medals as Broadway's Topsy—and a substantial in-plain-sight operation. However, Horne was so light-skinned and Montalban so dark that no one said anything.

House of Flowers, alone of this trio, owns a cult, and it was collecting enthusiasts even before it opened as, potentially, another of those quirky classics because of its array of Names: director Peter Brook, choreog-rapher George Balanchine, and designer Oliver Messel, with Diahann Carroll as the ingenue to Pearl Bailey's diva and the whole based on a short story by Truman Capote. Quirkiest of all, the show was to be written by Capote and Harold Arlen, though Capote was only barely a playwright, a failed adaptation of his own novel *The Grass Harp* his sole qualification. Capote had not only never written a musical but probably had never seen one; those who knew him noted how un-versed he was in The Knowledge typical of gay men ambitious to enter the Great World—especially in theatre and music. Capote and Arlen were to collaborate on the *House of Flowers* score, the two writing lyrics for the first time in their lives—and Capote the eternal wanderer would have to confer with Arlen at long distance. Musicals aren't written that way.

But the material itself was promising, if offbeat. In Capote's story, the house belonged to a young man named Royal who marries a girl from Port-au-Prince, Haiti. She is in fact a prostitute in a bordello called the Champs Elysees, but love draws her to his secluded house of flowers despite a huge drawback, Royal's evil grandmother. She tries to frighten the girl by leaving things in her sewing basket—a cat's severed head, a live snake, spiders. The girl cooks them into the old woman's diet and finally tells her of this, whereupon the old woman dies of shock.

The story is filled with such colorful incidents, but also with great charm and authenticity, as if a narrative of folklore perfected over the years by many tellers. Capote and Arlen used bits of the story—a cock-fight; the use of bumblebees to test one's love; the Houngan "in touch with [gods] of food, light, of death, ruin"; and a client of the bordello, Mr. Jamison. They left out the grandmother and kept their heroine, Carroll's role, innocent of bordello practice. Because Bailey's role was that of the bordello keeper, they had to shift the romance to secondary status and invent something for Bailey to do: have a feud with a rival bordello run by Juanita Hall.

Against all likelihood, Capote and Arlen turned out to be expert lyricists, at that to Arlen's most ravishing music. We hear the two shyly edging their way into composition with two numbers they discarded early on, "Can You Explain (the wave that's hitting the shore)?" and "Love's No Stranger To Me." Apparently meant for Pearl Bailey, they lack the worldly sass she was known for in both words and melody and leave no room for Bailey's patented "ad libs" of sly commentary. Then, getting into gear, the two authors accommodated Bailey in the racy "What Is a Friend For?" and, with her bordello girls, the mocking "Has I Let You Down?." For the romance, they wrote a trembling beauty of a ballad in "A Sleepin' Bee" and the evocatively jazzy title song, framed by woodwind curlicues suggestive of lazy teasing in the sun. *House of Flowers* would have above all atmosphere, the way *Carousel* was imbued with New England or *Guys and Dolls* with Damon Runyon.

Some musicals suffer tryout hell, but *House of Flowers* was damned in rehearsals and never redeemed itself. On the first day, Capote arrived with an armful of, naturally, flowers, handing a rose to cast members in the fluttery yet strangely confident charm for which he was becoming famous. "Hopping, skipping, jumping around the theatre" was chorister Geoffrey Holder's recollection: "Pearl, a rose for you . . . Diahann, honey, a rose for you." Brook's treatment of the nearly all-black cast was less engaging, addressing them so condescendingly that Equity had to demand an apology. Worse, producer Saint Subber exercised no authority over the factions that developed when Bailey seized control of the production. By the time *House of Flowers* opened in Philadelphia, director Brook, choreographer Balanchine, bordello attraction Josephine Premice, and the Mr. (now Monsieur) Jamison, Jacques Aubuchon, were departing and Capote was turning out multiple rewrites of scenes.

It was Bailey's fault, he thought. One of the most original shows of the decade was being corrupted into her star turn. However, others on the scene blamed not Bailey but Brook, for being not only a tyrant but inept at his job. Considering that he was later to be famed for staging the savage *Marat/Sade* and an impenetrable pageant in an invented language for audiences of two hundred at a time in Iran, Brook was arguably the wrong man for *House of Flowers*.

But Capote and Arlen were the right ones, reminding us that New Yorkist art mixes an alchemy of minority-group styles to create unique American forms. One gay and one Jewish author made with their black company a piece of rare sensuality: *House of Flowers* may still be the sexiest musical ever staged. Cole Porter must be the most risqué of lyricists, but Arlen's jazz palette splashes this show with the exotic. Listen to the raucous chorus with steel drums, "Smellin' of Vanilla (Bamboo Cage)," or the cathouse keyboard banging out "Waitin'" for three daughters of joy or Royal's gasconade on how, dumped into the ocean, he fought through sea monsters to safety, "Turtle Song." And note that Monsieur Jamison never sang a note: as the villain of the piece, he was locked out of music meant only for the enchanted.

In a way, *House of Flowers* was a Caribbean *Pal Joey*: filled with people with different morals than yours because they dwell in a different world.

Indeed, Bailey's establishing song, "One Man Ain't Quite Enough," is almost the autobiography of a jaded queen, as in "Let your lovely friends take their turn." This was a magically worldly-naive show, one centered on a relationship between a woman who has had them all and a girl who asks a bumblebee what love is, and it was too special for the era. Amid very mixed reviews, including a few raves, we note the *Daily News* accusing Capote of writing "out of a dirty little mind." Still, the show lasted five months on Broadway, long enough to admit anyone who wanted to see it—and to suggest that admissions policies at places like the Stork Club were ritzing the zeitgeist. It was time for New York's leadership caste to be open to talent without restriction.

Thus, as the 1950s wore on, Walter Winchell's career continued to sag. There was a new problem: he had no choice but to take his act from radio to television. As a visual, however, the Winchell of *Wake Up and Live,* tapping at his telegraph key in his fedora, was too high-pitched for the 1950s. Worse, he reached the air only after Sherman Billingsley had made a crazy kind of triumph with his own TV show, *The Stork Club.* It was a sort of failure d'estime: so terrible that folks tuned in to see what new gaffes Billingsley would commit. He would ask an admiral when he was graduated from West Point, beg for opening-night tickets of an actress whose show was in mid-run, or simply freeze. As with his reply to Josephine Baker's charge of racism, Billingsley lacked any skill in saying nothing in a persuasive manner. One night he was to interview the Shah of Iran and went absolutely blank. Finally he thought of something. "How's Iran?" he said.

In the freewheeling, partly improvisational days of live television, accidents were an element of the art, and *The Stork Club* did at least offer glamorous celebs as they "really" were, long before talk shows were common. For the incompetent Billingsley to succeed where the practiced showoff—and former vaudevillian—Winchell failed may have contributed to a tremendous falling out between the two. Further, Winchell's worst enemy, Ed Sullivan, had a smash doing on TV what Winchell had done in The Column—palling around with the madeits and putting his stamp on wannabes.

Winchell did achieve a nationally celebrated comeback, even so, at the end of the 1950s. As a voiceover on *The Untouchables,* Winchell's staccato delivery suited a narrative of Prohibition-era Federal agents battling the mob. Still, the liberals' rejection of Winchellism never let up. Then, in 1963, Winchell's home-page newspaper, *The Daily Mirror,* closed forever, crippled by an aggressive union action.

Oddly, considering the acrimonious nature of the Baker-Winchell controversy, the two communicants made up after two years. But the Stork Club barely survived the *Mirror.* It, too, was a victim partly of labor problems. Billingsley had long fought to keep the unions out of his place (the musicians were a necessary exception), and the latter half of the 1950s saw Billingsley empretzled in picket lines, threatening letters, and even assaults on his personnel. True, much of his clientele were not the sort to let picketing deter them from collecting the PR spike attendant upon a Stork visit. But union plants on the club staff were engaged in sabotage, from the old schoolboy's trick of loosening the top of the salt shaker to sawing partway through chair legs. Mysterious fires broke out, and someone even tampered with the elevator that served the upper floors of the building.

Through it all, at least a portion of the arts world's elect looked on unmoved. If one expressed sympathy for Billingsley's literally unending problems, someone else would fire back with the tale of how Lena Horne showed up one night with George Jessel and that incorrigible Stork door policy sent them away. It's a saucy tale:

SNOOTY MAITRE D': (to Horne) Who made your reservation?
JESSEL: Abraham Lincoln.

In fact, Horne did hobnob at the Stork. This scenelet actually occurred at "21."

But that was no more than a distracting technicality to those weary of the Stork Club's selective guest list, because it compromises progressive reform, restricts the free market of talent that the New York arts scene has thrived on. Did the Algonquin Round Table's defiance of tradition and respect for creativity lead to Ethel Waters' taking the black time to Broadway, or was the Round Table simply a jokebook waiting for The Column to replace Society with publiciety?

The Stork went into eclipse and began to empty out. The city authorities might have stepped in and eased Billingsley's problems, for the Stork Club was after all a New York institution. But while Billingsley palled with Winchell and J. Edgar Hoover, he had made no contacts in Fiorello La Guardia's administration. And after La Guardia left office, on January 2, 1946, Billingsley apparently continued to try to fight his battles alone. By the early 1960s, he had to do the unthinkable and advertise, offering a hamburger platter at a bargain price. The Algonquin Hotel is still with us, and it even retains a bit of literary flavor in lunching editors from the nearby *New Yorker*. But the Stork Club went out of business in 1965, and now even the building is gone, replaced by William Paley's pocket park. It's amazing to visit the site—at what once was 3 East Fifty-third Street—and see just how small a space the Stork's ground floor occupied. (The Cub Room in fact was set into an extension that Billingsley carved out of an adjacent address.) But then, the very crowding in the Stork was part of its brand, its equivalent of the Four Hundred filling Mrs. Astor's ballroom. Billingsley's gold chain opened upon a view of rich and famous jammed up together like Winchell's items, with no more than a bit of ellipsis between.

That's what made Winchell and the Stork Club hot: that leap-off-the-mark race to notoriety as one crowds one's rivals. Back when Tammany and the Irish were in league to tilt elections, the biggest b'hoys were employed as "shoulders," physically ramming into citizens at the polling places of "unreliable" districts to chase them away. As anyone who has had personal access to the famous can tell you, the aggressive nature of American celebrity-making favors the monster. Stars are like those shoulders, shoving their way to victory. But the 1950s favored embourgeoisement, in the Ozzie and Harriet manner. Winchell was essentially a Depression personality, synchronous with racy New York wisecracks. The Stork suited the 1940s best, as a romantic rendezvous in wartime and then, in peace, a guiltless pleasure. By the 1950s Winchell and the Stork were anachronisms.

Winchell did not die till 1972, of cancer, in California; writers love to point out that his funeral was attended solely by his daughter, Walda. The symbolism is irresistible: the man who knew everyone worth knowing proves in death that, with men of power, friendship is a sham, because power has no feelings. But some extremely powerful men have had very close friendships—Franklin Roosevelt, for instance. Further, some of Winchell's former associates would have made the trip to Arizona, where he was interred. Walda didn't want them there, handling the arrangements in secret.

Anyway, the point is not that Winchell died friendless, but that he died powerless—and, worse, on the coast, displaced in the most literal meaning of the word. Hate him or not, Winchell was the pride of New York, not because his vulgar petty stranglehold on how America perceives fame was admirable in even a perverse way, but because he got to there from nothing, a b'hoy who made good, the child of immigrants taking high position in the new state of influence without ancestors. Winchell achieved the unthinkable: he ran the chaos that followed Mrs. Astor. He *was* the chaos. And that chaos was New York as a style and a skills set that, for a time, told America what its art was.

The Stork Club's funeral consisted of tributes in the press after it closed, on October 4, 1965. Oddly, the Josephine Baker incident seems not to have come up much. Journalists were magnanimous in their victory over the place, perhaps because the Stork's last days had been so humiliating to Billingsley. Was ever a man so deserted by everyone he called "friend?" Yes, one, you'll say: Winchell. But Winchell knew he didn't have any friends. It came as a surprise to Billingsley.

He himself got a typical New York funeral, a year after the closing of the Stork. A parallel construction: Walda Winchell buried her father and Shermane Billingsley buried hers—but in a service at the Frank Campbell funeral home, attended by many prominent Storkgoers. However, the club's biographer, Ralph Blumenthal, recounts a more telling last rite. Remember when Edna Ferber looked in on the Algonquin and found nobodies where her crowd had held court? Ethel Merman dropped by the club one night after a long absence. It was in its last days, and instead of the hubbub of mediagenic faces, there were three people inside.

One of them was a wraith of a man, and Merman recognized him as Billingsley only after he began to speak to her. Yet they had been lovers for years in the late 1930s, an item in The Column!

Josephine Baker got two funerals. The first occurred in the middle of her Paris comeback, in 1975 (after an absence of six years), a sellout at the Bobino. This theatre, situated in Montparnasse directly between the railroad station and the cemetary, was one of Paris' great ones in terms of tradition. Yet to Baker it was, after all, the Left Bank: the black time, in cultural terms. Still, as *Le Figaro* put it, "For the second time in fifty years, Josephine Baker has conquered Paris." Le tout Europe attended the opening, and the show's emcee, Jean-Claude Brialy, read out a salute from the president of the republic, Giscard d'Estaing. "The fossils congratulate each other" was the comment of the leftwing *Libération;* the rest of Baker's press was rapturous.

Then, very suddenly, before the run was over, she was gone, aged sixty-nine. "As deaths go, this was a good one," writes Baker's biographer Phyllis Rose. "Quick, clean, at a moment of triumph. . . . Officially, she died of cerebral hemorrhage, but some thought she died of joy." The French gave her a state funeral, televised, the coffin drawn past the Bobino over the Seine to the Church of the Madeleine. So she made it to the Right Bank after all. The service was attended by even more celebrities than had assisted at the Bobino opening, convincing Princess Grace of Monaco, a Baker stalwart, that the funeral had belonged to the paparazzi rather than to Baker. The second funeral, at the princess' insistence, was held in Monaco. This time, the press was not admitted.

A good death, yes—a glamorous one, even, as befits one of America's most glamorous artists: here was one American life with a superb second act. And yet it wasn't truly an American life, was it? What kind of history she might have made if she had forged her career at home is a tantalizing counter-factual, but the answer might be "None." Baker was too unencountered in her native land in her time; she had to arrive as an exotic in an exotic place: a find, a wonder, an article of le chic. Her theme song was "J'ai Deux Amours (mon pays et Paris)," but Baker's two loves were not, as one might think, America and Paris. The number was introduced at the Casino de Paris, in 1930, in a scene laid on the African shore, where Adrien Lamy played a French colonist who wants to take native girl Baker back to France. Composer Vincent Scotto and lyricists Géo Koger and the Casino's producer, Henri Varna, wrote this number for Baker as a woman torn between Paris and Africa. Further, to the French, "mon pays" means "my province" as much as "my country." Thus, Baker's two loves never included America, and in time she became burdened with the number, impatient with it. What did it mean, anyway? Baker had a hundred loves, a thousand. She would never love where she came from, but rather wherever she was going. "Home," to Baker, the cultural nomad, was a place with no there in it.

The 1960s

11

Cole Porter: And You'll Rate With All the Great Swells

It wasn't so bad tonight. Both Arnolds came, and Whitridge got to the piano to play those ditties again. "Remember?" he urges me. When we were young and all in hats. Big floppy ones sur la plage. Something shy and banded for tea-dancing. Boaters and berets. Whitridge with his wistful eyes, dreaming us back to the college shows, the first one to show up at rehearsals. "They've booked us at the Yale Club, don't you know?" He likes "Shooting Box" especially, knows all the words even now:

> *If you care for hotter places,*
> *I've an African oasis*
> *On an uninhabited plain . . .*

And when he finishes, he turns to me and I say, "Did I write that?" in a wondering way. It makes him so tender and happy and sad.

*The other Arnold of course has to cut in. The Improbable Saint. "Play Kate,"
he commands, missing the point. He wants to own the remembering tonight. "Your most . . ." as he struggles to find les mots. "Your most exquisite creation, Coley."
Everything ends with "Coley," like a stuck clock. "Remember, Coley? Philadelphia, the infernal Bella, and then the cheers when we opened. Coley!" "*

And I tell him, "Next week, East Lynne."

No, it wasn't so bad this time. We had a full helping: queens, jam, and trade. The trade was first, as befits. The boy from Liberty Music Shop. A latest passing fancy. Married, of course. All the best beaux are. This time I found a wire inside the phonograph arm and gave it a yank. He must know, but he never says anything, and it does enliven one's afternoon. But when you offer them a drink, all they want is beer.

Whitridge and wife were the jam. They succeed better than anyone at not plaguing me with concern. Such fuss. It makes one cross. The Beard was like that, always so gleefully sympathetic. A lot of them have managed to drift away, I suppose. Easier. But a few stick. Whitridge, Ray. The others just come for dinner and talk frantically away. My, aren't they glad when it's time to part?

Not Saint, though. No, the queen must make her exit—after hovering so delicately over me. Geraldine was acting up most unforgivably tonight, and Saint asked, "It's the right one, isn't it, Coley? The bad one?" I sipped my drink, above it. But Saint persisted, of course. "Don't you have anything to take for the pain, Coley?" he asked, and I raised my glass and said, "I'm taking it."

Writers make much of the last song Cole Porter wrote, "Wouldn't It Be Fun!" Designed for the Emperor of China in the television musical *Aladdin* (1958), the song bounces merrily in 6/8 metre as the lyrics wonder what it would be like not to be "famous" and "rich," to live like one of the masses, even a "peasant" or "beggar." Anyone but "me, mighty me."

These writers discern a great irony here, as if surprising Porter in autobiographical confession. In fact, Porter was simply writing for a character who was giving him trouble. After all, what does an emperor do, he complained, but think up ghoulish executions? The real irony is that the number wasn't even used in *Aladdin* when it aired.* In any case,

---

* "Wouldn't It Be Fun!" may have been cut simply because the show's ninety-minute time slot couldn't accommodate the entire eight-number score or because the Emperor, Basil Rathbone, couldn't sing. The song appears on the cast recording, but it is performed by another member of the company, George Hall. Amusingly, the LP release never admitted as much on the album sleeve and indulged in obfuscation on the disc's label, where every number is credited to the real-life performer—"Vocal by Sal

Porter loved being rich and famous. He needed luxury to spare and avidly sought widespread recognition of his work; further, while he led the gay element in New Yorkism, he never thought of himself as part of a minority group or of lacking civil rights. After all, Porter headlined the elite: he attended the choice parties, wore the best clothes, knew everyone he wanted to know. To be elite, he thought, was to be smart, successful, and physically whole, which is why the horseback-riding accident in 1937 that smashed both his legs eventually killed him. For two decades, Porter lived in agony, naming the left leg Josephine and the worse of the two, the right one, Geraldine. When Porter's doctor finally had to cut the right one off, in 1958, Porter, no longer whole, never wrote again or even went to the piano. Life and work—and his membership in the elite—were now over. Porter set to some serious, silent, relentless drinking till, in 1964, his life ended.

It began beautifully, with a doting mother and a wealthy maternal grandfather, the kind that rages and decrees but cannot stop his daughter Kate from giving her son every cultural advantage. From prep school to Yale, from classical study in Paris to larking about on the Lido, Porter entered the elite in its older sense of the crowd with money and manners. As short as a woman, with big doll's eyes, Porter was not a looker. But he was clever, droll, and eccentrically well-dressed. He could charm at will. And his talent was astonishing.

In fact, Porter composed one of the very first of the classical-jazz pieces discussed earlier: *Within the Quota*. This was a commission for Les Ballets Suédois in 1923, to a scenario and designs by a Yale pal, Gerald Murphy. At the time, Porter scores had been heard on Broadway, and he had even had a song hit, "Old Fashioned Garden." Yet his name as such was unknown; he got the job only because of his friendship with Murphy, a painter with connections in the French art world.

One expects, then, a tentative or simply unseasoned work, one perhaps saved by the orchestration (by Charles Koechlin). On the contrary,

---

Mineo" or "Vocal by Dennis King"—except "Wouldn't It Be Fun!": "Sung by the Emperor." The 1992 CD transcription, thirty-four years later, finally identified Hall.

Within the Quota is almost confident to a fault, sixteen minutes of ceaseless invention, unification by leitmotifs, and a bit of flashy polytonality. The subject is that favorite European fantasy—America in a bliss of celebrity mania. Murphy's backdrop, in red and black, was a newspaper's front page: EX-WIFE'S HEART-BALM LOVE-TANGLE, BOYCOTT ALL SYNDICATE HOOTCH, GEM ROBBERS FOIL $210,000 SWINDLE, and, in the largest type, UNKNOWN BANKER BUYS ATLANTIC. The action followed an immigrant's meeting with iconic American character models—the heiress, the "colored gentleman," the "jazz-baby," and the cowboy, each encounter harassed by a control-freak do-gooder—a sheriff, for instance, who shadowed the cowboy. (The reformer always appeared to low brass and pounding tympani, the very sound of "this will hurt you more than it does me" aggression wearing the moralist's mask.) The last of the icons to appear, the "Sweetheart of the World," was Mary Pickford, the biggest movie star in the known universe at that time. With her approval, the immigrant was instantly naturalized and became a celebrity himself: an American, in other words.*

We do not know who conceived the scenario. Was it Murphy and Porter, or perhaps the choreographer, Jean Borlin? But the threat of the interloper who seeks to curtail liberty is elemental in the work of New Yorkists, as if the very production of art reflects the epic battle of the wets and the drys, or of Dorothy Thompson and Charles Lindbergh. Are there two Americas after all, one pushing and the other pushing back? The Column and Main Street?

Yet Main Street read The Column. It mistrusted and disliked New York while nourishing an obsession about it, which is why Hollywood emphasized New York as a setting for films during the first years of the talkie. Sound might have been invented to crackle with that smart talk, that mixture of Irish whimsey and Jewish cynicism that propelled the lingo of the Manhattan "character."

Oddly, an artist who was in every respect the opposite of a New Yorkist made the most substantial attack on the do-gooder at just about the

---

* The use of the immigrant figure explains the work's peculiar title: he has entered the country legally, standing within the demographic requirements of the immigration laws mentioned in Chapter Four.

time of *Within the Quota*. D. W. Griffith's background was southern, not northeastern and not even urban, though he came to New York to enter the theatre, as actor and playwright. Further, his worldview was thoroughly nineteenth-century in its love of good-versus-evil melodrama. Yet Griffith's masterpiece, *Intolerance* (1916), builds its most interesting plot line around the calamities caused by reformers. "We must have laws to make people good," says one meddler, a member of a ladies' sodality of the bored rich. "When women cease to attract men," a title card observes, "they often turn to Reform as a second choice." Men do it, too. In *Intolerance*'s Christian story, one Judean sage tells another, "There is too much revelry and pleasure-seeking among the people."

There was certainly a lot of it among Cole Porter, who was the outsider in the club of creators of Golden Age musical comedy. A moneyed Republican and, by Times Square standards, a foreigner, Porter was also a hedonist, an avidly practicing homosexual, and a teaser of social cautions, Puck in checks. Somehow or other, his talent delighted the other major composer-lyricist of the day, Irving Berlin. Thus, the most sophisticated songwriter had a special appeal for the populist songwriter. They met socially often enough, but there was a professional link: a piece from one of Porter's college shows had been interpolated into a Shubert offering called *Hands Up* (1915), billed as a "musico-comico-filmo-melo-drama." One of its authors was Berlin's brother-in-law by his first marriage, E. Ray Goetz, and the number, "Esmerelda," was published by Irving Berlin, Inc.

It was Porter's first list song, and, dating from 1913 originally, it may be the first list song, period. Boy gets girl:

> GIRL: *Now as long as we're united in the bonds of matrimony,*
> *You surely must have something to confess.*
> BOY: *To make the maxim suit the rhyme, "Qui mal y pense soit honi,"*
> *Of course there's naught to do but answer "Yes."*

And he confesses:

> *Esmerelda,*
> *Then Griselda,*

And the third was Rosalie.
Lovely Lakme
Tried to track me,
But I fell for fair Marie . . .

As Porter's mentor, Berlin gave him practical advice, such as becoming a fixture in the theatre community rather than spending his time in Europe: producers are wary of dilettantes. And as Ray Goetz was a producer as well as a writer, it was apparently Berlin who urged Porter upon Goetz when he was preparing a vehicle for Mrs. Goetz, the Latin cucamonga Irene Bordoni. The result, *Paris* (1928), was a play with songs rather than a musical, but one of the songs was "Let's Do It." It's absolute Porter—witty and risqué in its lyrics, cagey in its melody (beginning, improbably, on the sixth tone of the scale), and of an irresistible rhythmic address. And while the title includes a refining "(Let's Fall in Love)," the words *Let's do it* bear a single-meaning bluntness that Porter of all Broadway writers made his own.

Paris put Porter over at last, and several prominent shows later, in 1933, Elsa Maxwell fêted him with one of her specialty parties at the Waldorf-Astoria—the new one, in its present location on Park Avenue. Maxwell merrily told the press that the age of Mrs. Astor's Four Hundred was over; the count of the elite had been cut down to less than half the old number. Of course, the nature of the elite had changed as well. Yes, Mrs. Astor's crowd might have arranged for someone like Porter—wicked though he surely was—to show up and favor them with . . . how would they put it? A selection of his *cunning* little catches. But *Astorshchina*, as the Russians would put it (roughly, "the rule and attitudes of the Astor regime") would not have tolerated *socializing* with Porter. Still, it was Porter, not the Astors, who led Society now.

Maxwell's honorees that night included George Gershwin and Grace Moore as well. Like Porter, they had become the rage, yet, oddly, all three were just on the verge of going truly big. Gershwin was about to bond his two careers as Broadway tunesmith and classical-pop visionary with *Porgy and Bess*. Its world premiere, on its Boston tryout, was so electrifying that it seemed to many to change the course of

American music—to bend it to the new rules of interracial détente. As to Moore, she had ennobled Broadway with some of its most distinguished "legit" vocalism while bringing a touch of show biz to the Metropolitan Opera.

And Porter's next show would be his first smash hit and his first classic title. It was also the most typical of all his works: *Anything Goes* (1934). We've spoken of this work already in another context; for now, we need to underline its view of life as a lark as long as no reformers are nigh. The characters of *Anything Goes,* a mixture of socials and riffraff, dwell in a universe in which there are no penalties for being Different. Literally, anything goes. Just for starters, the potential puritan figure— Reno Sweeney, Ethel Merman's part—is a former evangelist. She still speaks the religion lingo, but she has gravitated to nightclub singing, reminding us how much show biz there was in the reform racket, from Billy Sunday to Aimee Semple McPherson.

In this context, we are not surprised to learn that a certain Dr. Moon, a clergyman (the Victor Moore part), is in reality Public Enemy Number Thirteen, with a tommy gun in his saxophone case. True, the show's hero, Billy Crocker (the William Gaxton part) is locked in the brig in one scene on some minor technicality. But this is a momentary snag, something you have to put up with if you work in musical comedy. The main thing is the way Cole Porter's world defeats the disapprovers, as it did the reformer figure in *Within the Quota*. Other Porter shows—*Jubilee* (1935), *Panama Hattie* (1940), *Something For the Boys* (1943), and especially *Can-Can* (1953)—deal also with the ultimately impotent threat of those who think they know better than you how you should live.

Anything Goes' prominence, with its cornucopia of hit tunes—five, the same number as *Good News,* and but one less than mighty *Show Boat*—led to an invitation from Hollywood, where Porter had a chance to delve into the ontology of songwriting. His instincts as a creator were too artistic for most listeners, throwing off verbally nuanced (not to mention morally advanced) lyrics in often ambitious musical settings. Then, too, one was so busy absorbing the words that the music evaporated at first hearing—a violation of the practice of pop, which demanded that a song be more or less immediately collectable. On Porter's first job writing a complete new score for a movie musical,* *Born To Dance* (1936), he wrestled with this problem while learning how MGM does business.

And that was: slowly and at great needless expense. When not coming up with inane ideas, the writers were constantly on holiday, and the producer, director, and choreographer could object to songs at whim. Just settling on a script and a final tunestack took over five months, with most of the participants on fat weekly salaries. *Born To Dance* was to be Eleanor Powell's first starring vehicle, opposite James Stewart in a "three girls and three guys" plot with a Navy background. Powell could not only sing and act but was a sensational looker—yet she broke Hollywood's rules of entry by arriving in California with a mother who wouldn't let her daughter alone with any male over the age of six. Of course, Powell's main attraction was her dancing, the best in Hollywood after Fred Astaire's. Thus, Porter's assignment, in effect, was to write three tiers of vocals: dance occasions for Powell, instant hits in the pop vein, and, finally, something in the sophisticated Porter style, for himself.

Porter did all this with brilliance, giving *Born To Dance* one of the best original scores in Hollywood history. Retrieving "Easy To Love," dropped from *Anything Goes,* and adding to it "Goodbye, Little Dream, Goodbye," he at first had the ballads down, though "Dream" may have been too gloomy for what was to prove a mainly effervescent score. Porter replaced it with "I've Got You Under My Skin." For himself, he wrote the daffy "Love Me, Love My Pekinese," the capstone of a musical scene as the film's vamp figure (Virginia Bruce) arrives on a Navy cruiser. The sequence begins in Gilbert and Sullivan style and exploits Bruce's too-too diction and Metropolitan Opera vocal tone. Then, addressing the mass public as MGM demanded, Porter added in "Hey, Babe, Hey" for the three couples, the

---

* One of the first talkies, *The Battle of Paris,* sported two Porter numbers and Gertrude Lawrence but a lame screenplay; *Photoplay,* using a term I thought was recently coined, said it was musical comedy enough to "just [miss] being a floperetta." The *Anything Goes* film lost all but three and a half of its tunes (the half is the title number, reduced to a snatch heard over the credits) and *Gay Divorce* (retitled *The Gay Divorcée*) retained just one, "Night and Day." But *Fifty Million Frenchmen* didn't sing a note, its music reduced to underscoring.

simplest of melodies in clog-dance rhythm tricked out in multiple tunes to be sung against each other. For Powell, Porter contrived the syncopations of "Rap Tap on Wood," approximating in music her uniquely slithery dance style. And for Powell's production-number finale, Porter wrote "Swingin' the Jinx Away," a raveup in the latest musical mode.

Unfortunately, the film's director and choreographer had their hearts set on a finale staged on whizzing motorboats, which Porter's swing number would not support. Although he was eager to please, finding Hollywood not only lucrative but congenial in its unbuttoned sexual mores, Porter refused to write anything else for the spot—and Powell sided with him. She didn't want to whiz about on motorboats. She wanted to go into her dance in mini-tux and top hat on the deck of a battleship with guns booming.

Thus encouraged, Porter explained to the MGM chiefs that, back in New York, when a director and choreographer didn't like a song, the song wasn't replaced: they were. Indeed, the choreographer was replaced. The director, Roy Del Ruth, could not properly be fired, as he had been in charge of Powell's previous film, *Broadway Melody of 1936*, and MGM was billing Powell as "The Broadway Melody Girl." Del Ruth provided continuity—and that previous film's choreographer, Dave Gould, was now brought in for extra hit security.

That was one important difference between stage and film musicals: Hollywood liked cycles, series, remakes, and knockoffs, while the stage sought novelty. Typically, Porter's show just before *Anything Goes,* in London, was *Nymph Errant* (1933), about a schoolgirl who goes globetrotting to find the perfect lay. A classy show—but a weird one. *Experiment!* was its advice to the public (and the title of one of its songs). And this was no risky little niche offering but a big West End production put on by the English Ziegfeld, Charles Cochran. Of course Hollywood bought the rights to film it, because it was classy. And of course Hollywood never made it, because it was weird.

They seduce you in Hollywood. They don't work with you, they lure you and flatter you and when they like what you wrote they really like it. Because it will make them a lot of money. On Broadway, you have the producer who wishes you were Jerome Kern, and the critic who says you aren't as good as you used to be, and intellectual Moss Hart, who's so wonderful to be around except when he's got a show on. Deck him out for opening night, and all he knows is "The second act's wobbly." Everyone loves it, and now he's drunk and loving. Then he'll start awake from a nightmare, crying, "But is it art?"

And Hollywood has those boy parties by the pool. All so Greek, one supposes. And everyone knows and nobody cares, as long as you keep it private. Such ingratiating youngsters, too. Everyone's on the make. We used to call them "gigolos." Here they're called "option babies." They've got six months to be Tyrone Power or they'll be serving from trays in some taverna.

The Hollywood problem is their mania for box-office. How they cram their stars into everything! High Society *could have been so tantalizing. Yes, the girl was pretty, but what old duffers with her! John Patrick got the studio to bring John Lund in, the boy from that war play. The only looker in the whole film—and he's the villain! In padding, I suspect, to make him cumbersome. What a beauty he was on stage!* The Hasty Heart. *Now, that title will play. That has merit, with its death and love and John Lund handsome. That line of his, at the end?* "What makes a man want to die despised and friendless?" *I never forget that moment, how angry he was at that other fellow. Oh, but I did give them a lively score. Young man's music. Shimmerin' sharps and flats, with jazz for Mr. Armstrong and the most joyful tunes I'd written in twenty years. A slow waltz for two sweethearts,* "True Love." "Who Wants To Be a Millionaire" *for the second pair, and they're in love, too. All in love in that picture. Everyone gets love.*

The most consistent of writers, Porter was actually under-appreciated in his day because his songs observed genre, from his college shows to his last work of all, *Aladdin.* Yet these forms were either Porter's inventions or his unique versions: list songs, Latin rhythm songs, woman's-viewpoint songs, mock-country songs, double-meaning sex songs, minor-key ending in major-key love songs. The reviewers thought he was repeating himself when in fact he was developing a personal style. He was ingenious in nuancing his subject matter, for instance flavoring pop music with archetypes of the great world—"The Extra Man" (to accessorize the comme il faut dinner setting), "The Cocotte," "The Physician" (not just any doctor, but the one who gives new meaning to "bedside manner"), "chaperons" (in the older spelling, "sporty, fat and forty" who manage young people's dances by taking the boys as "our toys"), and of course "The Gigolo." Then Porter turns around and hymns the field expedients of the outlaw and the vulgarian—"Love For Sale," "The Bandit Band" (they're girls), "It Ain't Etiquette," "Find Me a Primitive Man."

However, by the 1940s Porter's shows were starting to resemble each other, as if he had learned Hollywood's lessons too well. And the songs seemed *too* consistent now, overexploiting the Porter genres. There was a lot of Ethel Merman—Porter's personal Broadway Melody Girl—and his risqué was running to the vulgar side. *Mexican Hayride* (1944), about a con man (Bobby Clark) on the lam south of the border who gets involved with a woman bullfighter (June Havoc), was a smash hit but not a good show. Wartime audiences kept it going. The producer, Mike Todd, specialized in the oldtime girls-and-gags show biz, and *Mexican Hayride*'s book, by Herbert Fields, was the kind that spins out plot by having the jesters get into ridiculous disguises, a usage dating back to the late nineteenth century. But the more logical storytelling in *Cabin in the Sky, Pal Joey,* and *Oklahoma!* in the early 1940s had made anything-for-a-laugh plots like *Mexican Hayride*'s excrescent.

Worst of all, the score was by far Porter's weakest since he had become famous in the late 1920s. Credit for *Mexican Hayride*'s success went to Todd and Clark, not to Porter, and he didn't like the production or anyone in it. "It stinks," he observed. Later that year came the aforementioned *Seven Lively Arts,* with more lackluster Porter. The list song, Bert Lahr's endless toast, "Drink," was actually feeble. But then, Porter at his best wrote comic songs, not songs for comics. Lahr at least suited Porter's love of scalawags; the pair made important history together on *DuBarry Was a Lady* (1939). But *Seven Lively Arts*' other star, Beatrice Lillie, mystified Porter, and his work for her was savorless and academic, adding to the already dense backstage tension. Lillie finally threatened to leave the show on the day of the New York opening; Equity had to exercise considerable diplomacy to recall her to her obligations.

It got worse as the 1940s wore on. Orson Welles' adaptation of Jules Verne, *Around the World* (1946), didn't need Porter's gifts. It wasn't a musical at all, but rather a spectacle employing songs and incidental pieces. Nor did Porter's movie work maintain the juxtaposition of universalism and sophistication he had set up in *Born To Dance*. *The Pirate* (1948) shows some of Porter's flash, and "Be a Clown," given two wonderful stagings (first as a dance for Gene Kelly and the Nicholas Brothers, then for Kelly and Judy Garland as a comic finale) let Porter show his expertise in a kind of song he had never written before. Still, the film itself, though adventurously erotic (for MGM, at least) and pictorially splendid, did not succeed. As a major production viewed as a misfire, it marked a further deterioration of Porter's standing.

Back on Broadway later that year, Porter was thought so inadequate that his next show was exiled to the New Century Theatre, way off the thoroughfare, near Central Park. But this was *Kiss Me, Kate* (1948). Saint Subber, *Kate*'s co-producer (with Lemuel Ayers), said he got the idea for the show while serving as stage manager on a tour of *The Taming of the Shrew* starring Alfred Lunt and Lynn Fontanne. This famous production was a rococo riot of dwarfs, animals, grotesques, and—vastly bickering offstage as well as onstage—the two leads. What, Subber wondered, if we were to build a show around that? A musical *Shrew*, part Shakespeare and part dressing rooms, while "Petruchio" tames his "Kate" in real life. And who was literate yet bawdy enough to score it but Cole Porter?

No, said Bella Spewack, co-author of the book (with her husband, Sam). *She* conceived the piece. A musical *Shrew* is easily commissioned: the difficulty lies in the execution. Broadway had already seen two Shakespearean musicals, and each had found a different solution to the problems posed by the antique diction and setting. Rodgers and Hart's *The Boys from Syracuse* (1938), from *The Comedy of Errors,* retained the original place and characters but spoke and sang wholly in contemporary Broadwayese. That's one stunt.

Right after that, *Swingin' the Dream* (1939) placed *A Midsummer Night's Dream* in nineteenth-century New Orleans, with jazz, voodoo, jokey modern references, and a fully mixed-race cast. Louis Armstrong played

Bottom and Butterfly McQueen's Puck enchanted mortals by spraying them with a Flit gun—insect repellent dispensed from something like a bicycle pump. Staged at the Center Theatre, the legit equivalent of Radio City Music Hall, *Swingin' the Dream* was a gigantic explosion of New Yorkism, with black jitterbug next to a corps drilled by Agnes de Mille, a kind of Manhattan Hollywood in designs "quoting" Walt Disney, and even a producer-director, Erik Charell, who had fled Nazi Germany. It did not catch on and closed in two weeks. Still, that's two stunts.

And it was Bella—*she* said—who came up with the third stunt: not to adapt but include Shakespeare, in both songs and dialogue. Kate's action takes place on the night of the first performance of the *Shrew* in its Baltimore tryout. It is apparently a musical *Shrew,* put on by a figure that never really existed—an operetta actor-manager. His co-star, a soprano, is also his ex-wife: romance. She's irritated at his interest in the girl of the second couple: suspense. And while Porter wasn't exactly keen on all this—he didn't like legit sopranos in musicals—he had worked with the Spewacks on *Leave It To Me!* with great satisfaction.

Oddly, the Spewacks' marriage somewhat resembled that of the *Kate* couple, as it was crumbling to the point that Sam was no longer interested even in writing with Bella. Yet it seems that Sam was the one who came up with a strategic plot accellerator—the boy of the second couple gambles and just lost big in a crap game, and the two gangsters who come to collect end up in costume taking part in the show: comedy.

Romance, suspense, comedy, Shakespeare, putting on the show . . . and suddenly Porter saw it. The main couple sing grand and the fun couple sing pop. The onstage numbers can footle with the Bard, perhaps using lines from the original. And some of them, on the contrary, can sing in a sort of Shubert Alley Folio, especially "Tom, Dick or Harry," with its "A dicka dick" coda. And the Porter list song? "Brush Up Your Shakespeare" cites titles and characters from the Globe Theatre catalogue. As he wrote, Porter must have realized that Saint Subber and Bella Spewack—who hated each other, and not cordially—had given him the opportunity of his career.

In fact, Porter was determined to make *Kate* his masterpiece. First of all, he wrote a huge score, ending with eighteen separate vocal numbers—but second of all, he rewrote, replacing songs till he felt the plot and its people had been defined. To this point, Ethel Merman had done his defining for him; a torch song in one show might do as well for another. But not since *Jubilee*—another big score, incidentally—had Porter become so intimate with his characters. And every time he wrote for them, he got closer to not who would sing these numbers but whom the numbers were about.

Consider the lead couple's establishing duet, "It Was Great Fun the First Time," which starts as celebration and ends in quarrel. Instantly, we know these two: wonderful partners yet suspicious and contentious when the wrong button is pushed. Immediately after came her romantic solo, the ruefully tender "We Shall Never Be Younger." Then Porter suddenly realized that he hadn't *engaged* with this pair. They were already always quarreling in their book scenes—and "Younger," though lovely, failed to specify. Out went "It Was Great Fun," replaced by "Wunderbar," a mock love duet that is secretly a real love duet.* It's not just Great Fun: it's the real thing. And her following solo was changed as well, to "So in Love." *Now* Porter felt he had these two down, from comedy with a subtext to honesty so deeply felt it's masochistic.

Mirroring the "two" *Kates,* as they constantly alternate between the onstage harlequinade and the backstage of street clothes, Porter separated the score into halves. The onstage numbers game with classical stuff—tarantellas, a cadenza for the heroine at the end of Act One, even a quotation from the "Miserere" from Verdi's *Il Trovatore* in the orchestra at the very end of "We Open in Venice." The pop numbers actually game with each other, as in snatches of "Another Op'nin', Another Show" between the sung lines of "Why Can't You Behave" or in the use of "Behave" as a verse to "Always True To You In My Fashion."†

---

* It is also, amusingly, a parody of Swiss operetta, even though—or perhaps because—there is no such thing. Further fun is had in the first line of the verse, "Gazing down on the Jungfrau." From where, a satellite?

† For "Fashion"'s single song sheet, Porter wrote a utility verse ("I know a boy, my fav'rite gent . . .") that stands among the most overlooked of Porter compositions. It

Kate's casting also maintained this dual citizenship, with baritone and soprano leads on one hand and light-pop tenorino and belter in the secondary slots. With Alfred Drake as *Shrew*'s producer-director-star, his opposite was to have been a Met soprano to match his better-than-Broadway voice; Jarmila Novotna and Lily Pons both turned it down, and Dorothy Kirsten was considered. Ironically, Patricia Morison, who got the role, was not known for singing, though she had in fact played opposite Drake ten years earlier in *The Two Bouquets,* a jukebox operetta with music drawn from Victorian composers. Morison had a trick voice, the kind that can soar when necessary but generally sings in mezzo keys. Her "I Hate Men" has a range of just over an octave, rising to only an E—almost suitable for Ethel Merman, though the style of music has a tripping bel canto quality out of Merman's styles set. In Philadelphia, where *Kate* played its own tryout, the song was not going over till someone on the production team recalled the famous baritone solo from Victor Herbert's *Mlle. Modiste,* "I Want What I Want When I Want It." Indeed, Porter may have had that number in mind when he wrote "I Hate Men," for they share a vaguely classical and even ponderously vocal feel. The Herbert's title line was punctuated by the singer's pounding a table to a resounding orchestral crash, and that effect, repeated throughout the refrain, became a staple of the operetta repertory. The number could still be heard on radio in the 1940s, especially when someone like Nelson Eddy was in a crossover mood, and Morison was directed to pound a table with an Elizabethan tankard when *her* crash sounded, in "I Hate Men." Whether or not the audience flashed on the Herbert number, they could now "place" the song, and it became an essential *Kate* number.

Mention of the staging team brings us to *Kate*'s one great mystery. The production was, in its Shakespearean half, wonderfully lavish, and the all but excessive dance spots appear to have gone over well, even if choreographer Hanya Holm was not on the short list then headed by Balanchine, de Mille, Robbins, and Kidd. Drake and Morison were terrific

---

was not included in *The Complete Lyrics of Cole Porter* and, to my knowledge, has never been recorded.

together, his hammy ego and her cantankerous vulnerability bringing the fiction of the *Shrew* into a contemporary reality. The second couple, too, were a hit, Lisa Kirk coming off her star-is-born gig in Rodgers and Hammerstein's *Allegro* and Harold Lang celebrated as the Cute Ballet Dancer Who Also Sings.

No, the mystery is Kate's director, John C. Wilson. A Yale alumnus and then stockbroker, Wilson became Noël Coward's lover and financial manager in the 1920s. Moving into theatre work, Wilson produced for Coward and also the Lunts. Then, suddenly, he became a director as well, staging New York's *Blithe Spirit* in 1941 and then a musical, the 1943 revival of *A Connecticut Yankee*. The latter was put on by Richard Rodgers himself, and Rodgers, a theatre being from top to toe, knew directors. Why did he want Wilson? There were reasons not to. For one, Wilson had a drinking problem, and, for another, he does not seem to have been an able technician. In early 1948—the year of *Kiss Me, Kate*—Coward had to order Wilson to step aside as Coward took over the direction of a revival of his *Tonight at 8:30* one-acts with Gertrude Lawrence and Graham Payn. If Wilson couldn't stage these tidy (if various) little pieces, how could he keep a big musical like *Kate* in order? One presumes that it was Wilson's producing success that recommended him. *Kate* was struggling to raise its capital; hiring Wilson as director gave *Kate*'s producers access to Wilson's investors.

In the event, the show drew raves from the critics, especially—at last!—for the score. For the first time since *Anything Goes*, fourteen years earlier, no one suggested that Porter's work had disappointed his standard. *Kate* ran 1,077 performances, the mark of a super-smash in those days, and Porter got his *Time* cover, on January 31, 1949. Significantly, those following the recordings scene in the late 1940s noticed that it was the original-cast album of *Kiss Me, Kate* that persuaded the American middle class to invest in the brand-new 33 RPM machines. The long-playing disc had every advantage over the 78: it was unbreakable under normal use, and one didn't have to replace it with the next side every three or four minutes. Still, consumers resisted till the appearance of *Kate* (and of *South Pacific,* a few months later). In those pre-rock days, hit Broadway shows provided the music industry with its biggest sellers and made the people involved household names. The *Kate* album's success gave Porter, who had endured not only his medical problems but that long career slump, a rush of good feeling. Best of all, he had not written *Kate* "down," in his Hollywood manner. He wrote clever, dishy, and hot, and the public loved it. One facet of the New York style lies in the bending of the national will to one's own, seducing and educating.

The queens have been thicker than ever lately. Saint treats dinner as holy ritual, but he does show up faithfully. Not like Jimmy Donahue. We aren't madcap enough for him, I suppose. Some of them have to be entertained every second along or they're instantly away. Merely hosting them isn't enough. They want a show—a Ziegfeld production, mind, or they'll highhat you for someone of a higher order. Off to the Windsors, Jimmy, so a couple of wide-eyed peasants-in-law or someone like that will take you for the lover of the greatest Jezebel in history. Maybe they'll finally stop talking of the night you sneaked onstage in Irving's revue and got the stage manager sacked for letting you.

Jack's been by all of a sudden, looking very spruce and trim. Sober, even. He has the uncanny ability to shed not only pounds but years—when he needs money, that is. His eyes shine, too, as if he'd been taking intravenous neon. He arrived en famille *with Natasha, went on about some project. He's another one with that just loved* Aladdin *but isn't it time you were back on Broadway? I wasn't listening to any of it, and neither was Natasha. How much does she know, at long last? Palling around with men who had her husband for cake? Some of them were on the trick but others had Jack for a serial defiling of the Commandments. Noël took that boy to such outposts of passion that he'd wake up thinking he was the ghost of Clifton Webb. The* baybay, *Noël called him. Well, he did cut a splendid figure then. I like a man who knows how to dress when he's trying to pick you up. Make me yearn to unbutton the cuffs on your coat and feel the wool. Good lad. Making love is such an art, in the end—and don't feign shyness. Show me a chap who knows the ropes. It saves time and pays well. Right. And who's a handsome boy, then?*

Cole Porter's contribution to New Yorkism was another quality that sets him apart from other Golden Age writers of musicals. They were

Jewish: he was gay, abundantly and even openly so. He married, because a gentleman must, but he avidly pursued the stock of beautiful men that society, in every age and community in Western history, has made available to the rich and gifted. It serves as a release valve for energies that might otherwise fuel revolutionary impulses.

Living thus, in absolute liberty, enabled Porter to exploit his talent even as he worried how far beyond popular he dared go. His lyrics were too smart—but so was his music. At the utmost, he contrived "When Me, Mowgli, Love" (from *Jubilee*) to imitate the stirrings and lowings of a jungle in heat, atmosphere overwhelming melody as if devouring prey. But then, in *High Society*'s "True Love," Porter channels Schubert in purest song. He confounds you so cleverly you don't feel confounded. He's impish, you think, not subversive.

Further, the subject matter of Porter's shows redoubles his wicked side, treating socially and sometimes legally marginal characters. The folks represented by Ethel Merman, Jimmy Durante, William Gaxton, Victor Moore, and Bert Lahr in various Porter titles could be read as a rejection of "correct" citizenship: as a preference for the subculture of Different. Lahr's washroom attendant in *DuBarry Was a Lady* is virtually Mose the Fire B'hoy readjusted to a later century with all his attitudes intact. (And note that he wins the Irish Sweepstakes, recalling the days when Tammany Hall and Mose adopted each other.) Porter's music, too, is Different: the sensation of his tunes hungrily gliding over the steady 4/4 beat under them suggests a "special" existence floating above conformism. No other lyricist of his day sounded as worldly as Porter, as naughty, as vivacious—qualities particularly associated with the gay end of the great world of his time. Porter's truest true love isn't true at all but achingly hot and unencumbered by bourgeois cautions, and his double meanings can be so subtle that they lurk rather than leap at one.

On the other hand, "Two Little Babes in the Wood," from the 1924 *Greenwich Village Follies* (and re-used in *Paris*) is one great double meaning from start to finish. Storybookland is turned inside out as a pair of wee tots hits the metropolis to play for pay as go-to-hell kitties and the word "babe" undergoes a wrestling match of images. The maestro of the *Greenwich Village Follies,* John Murray Anderson, later the supervisor of *Billy Rose's Jumbo,* was as well a devotee of the arty chamber piece, *Jumbo*'s exact opposite. Anderson had developed something called the "Ballet Ballad," in which music, pantomime, and dance collided in the most chichi format imaginable, twee and demented at once. "Two Little Babes" was one such, as singers set forth the tale and others enacted it. Thus one could "watch" the song's central pun, as the two innocents left to die in a forest are picked up and "babed," so to say, by a rich old gent. "And the whole town's agreed that the last thing in speed," the song finally caroled, were—of course—those two little "babes" in the wood. Porter himself recorded the number (on a disc that was not released) during the run of *Anything Goes,* and he further textured the pun by playing the first verse and chorus as a fairy-tale waltz, the second in jazz romping with blue notes.

Images are inverted in Porter; love is useful but sex is Different. "I'm yours till I die!" the heroine cries of her lover in *Kiss Me, Kate*—but one hasn't quite collected the text of the piece till, later on, "Too Darn Hot" 's list of randy men on the prowl includes "a marine for his queen." As everyone says of the Porter years on Broadway, people knew but no one ever spoke of it. Porter spoke of it, and publicly, in crowded theatres. True, Porter's wealth and social standing generally insulated him from petty humiliations by homophobes. One exceptional moment occurred during *Can-Can*'s tryout, when the musical director, in the pit for a quickie orchestra rehearsal, forgot that Porter was sitting in his usual place in the third or fourth row and let pass a Remark. At Porter's insistence, the producers had to replace him that day, though entrusting to a newcomer the countless cue and tempo changes of a musical-comedy score was a disaster invited to happen.

Besides money and position, Porter had, of course, a wife. The consort he selected was preposterous yet strangely ideal, a divorced beauty significantly older than he, Linda Lee Thomas. Of notable pedigree, a millionairess habilitated to conspicuous consumption, Linda had good reason to marry—and to marry Cole Porter in particular. In 1920, when the couple wed (in Paris, typically, for both spent far more time in

Europe than at home), a woman of delicate background couldn't attend parties or the theatre or, really, go out at all after dark unless escorted. No, it wouldn't have stopped Edna Ferber, but Ferber embraced the new while Linda lived within the rules. Marriage solved Linda's problem—and, further, Porter gave her access to the slightly bohemian set whose company Linda enjoyed. She was devoted to old-fashioned customs but not to old-fashioned people; traditional Society as such had lost its fascination for everyone but itself by then. True, the bohemian's characteristic tolerance for parvenu strays of unreliable manners could be trying; Elsa Maxwell once caused Linda very nearly almost to lose her temper. But the bohemian tolerated also divorced women, treated with a shameful disdain in more conservative social loops.

There was this as well: Linda understood how gifted Porter was. Unlike Nora Joyce, generally indifferent to and occasionally scornful of her husband's art, Linda partook of the music, reveled in it. When she and Porter met, he was unknown. When they married, he had just enjoyed a modest success with *Hitchy Koo 1919* and was still unknown. *Within the Quota* came along a few years later, and Linda may have hoped that Porter would pursue classical composition. Nevertheless, once Porter became known—with "Let's Do It," "Night and Day," and *Anything Goes*—she saw him correctly as redeeming the at times crass business of Broadway with what those of Linda's background valued more than anything else: style.

But the gay thing came along *tout inclu,* and if Linda was prepared to deal with a little of it, life with Cole Porter meant dealing with a lot of it. She may have expressed her displeasure in hypochondriac or psychosomatic disorders, then, because Linda took ambulances the way others took taxicabs, and she seems to have been content only when inside an oxygen tank. Although the Porters were extremely social, their hosts took it for granted that, come the day of the dinner, Linda might well be unavailable for medical reasons, which completely throws one's table out. Among their kind, this marks a serious lack of decorum.

The story gets odder: Porter was sexually adventurous, yet his daily routine was vaulted on order and dependability. *Comme il faut,* to Porter, wasn't a matter of manners only. It comprised an on-the-dot regular-ity, and the normally ebullient Porter could get testy when the schedule was off by even two minutes. Once he was professionally established, he employed a secretary to attend to the paperwork—a gem, of course. Unpredictable behavior was amusing in an Elsa Maxwell, but Porter's business structures had to be kept in order, often through little slips of paper dropped on the secretary's desk, to leave nothing to chance. The man behind all that devil-may-care poetry of the Ritz and the devilish rhythmic horseplay was utterly humorless and unforgiving in the matter of personal responsibilities. He wrote about the world of Anything Goes; he didn't live there himself. Even sex, so often a se-ducer of souls, was compartmentalized in Porter's life, limited to certain acts of carousing passion at certain times with members of a certain class. There was too much of it for Linda's taste, yes—but it, too, was conducted in an orderly manner. When making art, one amuses oneself with the unconventional. But when one makes life, one behaves, above all, correctly.

Sooner or later, everyone reaches a moment of decision that he spends the rest of his life regretting. A trap—because you didn't know what was at stake. They warned me about the horse. Skittish, shies at a beetle. But you tell them no. Don't try to limit me, I'll take my pleasure. He's a handsome nag, and we'll trot along the paths of his life.

When was my moment, then? When we'd just reached the place, with its dashing little wooden sign at the turnoff? Piping Rock Club? So rustically simple for a lair of the powerful. Underplaying, the oldest art of them all.

That was when, I suppose. At the sign. As we came up the road, there where I could have told the driver to curl back around to Oyster Bay. And now I've been doctored and set and reset and carried about and pitied with those lying smiles till I can't recall when I wasn't. I still dress better than any of them. Spats to carnation, the picture of confidence. Robust. *A grin to hide what I think of them, hide what happened when my heels caught in the stirrups. Couldn't break out and roll free, but* you chose your moment. *Is my grief great enough for you at last? Why didn't the groom insist I take another ride? Because they all defer to the powerful? I'm powerful now. My armor is how much I hate the sign and the horse and the groom and you.*

The Welsh have a word for which English offers no equivalent, meaning, roughly, a longing to return to a state one was never in in the first place: *hiraeth*. The wish, one might call it, of a homesick orphan. *Hiraeth* began to seize Porter at some point after *Kiss Me, Kate,* when the burden of living in his physically compromised state overwhelmed him. Even before the accident, Porter's health had known some bad moments, but by the 1950s he was often in the hospital for weeks at a time, even when not enduring the latest operation on his legs. Linda died in 1954, and the next Porter show, his last new work on stage, *Silk Stockings* (1955), underwent a turbulent tryout.

The problem stemmed from a disagreement between the producers and the authors. *Silk Stockings* was to have been a beguiling romantic comedy, but the two men in charge of the production specialized in leggs-and-laffs shows. They had most recently put on *The Boy Friend,* a mild piece that was a mild hit; this time they wanted a smash, and they fired everyone who resisted. Another problem was an omen: while the ballads found Porter in trim—including his last hit for Broadway, "All of You"—the comedy numbers eluded him. Noël Coward and orchestrator Don Walker may have written some part of them, and still the results are the weakest set in Porter's output. It was as if he had lost his sense of humor.

But *Silk Stockings* was a smash. Indeed, its immediate predecessor, *Can-Can* (1953), for the same producers, had not only been a smash but offered one of Porter's very best scores. Oddly, its mixed reviews enthused only about Gwen Verdon, in a smallish speaking part with solo vocal lines in one ensemble number but a great deal of snazzy dancing. After the "Garden of Eden" ballet near the end of Act One, the opening-night public stopped the show with their cheers. Yes, we constantly hear of shows being "stopped," especially from the performers who claim to have stopped them. But this time it really happened.

"The audience held up the show in Miss Verdon's honor," wrote Walter Kerr, in the *Herald Tribune,* "causing the actress to take a breathless bow in even greater déshabillé than the producers of *Can-Can* probably intended."

It's a familiar tale. The "Garden of Eden" represented a presentation by the Montmartre arts set, for which choreographer Michael Kidd devised a pageant of inch worms, kangaroos, penguins, sea horses, frogs (each in their uniquely characterizing music), and at length a snake, to tempt Eve—Verdon, of course. Most often, when the soubrette shows signs of stealing the show, her role is cut back. It happened on a Porter piece, the aforementioned *Leave It To Me!,* when Mary Martin's interpolation of Arditi's "Il Bacio," in the coloratura soprano that Martin fielded in her youth, was dropped. She retained "My Heart Belongs To Daddy," however: an undroppable number. And Verdon's Eve could not be deleted, much to the dismay of *Can-Can*'s star, the authentically French Lilo. Waiting in the wings on opening night to enter for the book scene and its capping number that close Act One, Lilo had to watch *Can-Can*'s assistant stage manager lead Verdon back before the public for a special solo bow. As Verdon had been changing in her dressing room, the dishy ingenue was indeed "in even greater [*recte*] déshabillée." This only added to the impromptu excitement, and it completely spoiled Lilo's debut.

While glowing over Verdon, Kerr—who had one of the laziest ears on The Street—took Porter's work on *Can-Can* for granted. "No Porter score is hard to listen to," he observed. "But it couldn't have been hard to write, either."

On the contrary, for *Can-Can* Porter did something he'd never done before, shifting his compositional style into the very timeplace of the action. His plan was to channel *belle époque* Paris without doing any pastiche antiquing. The very first notes of the Overture, a clanging bell ripping into a galop à la Offenbach, announce a unique Porter: he will not rely only on an accordion in the pit to provide atmosphere, but will rummage through the contours of French popular song. "Allez-vous-en," with which Porter brought down the first-act curtain, turns on chromatic triplets of the kind that Josephine Baker might have fondled in her later, darker period. "If You Loved Me Truly" revives *opérette*. "Never Give Anything Away" turns back to the heavy downbeats of the turn-of-the-century Parisian waltz. "I Love Paris" is the typical Porter minor-into-major-key ballad, here sounding like pure Édith Piaf *air de Pigalle*. There is as well a very special (if not particularly French) Porter invention, "I Am In Love," a ballad for the judge who wants to outlaw the feverishly erotic can-can—yes, another of those reformers passing laws to make people be good. This number is built on repeated-note phrases rising by steps, undergoing bewildering harmonic transitions in the release, then leaping to a fierce conclusion: the sound of a Fundamentalist whose zealotry dissolves in confrontation with the sexual-emotional attraction of his enemy. A sensational composition, it is more or less the climax of Porter's work and life and was all the more arresting because it was introduced by Peter Cookson, a pleasant romantic lead (and husband of Beatrice Straight) who had never sung professionally before and revealed a stirring baritone.

Thus, *Can-Can* is not, as it may first seem, just an enjoyable score. It is a great score, a Cole Porter score in the extreme. Even more than the *Can-Can* libretto, it defines the show's theme: that the vital man's need for liberty will conquer the limited man's need for control. One song is even titled "Live and Let Live." If the critics didn't get it, the public did, and *Can-Can* ranks with *Anything Goes* and *Kiss Me, Kate* as Porter's three most popular scores.

As the 1950s wore on, however, Porter derived less joy from work, and after they cut off one leg at the hip he gave up. His *hiraeth* was almost knowing, because even as he longed for something he never had—the physical beauty that lets one live in endless laughter—he would have settled for simply being whole again. No longer charming because not willing to trouble to be, he summoned guests to his elaborate suite in the Waldorf Towers for ghastly dinners in which he was as silent and ungiving as something sealed up and hidden away. The luxurious Porter habitat had become that "uninhabited plain" he wrote of so long before, in "I've a Shooting Box in Scotland." Many of his closest friends dreaded the invitations or simply stopped coming altogether, fearful of his baleful eyes. What makes a man want to die despised and friendless?

Those soigné cahoots Sara and Gerald have been plying me with ideas for shows. Think Auntie Mame *would suit, with Ethel singing my songs.*

"Wrong for it" is all I said.

The Saint stayed on after the Murphys left, begging me to take an interest in something, Coley. Tiresome. And "Who would you miss, Coley? You know . . . when you . . . ? Isn't there someone?"

He wants me to say, "You, Arnold." I told him all I would miss was my Queen Anne chairs. It was the first thing I thought of. I should have said, "That boy from the Liberty Music Shop." No. I should have said, "I miss being a man. Now take me out of the agony of being unable to live."

But I just looked at him, and then my man came in with "Mr. Porter, it's your bedtime now." And he carried me away and left Arnold gaping.

12

Truman Capote and the War of the Writers

From the first day of it all, he commanded the words as few writers can, and nearly everyone said so: the chiseled sentences, flowing paragraphs, conciseness and clarity. He hooks and reels you in in his first lines:

> I know what is being said about me and you can take my side or theirs, that's your own business.

Sometimes it's the sheer confident address of the reader, as directly above; sometimes it's the revelation of the unexpected, grotesque, and whimsical at once:

> Yesterday afternoon the six-o'clock bus ran over Miss Bobbit. I'm not sure what there is to be said about it; after all, she was only ten years old, still I know no one of us in the town will forget her.

It's as if one heard him speaking, Truman himself, recounting his tall tales right to you; and they were all tall, even the real ones, as if an amusingly misbegotten world had been made just so he could invent narratives about it. A gossip? Not exactly: Walter Winchell was a gossip. Truman Capote was a historian of his own imagination. And he never asked to be left out of others' tall tales, either. "I don't care what anybody says about me," he would tell his friends, "as long as it isn't true."

Which makes him sound pert and mouthy, striking a paradoxical pose, good copy for publicists of the anecdote. But then, he was very, very good at the commercial aspects of the game. Capote's publisher, Bennett Cerf, tells how rival publisher Richard Simon phoned up a few days before Cerf's Random House brought out Capote's *Other Voices, Other Rooms,* in 1948. "How the hell do you get a full-page [photograph] of an author in *Life* magazine," asked Simon, "before his first book even comes out?"

"Does Macy's tell Gimbel's?" answered Cerf, wondering what this was about. Capote, twenty-three years old (and looking far younger), had earned a readership for some magazine stories, but in the general run of American fame he was not yet *Life* photography material. Had he actually wangled a page of the current-events-and-culture handbook of the American middle class?

Simon demanded to know what occult power Random House had over *Life*'s editors. "Dick," Cerf replied, "I have no intention of telling you."

Simon hung up, says Cerf, "in a huff," and Cerf hung up as well. "For God's sake," he shouted to his staff, "get me a copy of *Life*!"

Capote's is the saga of the creator as his own mythologist, the snitch as artist, the squealy gay guy who seizes power through courage and imagination. Yes, courage: it's very, very far from easy being short and effeminate, not to mention refusing to make kowtow to the cautions of the closet. "What chance have you got when there is always trickery in one hand, and danger in the other?"

It's a line from *Other Voices, Other Rooms,* and it's the challenge Capote faced every day of his youth. Like many gays, he compensated by becoming the indispensable entertainer—the storyteller, the partygiver, the one who says, "I know what we'll do" at the start of what turns out to be one of the most enjoyable times of your life. He wowed the kids in Monroeville, Alabama; he wowed the literary world when he got to

New York; he wowed movie stars and smart society belles and even their husbands who had always believed themselves to be homophobic. He fascinated everybody, except for one lifelong holdout whom I'll get to presently. And he did it by enhancing that imagination with what Terrence Rafferty called an "evident delight in being naughty," so that the gossip that dominated his conversation seemed to inform his fiction, with its real-life Gothic of precocious children and haunted grown-ups. It's gay life rendered as fantastical comic tragedy. Capote's gossip was fiction, but his fiction is an extravagated gossip. If Cole Porter textured New Yorkism with an encoded gay style, Capote outed it.

A line from *House of Flowers* is apropos here. When the show's young heroine tells the bordello ladies that she will know if she's in love if a bee sleeps in her palm—a typical Capote invention, pure bagatelle yet of an entrancing insight—the ladies are skeptical. One asks, in a silken Caribbean accent, "What you give the Houngan for this information?" Capote himself was a Houngan, passing information to the hetero universe that he understood better than they did, slipping as he did between the gay sensibility and the part of Creation that straights think of as real life: theirs.

So while Capote's later fiction documents actual experiences of folk familiar and unknown, things that happened, his earlier fiction is in flight from it, either as disguised autobiography or crazy yarns. Earlier in this book, we saw how much Edna Ferber and Dorothy Parker could put themselves into their work, in Ferber's pop-eyed epics of Americana and Parker's tidy little *complaintes*. The unloved spinster sweetens her life with romances unavailable to her personally; the party girl tells how it feels when they stop calling. There was I, waiting at the church.

Capote went both ways at once, telling how it feels by sweetening his life. His worldview in these early years is as violent as fairy tales yet as fey as a maiden aunt on her third sherry, which is why the six-o'clock bus runs over Miss Bobbit. "A wiry little girl in a starched, lemon-colored party dress, she sassed along with a grown-up mince, one hand on her hip, the other supporting a spinsterish umbrella." The leading lady of "Children on Their Birthdays," Miss Bobbit wakes up a sleepy town with her odd ways, her high style, and her tendency to dominate. She takes over the place just as Capote did, everywhere he went.

The story, one of the best Capote ever wrote, is a study in how the outsider sets the fashion by sheer force of personality—really, through artistry. That is what the subjects of the present volume have in common: the belief that having been born Different makes one sovereign among those born normal, or ordinary, or dull. It is a handicap, Different— unless used correctly. Then it's a gift. Miss Bobbit befriends a black girl, breaks up two best buddies who pursue her, wins a talent contest, and dies in her bus accident on the day she is to leave to seek her destiny in Hollywood. There is little plot per se; Capote fills his tale with character studies and grotesque little side trips with, for instance, a certain Mr. Henderson. Boarding in the same house as Miss Bobbit and her black friend, he shouts that "There were midgets in the walls trying to get at his supply of toilet paper." Again, it's gossip. But Capote presents it with his word-perfect ear for dialect and his ability to shift from deadpan to lyrical like a magician pouring colored drinks from a flask of clear water.

A mind so attuned to the artistic possibilities in gossip was bound to add journalism to his activity sheet, especially the fly-on-the-wall genre, detailing what people say and do in private. *The Muses Are Heard,* on a Russian tour of *Porgy and Bess,* and the much shorter "The Duke in His Domain," a profile of Marlon Brando, were mid-fifties *New Yorker* commissions made of tattle. Capote's devilish side, till then content to diddle fictionalized versions of folks, had at last led him to tell on real people by name, and he seemed to enjoy making them look foolish. He clearly has no interest in *Porgy and Bess'* standing as a linchpin in the popularization of minority cultures through a combination of their arts. One would never guess from *The Muses Are Heard* that *Porgy* created two generations of black opera singers, for the opera stage was strictly white till the cumulative influence of *Porgy* and *Carmen Jones* and the racial integration of the New York City Opera (in the years after World War II). Then came the emergence of Leontyne Price in an earlier tour of this same *Porgy* production and—in a final rubber-stamping by the toniest WASP stronghold—Marian Anderson's highly symbolic debut at the Met, in 1955.

Capote ignores the history to focus on how silly everybody is, from the *Porgy* players to the *Porgy* management and, taking in a few kibitzers in New York, columnist Leonard Lyons and Ira Gershwin's widow, Lenore. True, comedy is built into the very idea of Americans venturing behind the Iron Curtain in December of 1955, a bit more than two and a half years after Stalin's death, long before thaw and détente. There's more culture clash here than in all of *Gulliver's Travels*. But Capote has come to jeer. Worse, his Brando piece rips open the heart of this most secluded of public figures. "A real vivesection," Dorothy Kilgallen called it, and Brando considered suing Capote. But you can't litigate after you yourself told the truth. "That little bastard spent half the night telling me his problems," Brando fumed. "I felt the least I could do was tell him a few of mine."

Brando was simply unprepared for Capote's combination of art and PR. Once, Capote let a dust-jacket photo—you know the one, as he reclines staring at you, looking naked in schoolboy chic—stamp the brand. But now he avidly sought work that itself would make him notorious without his seeming to take part. Thus, the novella *Breakfast at Tiffany's* (1958) is a first-person narrative in which the author gets no character space. And yet at one point the narrator describes a story he'd written, "about two women who share a house, schoolteachers, one of whom, when the other becomes engaged, spreads with anonymous notes a scandal that prevents the marriage." Is this Capote describing Capote? In "Children on Their Birthdays," he was a totally disembodied narrator—except in one moment when someone addresses him as "Mr. C." It is as if Capote cannot rule himself out of anything interesting, whether in fiction or life.

Breakfast at Tiffany's is a transitional work. It caps the earlier part of his career, stabilized by "creative" writing, and leads on to the latter part, stabilized by journalism. There is a touch of the latter in *Tiffany's*, because heroine Holly Golightly seems to offer more of Capote's tattle. She is not unlike Christopher Isherwood's Sally Bowles: a party girl with some esoteric verbal tics ("quel rat," for instance, or getting depressed with the "mean reds"). She is shallow yet vital, and so persuasively delineated that everyone thinks she must be based on someone—Marilyn Monroe, perhaps.

One doesn't get that feeling about Gloria Wandrous, the so to say Holly Golightly of John O'Hara's *BUtterfield 8*. Gloria, too, is a party girl with a unique style, but she seems pure literary invention, and is not remotely as bewitching as Holly. Gloria is earthy and knowable. Holly is airy and mysterious—in fact her own invention, a former farm girl going Sophisticate in the City.

Perhaps this is because Capote was gay, with a gay man's x-ray vision into the inner longings of the human condition: one grows up overwhelmed by the knowledge that one is double-jointed, perhaps elite. One studies the patterns of "normal" behavior to pass among others as family—and, in studying, grows wise. "The theme in all of [Capote's] books," said novelist John Knowles, "is that there are special, strange gifted people in the world and they have to be treated with understanding." Like Miss Bobbit, for instance, and especially like the protagonist of *Other Voices, Other Rooms* and most of the principals of *The Grass Harp*. And Holly Golightly. But then, Capote celebrates the strange even in the ungifted, as if in relief from the O'Hara reports on Ivy Leaguers degenerating in middle-aged self-hatred. O'Hara frequently reduces his scene to conversations in real-life places your uncle would feel at home in; Capote orders up fantastical sets where everyone sings opera in his pajamas.

Although published a generation apart, *BUtterfield 8* and *Breakfast at Tiffany's* appeared in film versions almost simultaneously, respectively in 1960 and 1961. Immediately, we spot the difference between Capote's world and not only that of O'Hara but of just about any mid-century hetero writer: the straights see life as compromised by dreary and hostile relatives and business associates, very much in the manner of the current cable television series *Mad Men*. True, MGM had to leave much of O'Hara out of its *BUtterfield 8*—but what's left oozes tedium. Paramount's *Tiffany's* abounds in eccentrics like John McGiver's James Thurberesque Tiffany's clerk, lovably pompous. The *BUtterfield 8* movie also suffers from Elizabeth Taylor's dire heroine, so tense, so regal, so "They promised me an Oscar if I played a prostitute."* Audrey Hepburn's Holly Golightly has the innocent grace without which Capote's "strange gifted people" would seem cranky and destructive. Indeed, writer George Axelrod and director Blake Edwards transformed a downbeat tale with a sad or at least inconclusive ending into a screwball romance. One moment captures how Hepburn and company gave Capote extra fun while respecting his program: at one of Hepburn's wild parties, George Peppard (in a new version of the novella's narrator) looks out the window. He sees Hepburn, on the street, helpfully pointing out her place to cops who have come to raid it.

Peppard's role breaks with the original: he is a writer, but not one of stories about schoolteachers and poison-pen letters: a heterosexualization of the Capote figure. A comedy of 1961 could not get by without a love plot, especially not a movie imbued with the myths of Manhattan as a place where money and beauty make their bargain. Capote troubled to include one character in love with his Holly, a bartender named Joe Bell. But Capote gave Bell's passion little more than long walks through the city after Holly has vanished, in the hope of running into her somewhere. In Capote's tale, everyone suffers from terminal frustration. Paramount cures the ailment, liking or tolerating everyone. More than the novella, the film is an ultimate statement on the style and attitude of New Yorkers; even aside from the sheer geography of the location shots from Central Park to Tiffany's itself, it could not have taken place anywhere else. Just the notion of the author of one little-known book being kept by a beaming gargoyle of an older woman in a flotsam-filled brownstone is crazy, smart, fashionable New York to its utmost.

The huge success of the *Tiffany's* movie consolidated Capote's twin careers of artist and celebrity. People close to him in the early 1950s— after his first successes but before he emerged as a household name— would recall Capote's revealing to them his program as a kind of formula for the collection of fame. There was a certain amount of writing for Broadway and Hollywood, of befriending the influential, of getting

---

* They were right. Not only did Taylor win as Best Actress, but Shirley Jones, who also went daughter of joy that year, in *Elmer Gantry,* won as Best Supporting Actress.

photographed for outstanding media outlets, and so on. He had it all planned.*

Part of Capote's formula involved membership in an informal trio of writers with Tennessee Williams and Gore Vidal. Having famous friends enhances one's own fame through a sort of anecdote insurance: you appear in your stories but also in theirs. And of course, all three were more or less gay-identified. Vidal insists that the human is bisexual, tilting when needed to accommodate any of a host of stimuli, but his publication of *The City and the Pillar* (1948), the picaresque of a bisexual whose tilt intensely favors his own gender, marked Vidal as, at the least, politically homophile. And Williams and Capote were professional sissies. Even Cole Porter married, remember. This trio marked a breakaway in American culture, scorning the use of cover procedures.

Even in their work: as Williams wrote play after play exalting the spell of the Beautiful Male, as Capote specialized in heroes who tend to be sons or confidants rather than lovers of women. Noël Coward also lived openly, and was almost as much a presence in the U.S. as in his native England. But Coward also came to power during the age of Brittle Sophistication in the 1920s and 1930s. The Capote-Vidal-Williams group rose up after World War II, when being openly Different was a provocation.

This was not an alliance in any real sense, but simply an accident of chronology in which three Americans more or less launched an era of gay writing. One was principally a playwright (though all three saw production on Broadway), and the other two were very unalike in style and content. Nor were they a tight unit socially, for Williams could be insanely treacherous and Vidal realized early on that he hated Capote's guts.

Everyone says of Truman that he could charm anyone at need. He charmed *Life* into giving him a page of top American cultural real estate before his book had come out. He charmed Marlon Brando into a

---

* The one element that Capote could not control was the popular mispronunciation of his last name as two syllables, with a silent finale *e*. In 1958, Rodgers and Hammerstein made the mistake in a lyric in the song "Chop Suey," from *Flower Drum Song*. It took *In Cold Blood,* which thrust Capote's name into common usage, to correct the error.

scorching confession that Brando wouldn't have entrusted to a priest. He charmed those terminal heteros Humphrey Bogart and John Huston when they were all filming *Beat the Devil* in Italy. Huston liked Capote so much when they first met that he went out and bought one of Capote's books. *That's* charm.

But Capote couldn't charm Vidal, his one major failure known to record. The two became, one might say, best enemies. "A marvelous liar" was Vidal's eventual summation of Capote and his famous story-telling. Others mused fondly on the invocational "W-e-e-e-l-l-l" with which Capote would begin the lesson. Vidal was not fond: "When truly inspired, like Joan of Arc attending to her voices, [Capote] would half shut his eyes and start inventing stories about people whom he had often never known or, indeed, even heard of."

So it was art, storytelling in the sense of yarn-spinning; and it was gossip, less fabulous than malicious. Vidal found Capote's work indistinguishable from Capote himself: "a profound silliness on every level."

The trio that the two comprised with Williams broke apart quite early on, to whatever extent it even *was* a trio, and, to Williams' amusement, Vidal scorned Capote ever after. He went out of his way to caricature Capote, along with Vidal's other pet derision, Norman Mailer, in *Myron* (1974). This sequel to *Myra Breckinridge* takes place on the set of an imaginary Maria Montez movie, *Siren of Babylon*. Various characters are magically imprisoned there in a time warp, among them a prissy know-itall named Maude (the Capote figure) and a noisy idiot named Whittaker Kaiser (Mailer), who picks fights with other men and passes time shadowboxing, his ass "wobbling like a bale of live cats." Vidal ridicules him as an aggressively compensating hetero, the kind that misses the paradigm proposed by Randolph Scott or Clint Eastwood, too securely masculine to need to push. "My cock is bigger than your cock," Kaiser brags to Myron, as Maude "shrieked with delight."

Both Capote and Mailer tried to even the score. Mailer typically head-butted Vidal at a party; what a clown. Capote, also typically, applied the poison tongue, publicizing a tale he claimed to have heard from Lee Radziwill, one of Capote's "swans": the exquisitely classy ladies who formed, for a time, his court. Radziwill was, of course, the sister of Jacqueline Kennedy, and Capote's revenge was the famous White House Story, which he aired in *Playgirl* magazine in September of 1975. Laid out in a gourmand's sense of detail—one can virtually hear Capote smacking his lips after the "W-e-e-l-l-l"—the story supposedly told how a quarrel between Vidal and Bobby Kennedy at a high-hat function led to Vidal's being physically thrown out of the White House front door onto Pennsylvania Avenue. The image was that of an obnoxious cow-poke tossed through the doors of an Old West saloon, designed to finish Vidal as a figure of weight in American letters.

The story was not only wholly false but unbelievable. White House social events are ruled by WASP protocols; no one can be "thrown out." The removal of anyone creating disharmony is surgical, like the way drunks were eased out of "21" that we heard about a few chapters ago. You could be standing three feet away and miss the whole thing. As for anyone's being tossed onto Pennsylvania Avenue, the White House isn't a New York brownstone, fronting the road with a strip of sidewalk between. An Olympian couldn't put the shot from the doorway to the street.

Anyway, none of that occurred in the first place. Vidal happened to be kneeling next to the seated First Lady with a hand on the back of her chair. Bobby, who disliked Vidal, brushed it off, Vidal got up to confront him, the two traded testosterone snarls, and that was the end of it. Vidal left the party with other guests some hours later.

Again we see Capote making a whore of the media to accomplish his goal, as though writing in Communications the way he wrote in his notebooks. It backfired badly, because, when Vidal sued for libel, Capote's only source of defense, Lee Radziwill, denied that any such event had occurred.

Capote should have settled, but he fought the suit; after eight years of litigation, he gave in, publishing an apology and a confirmation that the White House Story was a hoax. Here was a rare act of career that had never been part of Capote's plan: to be unmasked as an author of evil lies.

So he was no Baron Munchausen, flighty and dishonest yet a maker of enchantments all the same. Libel is not a form of enchantment. Capote recalls the aforementioned dictum of Walter Winchell, "Never ruin a good story by trying to verify it." There's a more melodious way of putting it, as actor Carleton Young does at the end of the 1962 John Ford movie *The Man Who Shot Liberty Valance:* "When the legend becomes fact, print the legend." Or we can quote once more Capote's own version: "You can take my side or theirs, that's your own business."

It would appear that Capote never outgrew that troublemaker phase some people pass through in their teens and twenties. He remained for all his days what we might call the "also" person. Like Jerome Robbins, for example: he was socially difficult and professionally evil, but he also ennobled everything he worked on. Capote might spill your deepest secrets to strangers or, as with Vidal, invent spiteful flimflam, but he also was a wonderful writer. Diana Trilling praised an aspect of Capote that few remark upon—his rejection of the leftist pieties expected of writers from the 1960s on. "The greased path," Trilling called it, "of political, liberal, enlightened—supposedly enlightened—ideas. Truman's chic was . . . the chic of the homosexual smart world." In short: "He didn't just 'dress up' his books with a lot of . . . unexamined, regurgitated folderol from the left."

Trilling's reference to "the homosexual smart world" clues us into Capote's identity as fancy heteros' gay of choice. As Dotson Rader noted, "Since American art is to such a large degree a product of homosexuals and Jews, regardless of how anti-Semitic . . . and . . . anti-gay you are, you've got to hide it until they leave the room. You're dead socially without them." Rader even likened Capote to Ward McAllister, our social arbiter of that bygone New York when everyone agreed on who the elite were.

By Capote's time, *elite* was an almost indefinable concept, because social and political structures had become fluid and infinitely adjustable: an open homosexual was now running New York society. That is, the straights who in Cole Porter's time could pretend gay didn't exist (because it never came up in conversation) now had to confront it. Not only did it come up: it informed and perhaps even ruled social style. Cole Porter's age called it "sophisticated." Now it was "gay" or, to give it its rightful name, "fagtastic."

There's more. Porter's sex life, despite his closeted cover-ups, was classic gay: promiscuous and centered on handsome young men. Sometimes they were middle-class, scrubbed and sporty. Sometimes they were on the rough side. Porter even indulged in trips to the Harlem bordello famous for the two-way mirror through which one could watch two men on maneuvers.

Capote had no use for any of this. He cultivated a quirky interest in men who—everyone else agreed—were dreary in appearance and personality, and he could become obsessive about them. It was the one piece that didn't fit into the rest of the puzzle, because one looks to gays as arbiters of taste, especially concerning the attractiveness of men.

However, Capote had a lifelong partner, Jack Dunphy, who though socially awkward was at least presentable. In fact, he had been a chorus boy on Broadway, in dancing rather than singing ensembles.* He must have been good, because he worked for Agnes de Mille in the opening-night cast of *Oklahoma!* (1943). Dunphy married a fellow cast member, Joan McCracken, but when she left him for another man, Dunphy went into an on-the-rebound gay phase that lasted the rest of his life.

Antisocial and volatile, a great destroyer of dinner parties with non sequitur outbursts, Dunphy was the kind of man who owns noisy, aggressive dogs and takes them everywhere. Most people viewed him as the rudder to Capote's runabout, a steadying influence. Most straights, that is. They made the assumption that because Capote was fey and flighty and Dunphy masculine in demeanor that Dunphy would soothe the excitable Capote as a kind of hetero minder. A straightenouter.

In truth, however, if anyone needed steadying it was the unpredictable Dunphy. His most obvious faults—the uproars and clumsiness and tendency to dress like a beachcomber even at the opera—were viewed as hetero faults, those of a "normal" male who would calm down if only he had a woman to pick out his ties. The gay men new to Capote's circle were always hearing what an ace Dunphy was and how lucky Capote was

---

* Corps members, in those days of large casts, were auditioned and hired separately as singers or dancers and then blended in the staging of musical numbers to give the illusion that everyone more or less did everything.

to have him. However, gay men do not navigate around breeder myths on what constitutes manliness, and they tended to discover in Dunphy nothing more than a quarrelsome old woman with no sense of occasion and no ability to reason.

But then, even gay-friendly straights cannot comprehend gay culture or gay men. They try to see it through the usages and signifiers of hetero culture, which is completely different. Straights simply do not speak the language—as when various academics, poring over the life and work of Tennessee Williams, helpfully inform us that Williams' longtime partner, Frank Merlo, was nicknamed "Horse" because of "equine facial features." Right.

Jack Dunphy was a writer himself, a surprisingly good one, though his plays tended to close in tryout and he published six novels in relative obscurity. (There was a seventh "sort of" novel, *Dear Genius,* about his relationship with Capote.) Probably the best known of the fiction, *The Murderous McLaughlins* (1988), contrasts notably with Capote's work, for this look back at an Irish-American family in south Philadelphia* seems torn from Dunphy's past. So was much of Capote's early fiction—yet Dunphy gives us none of Capote's shimmering evocations, his whimsical phantoms. Remember, Capote treats those strange, gifted people. Dunphy treats a bleak world populated by the sad and angry.

Being close to Capote must have been professionally humbling for Dunphy. But Capote to an extent humbled all other writers with the publication of *In Cold Blood* (1965). And so began a *querelle,* like those agitating the Parisian intellectual scene when not only ideas and literature but even music and theatre were seen as central to the nation's destiny.

This controversy turned on a number of questions. Did Capote introduce, as he claimed, a new genre, the non-fiction novel? Was it simply a narrated form of journalism, or, by setting facts into a novelist's structure and voice, had Capote realized an innovation? Was *In Cold Blood* simply the latest in a slim tradition of works whose content was docu-

---

* Dunphy carefully never identifies the locale, confusing his publisher, McGraw-Hill, which placed the action in the dust-jacket copy in "long ago New York City." However, Dunphy repeatedly cites organizations and streets peculiar to Philadelphia.

mentary but whose style was art? And were those writing about *In Cold Blood* affirming Capote's self-aggrandizement or assessing a phenomenon? Terrence Rafferty called the book "a piece of third-person reportage of unsurpassable technical perfection," which suggests that it can't be journalism because journalism isn't this well written. Or does Rafferty mean that, finally, journalism *is* well written: by Capote in this book? What led Norman Mailer, three years later, to publish *The Armies of the Night* with the subtitle "History as a Novel/The Novel as History"? Does that explain something? *In Cold Blood* also bears a subtitle: "A True Account of a Multiple Murder and Its Consequences."

That brings us no closer to a successful act of taxonomy, but it does remind us how much those consequences added to Capote's success: because the work was originally to have discussed the crime but not the criminals. The two drifters who killed the Clutter family provide most of Capote's "story," but they had not been caught when Capote (and his next-door neighbor from his childhood in Monroeville, Harper Lee) arrived in Kansas to start the research. No, at that time Capote was writing a *New Yorker* piece investigating the homicides' impact on the folk who lived in the area. Law enforcement did not have any suspects, or even an idea about whether the guilt lay with a neighbor or a passing stranger. When the murderers were apprehended, the possibilities in their "characterization" changed Capote's driveline: from a mysterious disturbance in the prairie to what Capote called "a collision between the desperate, ruthless, wandering, savage part of American life, and the other [part], which is insular and safe, more or less." This is what journalism doesn't need and fiction must have: personal conflict.

Capote made this statement in an interview in *The New York Times*—a very lengthy one and thus a solemnization of how big a triumph he was enjoying. *In Cold Blood* was a colossal popular and literary success at once; that almost never happens. Every reader has his own favorite "couldn't put it down" title, from *Watership Down* to Mark Helprin's *Winter's Tale*. But *In Cold Blood* popularized the notion of the compulsive read, not least in Capote's suspenseful cross-cutting of the worlds of hunter and prey till they meet in violence. Of course, when Capote wrote the book, those consequences were unclear. Perry Smith and Dick

Hickock were convicted of the Clutter murders, but only after their appeals had been exhausted and the two were hanged did the "story" reach an "ending." There's a symmetry in it: which was done in colder blood, the slaughter of the Clutters or the execution of the murderers?

The *New Yorker* serialization, in four consecutive issues, added a twist to the "couldn't put it down," because subscribers had to wait for each next issue, and newsstand customers often found that the magazine had sold out. Put it down? They couldn't pick it up. By the time the Random House edition appeared, *In Cold Blood* had become one with its PR, the embodiment of "the most talked-about book of its generation." Short of the Bible, it may be the most talked-about book ever, and this time Capote could devise an opening passage unlike his others. There was no ten-year-old Miss Bobbit getting run down in the street, no seduction of the senses. As if playing against your knowledge that you were about to begin the book of books, Capote started in a voice new to him, that of the neutral spectator without quirks and takes. For once, pure narration:

> The village of Holcomb stands on the high wheat plains of western Kansas, a lonesome area that other Kansans call "out there." Some seventy miles east of the Colorado border, the countryside, with its hard blue skies and desert-clear air, has an atmosphere that is rather more Far West than Middle West.

Some thought Capote too neutral, battening on the fate of the killers to juice up his ending. The book's detractors generally resented the promotional whirligig and what they saw as an overpraising of Capote's talent. As "empty of significance as a dead snake," said the *San Francisco Chronicle*. A "Macy's Thanksgiving Day balloon," said *The New York Times,* moving "gigantically along the avenue to success." But the *querelle* grew especially heated when Kenneth Tynan accused Capote of virtually conniving at Smith's and Hickock's executions. Vivien Leigh's biographer Hugo Vickers called Tynan "perhaps the best example of the failed actor turned brilliant, if vicious, critic. He was also an anarchist. When attempting a revolution, certain heads must roll."

Leigh's did, and now it was Capote's turn. In his home paper, the

London Observer, Tynan coyly spoke of an unnamed "prominent Manhattan lawyer," who had assured Tynan that if the convicted pair had gotten life, *In Cold Blood* could not have been published. It's a ridiculous statement, and the anonymous attorney sounded like an invention. In fact, Tynan had baited a trap for Capote, whose reply to this very public *J'accuse* included the promise to donate five hundred dollars to any charity of Tynan's choice if he could produce the mysterious attorney. Tynan did—though this stunt distracted from the eventual rather telling revelation that the attorney had not read *In Cold Blood* when Tynan consulted with him. Tynan got his check, made out to the Howard League for Penal Reform, and he made a copy of it to mount on his study wall.

Thus Tynan took revenge on Capote for . . . what? His cultural prosperity? His having graduated himself from Vidal's "profound silliness" to artist of weight? For reminding us that some people are evil because they like to be evil? Tynan didn't believe in evil; he would have had the prisons opened to the last cell.

Capote, of course, nourished a revenge dream of his own: that Tynan would be kidnaped and imprisoned in a lavishly appointed private clinic where, day by day, doctors would amputate a limb or take out an organ. A schedule of treatments, exercises, and the like would follow each operation, but these would doggedly continue until there was nothing left of Tynan except for one eye and his genitals. "*Everything else goes!*" was Capote's final war cry, as he told and retold the tale; Tynan heard that it had become Capote's latest set piece at dinners. At last, the remains of Tynan would be tortured with showings of the most fabulous pornographic movies, running non-stop.

As with the uprisings of narrow-culture America, from Prohibition to the Birthers of 2009, this *querelle* never said what it really hated. So I will: it hated having to accept that a faggot had pulled off the literary coup of the age. Shouldn't that honor have fallen to one of the he-men of the Ernest Hemingway school,* perhaps a descendant of John O'Hara?

---

*It is almost standard "knowledge" that Hemingway was gay. However, his biographers generally believe this is a lie told by a personal enemy and spread by others. It seems plausible because of fleeting gay undercurrents in his work (especially the Nick

For some time now, Capote's detractors had been hoping that he'd be exposed as a crafty little whirlwind of show-off skills, a pansy putting on airs. During Vidal's lawsuit against Capote, Liz Smith tried to get Lee Radziwill to intercede on Capote's behalf, and, Smith recalls, Radziwill replied, "Oh, Liz, what does it matter? They're just a couple of fags."

Did she really say that? Never mind; we print the legend. Anyway, *In Cold Blood* crushed the dream of every Capote-hater in the business, because it seemed to mark a possible turning point in his career: from writing about himself to writing about the world. If Miss Bobbit was profoundly silly, the Clutters and their killers certainly weren't. And Capote not only wrote of the world but addressed it, speaking in particular to an American readership. This is what all my subjects have been doing in these pages, distilling from a temporarily unappreciated social status an art made of arts, a neighborhood made of neighborhoods. Irish, Jewish, Italian, black, gay: they became leaders on the national level, so much so that, even when they had no political power, they could influence those who did.

So there is something immense and symbolic in—just for example—the Metropolitan Opera's proposing to launch its 1961–1962 season with Leontyne Price as Puccini's Girl of the Golden West. It was to be the first time a black singer was given a season opening—the highest honor the Met can bestow—but it was threatened by contentious negotiations over the orchestra's contract. The Met's manager, Rudolf Bing, in his habitual us-versus-them mentality, decided to punish the union by cancelling the season. However, the affair had got so much publicity that President Kennedy ordered his Secretary of Labor, Arthur Goldberg, to settle the matter.

Through federal intervention, then, the season was saved: by an Irish-Catholic president, through his Jewish official, on behalf of (among many others, from artists to house staff) a black soprano. This is part of the

---

Adams stories); of the emphasis on hunting, bullfighting, and such, which suggests the overcompensation of the closet; and of the mysterious suicide. Nevertheless, there is no evidence that Hemingway was gay.

legacy of the New Deal, a connection running through the very center of New Yorkism back to Al Smith, the Triangle Fire, and Irving Berlin. It is the America that other Americans, coming from an impoverished social background, do not understand and deeply resent. This is why they continually stage backlashes against it under pretexts, screaming down the proofs that invalidate their positions. They run on an unappeasable, paranoid rage: single-issue fanatics without a cause. They don't know whom they hate, and they don't even know why. The enemy is nameless: someone is changing my life.

Conclusion: The Ball of the Century

The celebration that Capote staged in the Grand Ballroom of the Plaza Hotel at ten o'clock on the night of November 28, 1966 marked the high point of his life. True, the ball was nominally in honor of Katherine Graham, who had taken over the *Washington Post* as its publisher three years earlier, upon the suicide of her husband, Philip Graham. Nevertheless, Capote was the birthday boy, and everyone knew it. He had achieved a renown beyond the reach of almost any other American writer. Capote was famous even among people who don't read: Hollywood famous, event famous. He was more than an author of books now: an author of happenings. We started in hotels and we end in a hotel, at Capote's "Black and White Dance" (as stated on the invitation), the greatest ball ever given. And not arguably: it *was*.

In a way, the evening comprised a sum of the elements of Capote: everything but his art. There was Truman the junior partygiver of Monroeville, not simply throwing but directing them, as the master of frivolity, the one you have the best time with. There was Truman the socialite, bringing friends together but also Knowing Everybody Knowable, ecumenically exclusive. As he planned his guest list, Capote carried around one of those black-and-white-covered "composition" notebooks with the lined pages, writing in names and addresses as possibilities struck him, having as much fun as an eight-year-old deciding whom to leave out of a Halloween party.

Truman the mischief-maker directed the dress to include masks—black for gentlemen and white for ladies. He bought his own mask at F. A. O. Schwarz for thirty-nine cents; some of the women ordered theirs from Halston, Mr. John, or Robert Mackintosh, who had distinguished himself earlier that year with a pride of unique designs for Angela Lansbury in *Mame,* from gold pajamas to top-hatted black fox-hunt chic.

Interestingly, while the press had taken to underreporting or ignoring other balls given in New York in those years, it feasted on Capote, proving that Capote's formula for seizing and holding Fame Control, now in its third or fourth decade of maintenance, had been very clever indeed. The masks were a story. The guests were a story. The Plaza was a story. Bandleader Peter Duchin was a story, because his father, Eddie Duchin, had been so prominent in the same line that Hollywood had filmed his bio. Katherine Graham was a story, although no one could properly write the story behind that story, which was: Why is the dowdy Graham the honoree and not . . . oh, Marlene Dietrich? Or Babe Paley, everybody's favorite among Capote's swans?

Good old Truman: he knew that his guest of choice must be respectable and important yet relatively contentless. Graham had so little of the prima donna in her makeup that when she made her hairdressing appointment at trendy Mr. Kenneth's, she didn't ask for the honcho himself and had to be whisked out of the "and others" section of the salon by a solicitous assistant. No, Graham wasn't the headline: the ball was. Capote was. Who danced with whom? Lauren Bacall with Jerome Robbins? How's his fox trot? And what did they say? What was for dinner? And who of the guests declined to pass through the very public gauntlet of reporters, photographers, and celebrity stalkers and use the Plaza's secret security entry?

Not. One.

And who was actually there? Those Capote was close to, those he admired, those he felt loyal to for some act of generosity, and those he thought too significant to leave out. Many, desperate to be there, weren't asked. Some were asked and did not appear—Greta Garbo, Jacqueline

Kennedy, Elizabeth Taylor and Richard Burton. Tallulah Bankhead begged to be asked and got her wish. And then *The New York Times* printed the invitation list (in fact a composite of some kind, lacking some names and including last-minute additions who hadn't been formally invited), revealing how completely New Yorkism had replaced Society as the elite class. Here were wastrels and achievers, the social and the unaligned, the grandee and the upstart. Kitty Carlisle Hart and Candice Bergen. John O'Hara and Harper Lee. Ralph Bunche and Noël Coward. Leslie Caron and Marianne Moore. Arnold Saint-Subber, Cecil Beaton, and Virgil Thomson, all of whom worked with Capote on his first Broadway production, *The Grass Harp*. Cole Porter's old playmate the Duke of Verdura and Frank Sinatra. Leonard Bernstein and his wife, Irving Berlin and his wife, and Gian Carlo Menotti and *his* wife, Samuel Barber.

It was a playful combination, but also an expression of power: that he could cause them all to want to be there. Such gatherings used to obtain only in European capitals, where those of political power mixed with those of cultural power—though of course there is always the danger that a drunk Norman Mailer, roostering around as always, will try to pick a fight with McGeorge Bundy (Lyndon Johnson's national security advisor) over the war in Vietnam, which Mailer of course did.

Some guests felt, in the end, that the evening lacked adventure, as each clique partied within its limits, but it was the talk of the nation: that was its success. Even a year later, interest was keen; *Esquire* devoted a cover to it, featuring eight scowling celebs in full dress who hadn't been invited, among them Ed Sullivan, Tony Curtis, and Kim Novak. The caption was "We wouldn't have come even if you *had* invited us, Truman Capote!"

Then came Capote's crash, as he slowly retreated from his roles as world-on-a-string V.I.P. and master writer. Calamities, calamities: the Gore Vidal lawsuit; dazed and incoherent television appearances; the almost unanimous rejection by his swans because he disclosed their secrets in his fiction. And it wasn't just they—the New Society that he had helped define shut its iron door altogether. Some Capote intimates recall his saying that his victims were so stupid they'd never recognize themselves (and their husbands, for the exposé was comprehensive) under different names. Others thought he wanted revenge on them for "what

[they] say about me as soon as I leave the room." Perhaps he suspected that they were all guilty of the words Lee Radziwill supposedly uttered to Liz Smith. Or he may have been living under the instruction of Tom Wolfe, who once pepped him up with "What does it matter what anybody says? Don't you realize you're one of the few people in the world who are absolutely fireproof?"

Capote's revelations were unveiled in what was announced as early chapters in his promised masterpiece, *Answered Prayers*. Everyone thinks of this as Capote's Proustian entry, dissecting a culture through its social life. However, in an interview with Charles Ruas, Capote himself said, "Proust, no. If I had any model at all, it was Flaubert."

Still, Flaubert didn't concentrate on the kind of people Capote wrote about. Reynolds Price points out that "Proust's society was one of *blood,* unshakably founded on positions of French social eminence that were reared upon centuries-old money, property and actual power over the lives of other human beings." One thinks of Lotte Lenya, as the procuress contessa of *The Roman Spring of Mrs. Stone,* telling Warren Beatty, "There is no such thing as a great American lady. Great ladies do not occur in a nation less than two hundred years old." It's that concept of a class bred to rule, one that New Yorkism wiped away with its regime of upstarts. What, then, was left for Capote to write about? Epic fiction devoted to society as Capote found it, Price goes on, "would likely implode upon the ultimate triviality of its subject."

Further, at its dark heart *In Cold Blood* treats large ideas. It's not far removed from a religious mystery, filled with questions about how six lives became so fiercely entangled, as black-Sabbath evil pays a visit on the everyday. Capote may have sensed that *Answered Prayers* would compromise this achievement—that it would indeed prove trivial after *In Cold Blood.* Yet he talked of his work-in-progress incessantly, and very publicly. "Even if I never finish *Answered Prayers,*" he said, "it's better known than most books that are published." Alluding to Capote's supposed invention of the non-fiction novel, Donald Windham declared that Capote was inventing another genre: "the nonwritten novel."

In the end, some chapters of *Answered Prayers* did appear, unimpressively; it is rumored that there is—or was—more. Was the manuscript stolen, as some suggest? Is it sitting in some secret place, as Capote himself hinted? The years leading up to his death, in 1984, just shy of sixty, found him so lush and vague that he may simply have lost track of the book. One speaks of "dependence" on drugs and alcohol, but Capote made a determined assault on stimulants, using them to penetrate to an affectless oblivion. One's entire existence becomes slurred; the world dissolves around one. As with Cole Porter's drinking, "dependence" is really a feeble euphemism for the suicide of the personality, in which one has only to wait for the flesh to catch up.

The Black and White Ball, then, marked the high point of Capote the celebrity just as *In Cold Blood* was that of Capote the artist. The ball marks as well the high point of New Yorkism, because crucial elements of the movement began to evaporate or lose favor in the 1960s. The sound of Broadway, engulfed by rock, ceased to be the national music. The Left's embrace of divisive identity politics crowded out the equality democracy of the New Deal. The Irish-Jewish New York wisecrack humor gave way to Los Angeles slacker nihilism jokes, literally remarks made of nothing. The collapse of effective public education has left most high school and even college graduates without the key ingredient in learning, the skepticism that equips one to reality-test what one hears. Without it, one can believe anything, which is why loony conspiracy theory is so popular and the heartland backlash so shrill, energized by not reason but rage. Embracing these ravings, the Republican Party has become the party of Elvis sightings. Republicans have even created a new genre of hypocrite, the "pro-family" Republican exposed in adultery scandals or outed in toilets by the vice squad.

It is odd to look back on Capote—or Ethel Waters or Fiorello La Guardia or even the Algonquin Round Table—and realize that they are not nostalgia any more: they're ancient history. New York isn't even the cultural capital today. Los Angeles took over at some point after World War II, and we may be living through a transition in which Las Vegas assumes the seat of power. We are left with mere echoes of a time when the art, politics, and social mores of The City of New York—to use its official title—virtually ran American culture, and when smart folks lived on the jazz of it all. Print the legend.

Sources and Further Reading

We start with the Astors, because when the notion of a leadership class headed by blue bloods took hold in the late nineteenth century, the Astors were The Clan. Justin Kaplan's *When the Astors Owned New York* (Viking, 2006) treats the family and its eccentricities in fine style. Kaplan knows how hard it is to keep one's Astors straight: directly after the dedication, table of contents, and half-title, he gives us a family tree, from founder John Jacob through the fifth generation. Eric Homberger's *Mrs. Astor's New York* (Yale, 2002) glides fascinatingly through the backstory of Social New York before getting to Caroline Schermerhorn Astor herself, with plenty of illustrations, some in color. Homberger includes quotations to catch his subjects in accidental self-revelation. They think they're sporting, but they're giving away trade secrets. For example, Ward McAllister: "Everyone realizes that the one end and aim of life here is to make money." McAllister's own *Society As I Have Found It* (Cassell, 1890) is available for browsing on-line in its original format.

On historical views of the role of an elite, see Crane Brinton's *The Anatomy of Revolution* (Prentice-Hall, 1938) and George Lefebvre's *Quatre-Vingt-Neuf* (which in French denotes 1789, the first year of *La Révolution*), published in English as *The Coming of the French Revolution*

(Princeton, 1947). Brinton compares the English, American, French, and Russian revolutions, in such chapters as "The Old Regime," "The Rule of the Moderates," and "The Accession of the Extremists." Cleveland Amory's *Who Killed Society?* looks at what was left of America's social elite after Walter Winchell, Elsa Maxwell, and Barbara Hutton got through with it; the book was bound in black cloth with flame lettering, to match the *Social Register.* When I was an undergraduate at the University of Pennsylvania, Professor E. Digby Baltzell popularized a revisionist look at what we might call "the caste." Baltzell uses specifics to comprehend generalities in *Puritan Boston and Quaker Philadelphia* (The Free Press, 1979), but his classic is the shorter yet even more comprehensive *The Protestant Establishment* (Vintage, 1964). The latter is dedicated to "my undergraduate friends."

The subtitle of Robert F. Martin's *Hero of the Heartland* (Indiana, 2002) is "Billy Sunday and the Transformation of American Society, 1862–1935." This reminds us that much of the evolution of the Manhattan-based elite that I treat in the present volume turned on the explosion in Communications. Suddenly, there was more theatre, more music, more printing—the very basis for the impact of an Irving Berlin, an Ethel Waters. Sunday's constituency gets into mob mischief in Richard Hofstadter's *Anti-Intellectualism in American Life* (Knopf, 1963). The author states at the outset that this is "largely a personal book" rather than "a formal history," with a theme "developed in a manner that is by choice rather impulsive and by necessity only fragmentary." I could say as much about my own book. Hofstadter's chapters include "Evangelism and the Revivalists," followed by "The Revolt Against Modernity," and, with a change of proper names and years, Hofstadter could be describing Republican culture wars of the millennium.

Of all the works on American social history that I consulted, the most readable was J. C. Furnas' three volumes for Putnam: *The Americans* (1969), which runs from 1587 to 1914; *Great Times* (1974), moving through the twenties; and *Stormy Weather* (1977), which closes the series in 1941. With a dry wit and the ability to turn up in the right place at a moment of discovery, Furnas juggles an amazing amount of data while never drifting into the trivial. In little more than five pages, he analyzes

Walter Winchell as thoroughly as any biographer with a whole book to work in. Furnas is brilliant, and he expects you to be as well. At one point in the Winchell survey, he speaks of "the hix in the stix," calling it "*Variety*'s second-greatest headline" without elaborating further. His readers are supposed to recall STIX NIX HICK PIX* (on rural movie audiences' preference for urban stories), and the superior headline is of course WALL STREET LAYS AN EGG. Incidentally, Furnas dates his chronicle from 1587 because of Virginia Dare, "the first child born of English parents in America," on August 18 of that year.

On the history of The City of New York, there are titles beyond count on various sub-topics but relatively few complete single volumes. George J. Lankevich's *American Metropolis* (New York University, 1998; second ed., as *New York: A Social History,* 2002) is useful, the epic laid out in fewer than three hundred pages. The unabridged modern classic is Edwin G. Burrows and Mike Wallace's *Gotham* (Oxford, 1999), a compulsively readable monster that stops, after some 1,200 pages, when the separate cities of New York and Brooklyn merged, in 1898.

Oliver E. Allen's *The Tiger: The Rise and Fall of Tammany Hall* (Addison-Wesley, 1993) and Seymour J. Mandelbaum's *Boss Tweed's New York* (John Wiley, 1965) treat the city when its flavoring was tilting to the Irish style, as befits the most favored minority. Mandelbaum emphasizes this New York's lack of "communication," in for example a postal service so inadequate that a local letter might arrive in one day or three weeks, if at all. Or consider its layout of streets leading to nowhere in mile after mile of monotonous straightaway, as opposed to the parks and plazas that decorate the towns of Europe. In Mandelbaum's view, Tweed was "a master communicator," in effect uniting the disjunct city energies through a corruption intricately yet comprehensively applied. What brought Tweed down was less the exposure of his tactics than the hole he left in the city's credit status. It was not a question of ethics, but of bankers' misgivings.

---

* This has entered the vernacular as STIX NIX HIX PIX, which sounds more like authentic *Variety*ese. But I have seen the actual front page of the paper, dated July 17, 1935: it's HICK.

On the other hand, Leo Hershkowitz's *Tweed's New York* (Doubleday, 1977) sees Tweed as "more a victim than a scoundrel or thief." He was surely corrupt. But he was expanding the processes of democracy at a time when power was generally passing from the oligarchy to the masses—and, says Hershkowitz, therein lay the basis for the war on the so-called Tweed Ring. The book is a very lively read.

For the B'hoy figure that gave New York its first immigrant "star," see Tyler Anbinder's *Five Points* (The Free Press, 2001), on "the most notorious neighborhood in nineteenth-century America," and Nigel Cliff's *The Shakespeare Riots* (Random House, 2007). Cliff's subject is the class war that erupted around the Astor Place Opera House in 1849, on the night Charles Macready played Macbeth. As many writers have noted, Astor Place was where fashionable Broadway and the rufftuff Bowery—parallel opposites moving north from downtown—came to a meeting point, and a feud between the native Edwin Forrest and the English Macready was turned, literally, into a battle. Cliff gets quite a saga out of it, taking in America's early-nineteenth-century Shakespeare mania, the at first separate and then intertwined careers of the two actors, and the gigantic antagonism between America and England because of military and financial matters. (And, even, because of Charles Dickens' unflattering *American Notes* and the protagonist's unhappy trip to the U.S. in *Martin Chuzzlewit*.) Working in a graceful style that is not afraid to let a sentence run on to accommodate interesting data, Cliff finally reaches his *pièce de résistance*, the riot itself, with a grand theme: "a contest to decide who controlled American culture."

All these books on nineteenth-century New York point to a contention about the very bloodlines of America, a "Whose country *is* this?" that has been raging ever since. It rages today, it would appear, simply because we elected a black president. Yet we inadvertently reduce this national uproar to a single individual whose New York was thought to be the very melting pot itself, and that individual is Boss Tweed. Is he in fact a bogeyman whose real sin was sharing power with the masses? On Tweed the human being, the standard modern biography is Kenneth D. Ackerman's (Carroll & Graf, 2005). In Ackerman's subtitle, Tweed is "the corrupt pol" who nevertheless "conceived the soul of modern New York." Truly a fascinating story.

Tweed was only the "boss" of his New York; A. Oakey Hall was its mayor. On a later mayor, see George Walsh's *Gentleman Jimmy Walker* (Praeger, 1974), and, on a later boss, Christopher M. Finan's *Alfred E. Smith* (Hill and Wang, 2002). Walker seems an ephemeral figure despite his continued fame as one of New York's great Characters, but Smith was a genuinely influential politician. It may be that FDR would never have reached the presidency in 1932 (or ever) but for Smith's early mentoring and easing Roosevelt into the governor's chair, in 1928. Frances Perkins, an important link between the two men, was to have followed her book on FDR with one on Smith, but she died during its composition. Her notes were passed to Matthew and Hannah Josephson to consult while writing *Al Smith: Hero of the Cities* (Houghton Mifflin, 1969). To an extent, Perkins' voice informs the book. Though the Josephsons did all their own research in the end, the work nevertheless speaks with a lively witness that is quite disarming. Finan's Smith offers more detail. Still, comparing his and the Josephsons' account of Smith's single greatest speech—his deconstruction, in Carnegie Hall in 1919, of the lies behind the "news" in the Hearst press—both books rise to the occasion more or less equally.

Walker and Smith play major roles in Herbert Mitgang's *Once Upon a Time in New York* (The Free Press, 2000), on how the Arnold Rothstein murder led to Roosevelt's removal of Walker. Mitgang calls it "the last great battle of the jazz age." He posts six epigrams in the front matter, all *mots* by figures in the present book, from Franklin P. Adams to Damon Runyon ("All life is nine to five against"). Fiorello La Guardia is here as well, with "If you were any dumber, I'd make you a commissioner."

La Guardia was both mayor and boss, and a great subject for biography, in personality and achievement. Two very useful guides are Thomas Kessner (McGraw-Hill, 1989) and Alyn Brodsky (St. Martin's, 2003). Kessner gets around more in a longer text, while Brodsky is concise and compelling. A typical touch: Brodsky's chapter titles are La Guardia quotations, from "I loathe the professional politician" to the subtly moving "You can't stay in office indefinitely." Both authors use the image of La Guardia as a "maker" of New York in their subtitles—in his break with Tammany Hall and its Irish favoritism but also as the chief of the city when it was a crucible of American arts and social culture. For a personal view, try Ernest Cuneo's *Life With Fiorello* (Macmillan, 1955).

Of several books on the Triangle Waist Fire, I think David Von Drehle's *Triangle: The Fire That Changed America* (Atlantic, 2003) is the best. The author sets out a solid account of the garment workers' struggle— before the fire—for basic human rights in an industry made of sweatshop firetraps. He then gives a moment-by-moment report of what transpired inside the building during the fire that is unbearably persuasive. Finally, he looks in on the trial of the Triangle owners, Max Blanck and Isaac Harris, who were acquitted. They had to be smuggled out of the courtroom into their limousine lest they be assaulted by a crowd of the victims' loved ones. Van Drehle also is the only source of the full list of the victims' names.

Switching over to the Algonquin Round Table creates an offensive non sequitur after the loss of so much life. Yet the workplace reforms inspired by the fire were related to the Algonquin's nonconformist wits, because both situations emphasize the New Yorkist conception of a society in which no one would be treated as utility, victim, or discard. There aren't as many books on the Round Table as one might think. I prefer James R. Gaines' *Wit's End* (Harcourt Brace Jovanovich, 1977), not least for the many unusual illustrations: Robert Benchley and his two sons out shoveling snow, the younger boy leaning wistfully against Daddy; Robert E. Sherwood so towering over wife and daughter that they seem to be Munchkins; the co-authors of *What Price Glory?*, Laurence Stallings and Maxwell Anderson, the latter looking surprisingly debonair for someone who's about to spend a decade pestering Broadway with verse plays and Stallings' muscles bunching up under his coat.

Among biographies, Malcolm Goldstein's *George S. Kaufman* (Oxford, 1979) should be noted as the one that Anne Kaufman Schneider thinks does the best job on her father. Edna Ferber's great-niece Julie Gilbert offers *Ferber* (Doubleday, 1978), which runs backward in time, like

Kaufman (and Hart's) *Merrily We Roll Along.* Dorothy Parker's two bios bear Parker lines as titles: John Keats' *You Might As Well Live* (Simon & Schuster, 1970) and Marion Meade's more detailed *What Fresh Hell Is This?* (Villard, 1988). While we're at it, *The Viking Portable Dorothy Parker* (1944) catches in one volume all of her major work and a great deal else. A later edition added in Parker's *New Yorker* book reviews, writing as Constant Reader. Here's a third great Parker line: digesting A. A. Milne's *The House At Pooh Corner,* "Tonstant Weader Fwowed Up."

Keeping for the moment to biography, our Algonquin pal Alexander Woollcott wrote the first one on Irving Berlin (Putnam, 1925), though it appeared less than halfway through his career. The standard modern life is Laurence Bergreen's *As Thousands Cheer* (Viking-Penguin, 1990), and the coffee-table volume is *Irving Berlin's Show Business* (Abrams, 2005), with text by David Leopold. There are some very unusual illustrations in the latter—full-stage views of *Annie Get Your Gun* to be found no-where else, a magazine page with shots of *Face the Music* snapped during performance. The curious can also take a look at the famous transposing piano.

Ethel Waters is best served by her own *His Eye Is On the Sparrow* (with Charles Samuels, Doubleday, 1951), at times reticent about her own backstage geschrei but otherwise plain and honest. The Classics label has CDed a complete run of her 78s on separate discs, from 1921–23 to 1946–47; these now fetch collector's prices on the online *Antiquariat* sites. A good single-disc sampler is *Am I Blue: 1921–1947,* on Jazz Legends (not to be confused with another Waters *Am I Blue* on ASW). The disc routes one through Waters' golden age, from blues "shouter" in the 1920s through her emergence into mainstream pop and on to Broadway stardom. Alas, the "You Can't Do What My Last Man Did" is the acoustic cut, less dra-matic than the electric remake with its dialogue interlude in black-vaudeville "foolnish." However, this CD does offer "Maybe Not At All," with Waters' dead-on imitations of Smiths Clara and Bessie. *Ethel Waters on Stage and Screen* (Sony) presents all her cuts from *As Thousands Cheer, At Home Abroad,* and *Cabin in the Sky,* along with—what else—"Am I Blue?"

There is more on just who formulated the musical attitudes of

American popular singing in Gary Giddins' *Bing Crosby: A Pocketful of Dreams: The Early Years 1903–1940* (Little, Brown, 2001), an exhaustive early-life-and-work, and in his shorter *Satchmo* (Doubleday, 1988), both enlightened by Giddins' you-are-there evocations and musical expertise. Giddins is also one of the modern guides in Ken Burns' PBS documentary *Jazz*. The lavish tie-in book (Knopf, 2000) amplifies the saga.

A BMG reissue of the 1960 LP *The Fabulous Josephine Baker* offers the later Baker, in deeper voice and better French. Earlier, she sang what they put in front of her; now she chooses her material. She has rivals but no superior—not even Piaf. A more synoptic disc is *Hommage à Joséphine Baker* (Sepia), which carries her from 1930 to 1953. Sepia is an enterprising newish English firm that reissues performances freed by European copyright law after fifty years. Sepia's physical presentations are impressive, and programs run up to the timing limits of CD technology. This one plays at 79:24, and the booklet includes English translations of most of the numbers, which favor French. Note, too, that BMG doesn't include Baker's haunting theme song, "J'ai Deux Amours." It's in the Sepia collection. Interestingly, Baker recorded it in 1930 in E Major. The Sepia cut, from 1953, takes the key down only a half step. The big transpositions that, we are told, lowered Baker's range by as much as a fifth presumably date from her very last appearances.

There are many Baker books, including her own, but the reader may be best served by two complementarily different ones, Jean-Claude Baker's *Josephine* (Adams, 1993) and Phyllis Rose's *Jazz Cleopatra* (Doubleday, 1989). Baker, writing with Chris Chase, offers a very personal reading, based on a zillion interviews but also on his own knowledge of his subject: he is one of Baker's many adoptees, though not strictly of the Rainbow Tribe. Like everyone else, he finds her as fascinating as maddening. Rose takes the long view; her subtitle is "Josephine Baker In Her Time," and she adduces much social content to explain not only what Baker was but what she *meant*. As writers, Rose is the insightful stylist, Baker the restless gossip. Both books are wonderful reads.

Ethel Waters' key film performances are *Cabin in the Sky, Pinky,* and *The Member of the Wedding,* all on DVD (the last in a Stanley Kramer box set). As for Baker, two years after she arrived in Paris, she appeared in a silent for Pathé, *La Revue des Revues* (1927), in hand-tinted color. This is a Cinderella backstager interrupted by theatre numbers of the kind seen at the Folies Bergère or Moulin Rouge, with showgirls in mad getups, strolling or posing. But Baker appears in two spots, a "plantation" bit with a black band and, to a dressy crowd in funny paper hats, a number in the "American Bar." The film must be a rare item, because neither Phyllis Rose nor Jean-Claude Baker mentions it; Kino has now issued it on DVD. An anachronistic modern soundtrack distracts, but Baker's solos preserve her unique art as her talkies do not. At this writing, both numbers can be found on YouTube.

Now to the wise guys. Patrick Downey offers *Gangster City: The History of the New York Underworld 1900–1935* (Barricade, 2004), its cover adorned, front and back, with mug shots. Burton B. Turkus and Sid Feder tell *The Story of "The Syndicate"* (1951; second ed., Da Capo, 1992), and for Hollywood's bad guys there is Eugene Rosow's *Born To Lose* (Oxford, 1978), richly illustrated with stills and frame enlargements. Rosow deconstructs the elements of the crime film, from the "takeover" (of the gang by an audacious underling) to the hideout. Stills of the nightclub so essential to the form include a great one (on page 129) of our jazz classic *Broadway,* so art deco that the chorus girls wear huge "skyscraper" headgear.

Now Winchell and Runyon. They come as a set in John Mosedale's *The Men Who Invented Broadway* (Richard Marek, 1981), lively and anecdotal. Edwin P. Hoyt tackles Runyon alone in *A Gentleman of Broadway* (Little, Brown, 1964), and Jimmy Breslin treats not only Runyon but Breslin in his *Damon Runyon* (Ticknor & Fields, 1991). If *In Cold Blood* is a non-fiction novel, Breslin's Runyon volume is fiction biography. Or something. Here's Breslin on the Round Table:

The Algonquin had Ring Lardner and George S. Kaufman and after that a collection of overrated misfits and half-talents, such as Robert Benchley, and I never did quite understand what it was he actually did, and Wolcott Gibbs, who wrote nothing more than reviews, and a half-poetess, Dorothy Parker. Their fame would extend all the way to Connecticut.

More truly, Wolcott Gibbs would have been as likely to attend Algonquin lunches as to lurk in toilets, tapping his foot. Breslin may have confused *The New Yorker,* Gibbs' haunt, with the Round Table because so many Tablers wrote for the magazine.

Of the several books on Winchell, Neal Gabler's biography, with the subtitle "Gossip, Power, and the Culture of Celebrity" (Knopf, 1994), is the clear favorite for its wealth of research. Of interest as well is *Winchell: His Life and Times* (Praeger, 1976), by Herman Klurfeld. WINCHELL'S NO. 1 GHOST was the headline on the front page of the *New York Post* on January 10, 1952, and here the ghost fleshes himself out. His writing has a bit of the jumpy Winchell style; one expected as much. Klurfeld was in the Stork on the night of The Happening, and he states unequivocally that typical bad Stork after-theatre service and not racism was at fault—indeed, the food did arrive but Baker had stomped out. In other words, she was treated no differently than anyone else, though I'm guessing that Billingsley did not present Baker with a box of Sortilege. Klurfeld also points out that, long after, Baker admitted in an interview (with "Hollywood columnist Shirley Eder") that "she had been used as a pawn in the matter, and Walter had done nothing to hurt her." Klurfeld points out also that Winchell and Baker, each in their way, completely mismanaged their responses.

Like Runyon and Winchell, John O'Hara nourished an interest in characters who cheat and steal to live, though O'Hara's were of the Ivy League class. Geoffrey Wolff's bio has the perfect title: *The Art of Burning Bridges* (Knopf, 2003). The rather "literary" writing can distract, as if Wolff, a novelist himself, is reluctant to disappear in someone else's life. But he seems to understand that O'Hara was less "difficult" than unwilling to be abused. A fine set of photos includes a couple taken at the Stork Club, one with Winchell and the other with Billingsley.

There are three excellent works on Dorothy Thompson. The two bios are Peter Kurth's *American Cassandra* (Little, Brown, 1990) and Marion K. Sanders' *Dorothy Thompson: A Legend in Her Time* (Houghton Mifflin, 1973). Both are scholarly and very readable, and while they can't avoid sharing material, you almost won't enjoy one without the other. Vincent Sheean's *Dorothy and Red* (Houghton Mifflin, 1963) is a personal reminiscence, and Red, of course, is Sinclair Lewis. Sheean, who for a time lived with the couple, notes that it was a true love match yet intolerably vexed by Lewis' "stormy sadness and his ungovernable temperament." Sheean thinks the two "were fonder of each other when there was an appreciable distance between them, when they could grieve over the separation ("how I miss you!" they never stop saying) without any of the rasping little dangers of propinquity."

Thompson's *Herald Tribune* columns are collected in *Let the Record Speak* (Houghton Mifflin, 1939), a look back at a time when Thompson seemed the only American not in government who knew just what risks we were running. "Write it down," she says, on February 18, 1938, even before the Munich crisis, "that the [Nazi] world revolution began in earnest—and perhaps the world war." Though he doesn't mention Thompson, Phillip Knightley does an exemplary job in exploring the world of the war correspondent, "From the Crimea to Vietnam" (as his subtitle tells), in *The First Casualty* (Harcourt Brace Jovanovich, 1973). Meanwhile, on Sinclair Lewis alone we have Mark Schorer's monumental biography (McGraw-Hill, 1961), 814 pages before the list of Lewis' works and index. Schorer has a great solution to the problem of keeping the reader abreast of what year the life has reached. Most biographers will place an event in "the following June" or "by that autumn." Yes, but *when?* Schorer's running heads, on either side of the page divide (e.g., 1941/1942) tell one at a glance.

Prohibition, the great nineteenth-century rebellion against diversity in American life, has inspired a miniature library of its own. One can start with Andrew Sinclair's *Prohibition: The Era of Excess* (Atlantic, 1962) or John Kobler's *Ardent Spirits* (Putnam, 1973). The colorful art of a foaming mug, a gangster's "getaway" sedan, and a tommy gun on Kobler's cover warns that his will be the lively account. Incredibly, Norman H. Clark's *Deliver Us From Evil* (Norton, 1976) attempts to defend Prohibition some fifty years after it proved to be catastrophic. Deliver us from Norman H. Clark.

The mid-twentieth-century uprising motivated (to a degree) by cultural politics was isolationism. The movement needs its historian, at least for an investigation on the grand scale, though isolationists of course pepper books on Charles Lindbergh and FDR. In the present volume, Roosevelt is an enabling eminence grise. His appointment of minorities to cabinet posts reminds us how much of New York's tolerance moved from the local to the national level, and why so much of the nation hated him. If we leave aside works by court historians, Roosevelt comes most alive in Kenneth S. Davis' five volumes called *FDR* (Putnam, Random House, 1972–2000), from *The Beckoning of Destiny 1882–1928* to *The War President 1940–1943*. The latter actually stops at the end of 1942, over two years before Roosevelt's death; Davis himself died without completing the manuscript. My quotation of Davis' rating of America First as partly pro-Nazi is from that volume.

The Lindbergh biography business was capped by A. Scott Berg's massive *Lindbergh* (Putnam, 1998), written with the family's cooperation and with access to the extensive Lindbergh archives. No restrictions limited Berg, but none was needed: the tone is respectful, tilting to the "naive" interpretation of Lindbergh's politics. Wayne S. Cole's *Charles A. Lindbergh and the Battle Against American Intervention in World War II* (Harcourt Brace Jovanovich, 1974) is downright worshipful. Cole's treatment of Lindbergh's testimony before the House Committee on Foreign Affairs on January 23, 1941 carefully avoids any mention of Lindbergh's insistence on viewing Great Britain and Nazi Germany as morally equal.

On the other hand, Max Wallace, in *The American Axis: Henry Ford, Charles Lindbergh, and the Rise of the Third Reich* (St. Martin's, 2003), quotes from previously classified documents to prove how close the Nazi government was to the American isolationist movement and even to Lindbergh himself, apparently through intermediaries. Further, Wallace shows how the American military attaché to Nazi Germany, Truman Smith, used a very willing Lindbergh to discourage France and Great Britain from confronting Hitler. In 1936, Smith invited the celebrated American aviator to have a look at the Luftwaffe, timing the trip to the Berlin Olympics. Lindbergh could assess the Germans' air force capability and inform our military; in fact, Lindbergh and Smith went on the equivalent of those mad shopping sprees popular on fifties television game shows, where contestants race through stores, grabbing everything in sight. The Luftwaffe's chief, Hermann Göring, lied about the size and readiness of his bombers in particular. As Wallace notes, it was "one of the greatest disinformation feats in history," because "neither Lindbergh nor Smith had ever sought to verify independently what they were told." And Telford Taylor, the exhaustive historian of Munich (Doubleday, 1979), calls the consequent appeasement of Hitler in 1938 "the only victory of strategic proportions that the Luftwaffe ever won."

Richard M. Ketchum's *The Borrowed Years 1938–1941* (Random House, 1989) is structured around the personal lives of Ketchums young and old in those years. Richard himself was at Yale, where one of his professors was Arnold Whitridge, a classmate of Cole Porter (though Ketchum does not speak of this and may not have known it). This is the same Whitridge who appears in the present book in the Cole Porter chapter, recalling songs from his and Porter's college shows. Ketchum heard Lindbergh's isolationist speeches as an undergraduate. Of the Madison Square Garden rally on October 30, 1941, Ketchum quotes a British journalist who thought the audience as "hysterical as any Hitler mob," and, reading Lindbergh's address later, the Englishman "realized that— the war having been on for a year, France and much else of civilization enslaved, London bombed, that march to the death camps under way— it contained no word of even mild disapproval of Hitler."

Indeed, another historian, Albert Fried, sees Lindbergh as virtually dismissing France and England as unworthy of survival in the Darwinian sense. Fried quotes Lindbergh: "The war in Europe is not so much a conflict between right and wrong as it is a conflict between differing concepts of right." By this thinking, the enslavement of European youth in labor camps, the systematic extermination of Slavs, and *Auschwitz-ismus* are all morally "right." This thinking is not what any reasonable person calls "naive."

I quote Fried in his *FDR and His Enemies* (St. Martin's, 1999). Joining Lindbergh on the slate are Huey Long, Al Smith, labor leader John L. Lewis, and anti-Semitic radio ranter Father Coughlin. Fried holds to the Tolstoyan view of the so-called Great Man as an instrument of irresistible sociopolitical forces—not a self-willing creator of history but a tool of history's will. Roosevelt serves as the protagonist of destiny's theatre, cast to fashion "the modern American state, centralized and ever-expanding, as guarantor of social justice and national security." Thus, Roosevelt's enemies were battling not a man but the inexorable turning of fortune's wheel, very much like the Prohibitionists before them and, I hope, the "tea baggers" after.

One wonders if Fried gave any thought of including among Roosevelt's enemies his ambassador to England, Joseph P. Kennedy, John Kennedy's father and another "isolationist" who was really pro-Nazi. Ronald Kessler's *The Sins of the Father* (Warner Books, 1996) emphasizes Kennedy's assuring the German government that England couldn't defend itself and the U.S. wouldn't protect it. He habitually waved away criticism of Hitler with a sneer at the "Jew media," and even decades later blamed the Second World War not on Hitler's insistence that there be one but on "a number of Jewish publishers and writers." Yes, remember when they invaded Poland? Among other Kennedy biographers, Kessler offers the most complete version of an anecdote involving Nancy Astor, hostess of the salon of English fascists, semi-fascists, and defeatists known as "the Cliveden set" after the estate owned by her husband, Waldorf Astor. (The correct pronunciation rhymes with "lived in.") "A perfection of a place" was Queen Victoria's opinion when the Duke of Westminster owned it. Given Roosevelt's disgust for fascism, Cliveden should have been marked *Here Be Dragons* on Kennedy's map; he was instead a habitué. The Nancy Astor story takes us to Parliament, when she was the first woman seated in the House of Commons. After MP Alan Graham remonstrated with her for bad manners, she replied (the phrasing varies from version to version), "You must be a Jew to dare to speak to me like that." The tale usually ends there, but Kessler goes on to quote Winston Churchill: "I have never before heard such an insult to a member of Parliament as the words just used by that bitch."

On the blending of classical and popular art, a CD from Naxos entitled *Skyscrapers: Symphonic Jazz* brings back old 78s from the Victor vaults, conducted by the house's pop Toscanini, Nathaniel Shilkret. The performances, from 1928 to 1932, include one of the outstanding titles in the repertory, John Alden Carpenter's *Skyscrapers,* subtitled "A Ballet of Modern American Life." Note, though, that it's *urban* American life, with its leading man billed as "The Strutter" and its "Negro Scene," a *Lento Cantabile* in Gershwinesque ballad style. Jazz is the sound of the city.

There are Walt Disney biographies both critical (Richard Schickel's *The Disney Version,* Simon & Schuster, 1968) and accommodating (Neal Gabler's *Walt Disney: The Triumph of the American Imagination*, Knopf, 2006). And, lo, *Fantasia* claims two books all its own. Deems Taylor, the film's narrator, wrote *Fantasia* (Simon & Schuster, 1940), a coffee-table entry with tipped-in color plates and, in the "Dance of the Hours" chapter, a dialogue between an opera buff and a non-believer that is quite funny. John Culhane's *Walt Disney's Fantasia* (Abrams, 1983) is an eyeful, with story boards, roughs, and cels used in the film itself. The first pages are a mini-history, with the original poster (giving Stokowski prominent billing, for culture cred), a psychedelic sixties rerelease poster, and a later one centered on The Mouse. Then one turns the page and sees the original title screen, in shades of blue with *Fantasia* in yellow-green, exactly as it appeared to its very first audiences.

On Toscanini, I prefer Harvey Sachs for biography (Lippincott, 1978) and Joseph Horowitz's *Understanding Toscanini: How He Became an American Culture-God and Helped Create a New Audience for Old Music* (Knopf, 1987) for deconstruction. Harvey Sachs does not prefer Horowitz, and replied with irritation in a book review in *The New Republic,* preserved in Sachs' *Reflections on Toscanini* (Grove Weidenfeld, 1991). A kind of parergon to the biography, this smallish volume goes into greater detail on such topics as "Toscanini and Mussolini" and that strange Franco Zeffirelli movie about the young Toscanini with Elizabeth Taylor in blackface as Aida. Few have seen it, and Sachs explains why. Even more irritated than Sachs—not with Joseph Horowitz but with Toscanini—is Charles O'Connell, Victor's artists and repertoire chief during the Toscanini years. O'Connell's *The Other Side of the Record* (Knopf, 1947), written in a hifalutin, mannered style, brings us behind the scenes with Lily Pons, Lauritz Melchior, Jascha Heifetz, and so on. There really was an audience for this in those days; my copy of the book is a seventh printing. Although O'Connell has high praise for Kirsten Flagstad and Helen Traubel, he is impatient with almost everyone else and scathing about Toscanini, whom he calls "as simple, as selfish, and as savage as a child."

For a taste of the Toscanini style, one might try his *La Traviata* with Licia Albanese, Jan Peerce, and Robert Merrill—but not the NBC broadcast, which Victor issued commercially. The Music and Arts label has released a complete set drawn from the dress rehearsals, where the first act breathes more than on the radio performance, with a wonderful spring in "Libiamo." The opening of Act Two is unusually exciting, as Toscanini hurries the first "dialogue" scene with slashing chords and breakneck recits. Then the agent of the heroine's destruction—the senior Germont—makes his entrance sounding like the materialization of destiny. What other conductor thinks of these things? Most arresting is Maestro's voluble role in this sequence, cautioning with "Legato!" just before the violins launch the accompaniment to Peerce's aria and exploding with curses when they don't supply what he wants. Later, during the Albanese-Merrill duet, at the climax of the *Andantino Cantabile,* Toscanini urges his players with "Molto crescendo! So! So! So! So!" Some listeners may feel uncomfortable with such ferocious precision; this is an intimate bourgeois romance, not *Otello*. Still, it is fascinating to hear the music so intently lived in, and, as always, Maestro hums along and even sings. It's the singing of history.

The cover of Earl Conrad's *Billy Rose: Manhattan Primitive* (Popular Library, 1969) shows a very little guy next to a towering bare-breasted showgirl, amplified by headgear shaped like a pagoda topped by an explosion of feathers. This was burlesque: the big beauty and the little clown. But Rose knew that membership in the elite meant rising above "girls and laffs" show biz into producing *Carmen Jones* and collecting art. Rose's own *Wine, Women and Words* (Simon & Schuster, 1948) is illustrated by Salvador Dalì.

On Barbara Hutton, Jean Maddern Pitrone offers *F. W. Woolworth and the American Five and Dime* (McFarland, 2003). I wish she had spent more time on the chain's inventory, pricing, and so on. Shopping at Woolworth's was an experience shared by millions of Americans that is now terminated without replacement, and one is curious about how it worked. C. David Heymann's *Poor Little Rich Girl* (Random House,

1983) gives us not only the life but the legend of Hutton. A misidentification of one figure in the book led to the threat of civil action, and, according to an article in *Time* on January 9, 1984, the publisher recalled all fifty-eight thousand copies in print. The work is readable nevertheless, and surely preferable to Philip Van Renssalaer's *Million Dollar Baby* (Putnam, 1979), though the latter author knew Hutton very well. There is at least the odd arresting moment, as when novelist Louis Bromfield starts screaming at Hutton in the bar of the Palace Hotel in St. Moritz, Switzerland, shortly before the start of World War II. "Your London palace will be bombed to smithereens!" he shouts, on his third brandy stinger. Even more bemusing is the Duchess of Kent at one of those too-too soirées, who says, "I can hardly wait to see you do the rumba, Barbara."

Stork Club (Little, Brown, 2000), by Ralph Blumenthal, is a fascinating look at another experience we no longer undergo: feeling exclusive in a celebrity joint. There are plenty of illustrations, from the little Oklahoma house where Sherman Billingsley first lived to his *Daily News* front page, when he was arrested after driving threatening strangers away from his house at gunpoint. That ubiquitous monster of the 1950s, Roy Cohn—Billingsley's lawyer—is in the photo, too. Most amusing of all is a shot of Elsa Maxwell and party at a table, the cigarette fumes so heavy that one of the four can scarcely be seen.

The three major Cole Porter bios reflect the increasing openness about gay material in the Stonewall era. George Eells' *The Life That Late He Led* (Putnam, 1967) is tactful on the sex life of one of the most rampaging *galants* in gay history. Charles Schwartz's *Cole Porter* (Dial, 1977) gets somewhat graphic, and William McBrien's (Knopf, 1998) not only names names but shows their photos. Eells, who knew Porter personally, includes Porter's journal on his first extended Hollywood experience, writing *Born To Dance*. Schwartz includes Porter's detailed account of the pain in his legs. Still, McBrien is the most comprehensive of the three, and his volume will likely be the reference Porter life from now on.

David Grafton's *Red, Hot & Rich!* (Stein and Day, 1987), supplies chronological cement matter threading together oral-history remarks from Porter intimates (such as Monty Woolley), colleagues (Mary Martin), employees, Indiana relations, and critics. One of Grafton's guest speakers,

Gwen Verdon, mystifies with the complaint that the dance music in a Porter show simply ground out the Porter tunes over and over. Yet the only Porter show that Verdon played in was *Can-Can*, and her dances—the Quadrille, the second-act Offenbachian Apache, and, especially, the "Garden of Eden" ballet—were all original compositions by Genevieve Pitot, Porter's regular dance arranger in his *Kiss Me, Kate* comeback period. True, at the climax of the very long "Eden," Pitot rings in the refrain of the preceding vocal, "Montmart'." But *Can-Can* is notable for its inventive dance music—as were all of Verdon's shows from *Can-Can* on. In earlier decades, dance arrangers did plug the preceding vocal, at least in the less ambitious works. However, starting in the 1930s and almost as a rule by the 1950s, those arrangers were encouraged to compose. Verdon's *Redhead* (1959), no one's idea of a breakaway show in its writing, nevertheless offered a dream ballet made of variations on a theme. In Roger Adams' charts, Verdon's establishing solo, "I Feel Merely Marvelous," was treated as a can-can, as a *Giselle*-era ballet movement, in a D Minor Lisztian gypsy fling, and finally as a *marche militaire*.

We should also look in on *Cole,* a coffee-table book edited by Robert Kimball (Holt, Rinehart & Winston, 1971), because its illustrations fill in much of the saga. Some of the rarest inclusions are a page of key sheets to Porter's first Broadway show, way back in 1916, *See America First* (the sets look very cheap); two full-stage shots of *Fifty Million Frenchmen;* an example of one of the many bejeweled cigarette cases designed by the Duke of Verdura that Cole and Linda were always giving each other on Porter's opening nights; a copy of the printed road-trip directions from Manhattan to Porter's Williamstown estate, Buxton Hill, given to weekend guests; a shot of Charlotte Greenwood performing her trademark leg kick in *Out of This World* and, facing, a shot of her doing exactly the same thing forty years before; and that *Life* photograh of the audience at *Seven Lively Arts'* premiere. The cropping obscures maestro Abravanel's carnation, but if one looks about two inches northwest of the direct center of the shot one can see Oscar Hammerstein, with his wife (her face partly hidden) to his right. Also to be glimpsed, even in the sepia that constitutes the book's color scheme, is a bit of the mural with which Joseph

Urban covered the walls and ceiling of the Ziegfeld Theatre when it opened, and which Billy Rose left intact when he bought the house.

Despite getting to Broadway earlier than most others of the Golden Age, Porter lived long enough to enjoy the definitive original-cast-album preservations that Jerome Kern, George Gershwin, and Vincent Youmans never got. (The trio did enjoy cast-album treatment on at least three shows each in London.) Some Porter titles come to us by other means. EMI's *Nymph Errant* records an all-star London charity concert (with irritating fanfares every time one of the women makes an entrance; enough already), but the eighteen numbers include dropped songs, and one original cast member, Elisabeth Welch, repeats her "Solomon." New World's *Fifty Million Frenchmen,* from another concert, is more theatrical and boasts along with the usual revived cut numbers the 1929 orchestrations. Like *Nymph Errant,* this one offers a lot of out-of-story numbers suggestive of revue, but there is a plot: Boy bets he can get Girl without spending a cent. Setting: Paris. Support: eccentric American tourists. Funniest lyric: I won't spoil it, but it concerns Kim Criswell's date at a John Gilbert movie, and at the performance I saw, when Criswell sang it, she and Porter took the biggest laugh I've ever heard a song lyric get in all my theatregoing.

A small San Francisco outfit devoted to producing out of the canon, 42nd Street Moon, not only staged but recorded *Leave It To Me!,* on their own Music Box label. The cast is game, the small band delightful, and the score one of Porter's best. As for archeological restoration, John McGlinn's of the original *Anything Goes* (EMI), with Cris Groenendaal, Kim Criswell (a fixture of these outings), and Frederica von Stade virtually sits us in the Alvin Theatre in 1934, for Miles Krueger's detailed plot synopsis allows us to attend the entire show. Krueger also explains the show's now dated references and interviews the original co-author and director, Howard Lindsay. This is especially useful in correcting the two *Anything Goes* factoids, the old one that it was at first about a shipwreck and the new one that Lindsay and Russel Crouse rewrote Guy Bolton and P. G. Wodehouse's script because it wasn't good enough. Lindsay confirms that "the book had to be changed" because of the sinking of the Morro Castle; he says nothing about its not being good enough. As it happens, once Lindsay and Crouse started rewriting, they simply improved the entire script, because in fact it *wasn't* good enough. However, that is what they chose to do, not what producer Vinton Freedley hired them to do. As for the shipwreck (Lindsay: "There was something in [the Bolton-Wodehouse] book that suggested that sort of thing at sea"), it was, on the contrary, a mad bomber thought to be running wild on board, as one can read in Bolton's *Anything Goes* treatment, which survives in the archives at the Library of the Performing Arts at Lincoln Center.

McGlinn also made a CD of Porter overtures and ballet music (EMI). This includes Porter's excursion into Symphonic Jazz, the ballet *Within the Quota,* heard in its original Charles Koechlin scoring. Other curiosities take in the overture to *Out Of This World,* recorded for the cast album but missing a bizarre fanfare meant to suggest a primitive erotic rite (which three words could describe the entire show). McGlinn of course reinstates it. His *Gay Divorce* overture, amusingly, stacks "How's Your Romance?," "After You, Who?," "You're In Love," the hotel-suite door chimes that turn into "I've Got You On My Mind," and the rousing "Salt Air" (near the end of which, by the way, the curtain rose on Act One, as *Gay Divorce,* like many thirties musical comedies, has no opening number). What's missing? The show's hit, "Night and Day." This is presumably because the dance for Fred Astaire and Claire Luce following his vocal repeated the refrain over and over. So Gwen Verdon was right about dance music—when she was six going on seven, not when she was on Broadway.

Of the many books on Truman Capote—some by those who knew him—the outstanding title is another oral history under George Plimpton's editorship (Doubleday, 1998). Witnesses take in such as John Huston; Diana Trilling; Stephen Sondheim; Ned Rorem; Kurt Vonnegut; Candice Bergen; Eleanor Perényi (the author of a superb biography of Franz Liszt and a Capote detractor for his cultural ignorance: "an empty, silly little man sitting around in Mona Williams' villa on Capri"); Neil Simon; that disgusting homophobe and, even worse, terrible writer Willie Morris; Alfred Kazin; and of course Gore Vidal. This truly fascinating read is organized chronologically and by event—Capote and Jack Dunphy (one of the contributors); Capote goes to Kansas; the swans; the whereabouts, if any, of the complete *Answered Prayers*.

Capote's ball at the Plaza gets its own book, Deborah Davis' *Party of the Century* (Wiley, 2006), which includes the one thing Capote felt we must know about the event: the guest list, from Leroy Aarons to Darryl Zanuck. More academically, there is *The Critical Response to Truman Capote,* edited by Joseph C. and John C. Waldmeir (Greenwood, 1999). The essays include reviews of Capote's books and plays when they first appeared, Peter G. Christensen on "Capote as Gay American Author," and John J. McAleer's comparison of *In Cold Blood* with Dreiser's *An American Tragedy.* Most interesting is Terrence Rafferty's *New Yorker* review of *Answered Prayers,* "an enigmatic ruin." By this time, Capote's immersion in the art of gossip ran so deep that the book was not only made of tattle but designed to excite it. "Capote," Rafferty tells us, "started spinning that feathery stuff around his own work, mystifying it thoroughly, as if the mystification were the art itself."

Thus, even when Capote's abilities as a writer faltered, he could call on his abilities as a PR huckster. There have been other wonderful American writers. But there has been no wonderful American writer's *career* to match Capote's—no comparable traversal of the culture, conquering every section of it that he wanted to conquer and even getting an important role in a Hollywood movie despite being the worst actor ever filmed. Moreover, it is impossible to imagine anyone but a gay fantasist making that trip. Capote knew what no straight man ever will: life is an art, and most poor sons-of-bitches are boring to death.

Index